EDEXCEL
A LEVEL
HISTORY

*Active*Book included

endorsed for
edexcel

Paper 3:

Britain: losing and gaining an empire, 1763-1914

Nikki Christie | Brendan Christie

Series editor: Rosemary Rees

PEARSON

Published by Pearson Education Limited, 80 Strand, London, WC2R 0RL

www.pearsonschoolsandfecolleges.co.uk

Copies of official specifications for all Edexcel qualifications may be found on the website:
www.edexcel.com

Text © Pearson Education Limited 2016

Designed by Elizabeth Arnoux for Pearson

Typeset and illustrated by Phoenix Photosetting, Chatham, Kent

Produced by Out of House Publishing

Original illustrations © Pearson Education Limited 2016

Cover design by Malena Wilson-Max for Pearson

Cover photo © Bridgeman Art Library/Leeds Museums and Galleries (Leeds Art Gallery) UK

The rights of Nikki Christie, Brendan Christie and Adam Kidson to be identified as authors of this work
have been asserted by them in accordance with the Copyright, Designs and Patents Act 1988.

First published 2016

19 18 17

10 9 8 7 6 5 4 3

British Library Cataloguing in Publication Data
A catalogue record for this book is available from the British Library

ISBN 978 1 447 985341

Copyright notice

Printed in Slovakia by Neografia

Websites

Pearson Education Limited is not responsible for the content of any external internet sites. It is essential for
tutors to preview each website before using it in class so as to ensure that the URL is still accurate, relevant
and appropriate. We suggest that tutors bookmark useful websites and consider enabling students to access
them through the school/college intranet.

A note from the publisher

In order to ensure that this resource offers high-quality support for the associated Pearson qualification,
it has been through a review process by the awarding body. This process confirms that this resource
fully covers the teaching and learning content of the specification or part of a specification at which it is
aimed. It also confirms that it demonstrates an appropriate balance between the development of subject
skills, knowledge and understanding, in addition to preparation for assessment.

Endorsement does not cover any guidance on assessment activities or processes (e.g. practice questions
or advice on how to answer assessment questions) included in the resource, nor does it prescribe any
particular approach to the teaching or delivery of a related course.

While the publishers have made every attempt to ensure that advice on the qualification and its
assessment is accurate, the official specification and associated assessment guidance materials are the
only authoritative source of information and should always be referred to for definitive guidance.

Pearson examiners have not contributed to any sections in this resource relevant to examination papers
for which they have responsibility.

Examiners will not use endorsed resources as a source of material for any assessment set by Pearson.

Endorsement of a resource does not mean that the resource is required to achieve this Pearson
qualification, nor does it mean that it is the only suitable material available to support the qualification,
and any resource lists produced by the awarding body shall include this and other appropriate resources.

Contents

How to use this book

STRUCTURE

This book covers Paper 3, Option 35.1: Britain: losing and gaining an empire, 1763–1914 of the Edexcel A Level qualification.

You will also need to study a Paper 1 and a Paper 2 option and produce coursework in order to complete your qualification. All Paper 1/2 options are covered by other textbooks in this series.

EXAM SUPPORT

The examined assessment for Paper 3 requires you to answer questions from three sections. Throughout this book there are exam-style questions in all three section styles for you to practise your examination skills.

Section A contains a compulsory question that will assess your source analysis and evaluation skills.

A Level Exam-Style Question Section A

Study Source 1 before you answer this question.

Assess the value of the source for revealing the reasons for the choice of Botany Bay as Britain's first settlement in Australia and the hopes the government had for the colony.

Explain your answer, using the source, the information given about its origin and your own knowledge about the historical context. (20 marks)

Tip
Consider the influence that Banks was likely to have on the debate surrounding the establishment of such a colony in Australia.

Section B contains a choice of essay questions that will look at your understanding of the studied period in depth.

A Level Exam-Style Question Section B

'By 1829, British settlement in Australia had effectively been transformed from an outdoor prison into an imperial colony.'

How far do you agree with this comment on the Australian colonies in the late 1820s? (20 marks)

Tip
Include changes in the economy of the colony as well as political developments.

Section C will again give you a choice of essay questions but these will assess your understanding of the period in breadth.

A Level Exam-Style Question Section C

How far do you agree that the role of the Royal Navy did not substantially change in the years 1763–1914? (20 marks)

Tip
When answering this question, you should consider the whole timeframe carefully and think about the context of the changing world. What is the primary role of the Royal Navy and does this change over the period?

The Preparing for your A Level Paper 3 exam section at the end of this book contains sample answers of different standards, with comments on how they could be improved.

FEATURES
Extend your knowledge

These features contain additional information that will help you gain a deeper understanding of the topic. This could be a short biography of an important person, extra background information about an event, an alternative interpretation, or even a research idea that you could follow up. Information in these boxes is not essential to your exam success, but still provides insights of value.

EXTEND YOUR KNOWLEDGE

Thomas Paine (1737–1809)
Tom Paine was an English radical who emigrated to the American colonies in 1774 with the help of Benjamin Franklin. His *Common Sense* pamphlet, published in 1776, was one of the most important documents of the revolution and its central demand was for independence from Britain. Paine moved to France in the 1790s and wrote the *Rights of Man* defending the French Revolution. He survived the French Revolution, despite spending some time in prison and returned to America in 1802.

Knowledge check activities

These activities are designed to check that you have understood the material that you have just studied. They might also ask you questions about the sources and extracts in the section to check that you have studied and analysed them thoroughly.

> ### ACTIVITY
> #### KNOWLEDGE CHECK
>
> **Mapping the world**
>
> 1 Read Source 8 and write down what you feel it says about the motivations for British exploration.
>
> 2 How might the source support the suggestion that exploration helped to enhance Britain's standing in the world?
>
> 3 Why was exploration so important to the development of the Royal Navy?

Summary activities

At the end of each chapter, you will find summary activities. These are tasks designed to help you think about the key topic you have just studied as a whole. They may involve selecting and organising key information or analysing how things changed over time. You might want to keep your answers to these questions safe – they are handy for revision.

> ### ACTIVITY
> #### SUMMARY
>
> **The birth of British Australia, 1788–1829**
>
> 1 Write a description explaining the reasons why the nature and function of British settlement changed between 1788 and 1829. Include the following:
>   - the original purpose of the colony
>   - the economic basis of the colony
>   - the political developments following the Bigge Report
>   - the indications for the future implicit in the way in which the settlement of Western Australia took place.
>
> 2 What were the key turning points in terms of the fate of the Aboriginal people of New South Wales and Van Diemen's Land?

Thinking Historically activities

These activities are found throughout the book, and are designed to develop your understanding of history, especially around the key concepts of evidence, interpretations, causation and change. Each activity is designed to challenge a conceptual barrier that might be holding you back. This is linked to a map of conceptual barriers developed by experts. You can look up the map and find out which barrier each activity challenges by downloading the progression map from this website: www.pearsonschools.co.uk/historyprogressionsapproach.

progression map reference

> ### THINKING HISTORICALLY   Cause and consequence (6c)
>
> **Connections**
>
> Look at Extracts 2 and 3 and Sources 7 and 8. Work in groups or individually and answer the following questions.
>
> 1 Read Extract 2. How might this be seen as similar to problems the British faced in governing the Canadas in the 1820s and 1830s?
>
> 2 Read Source 7.
>   a) What did Dalhousie believe about the French–Canadians?
>   b) How is this similar to James I's ideas about the Irish?
>
> 3 Look at Extract 3 and Source 8. What did the British in Lower Canada in the 1820s and 1830s copy from the English methods of subduing the Irish?
>
> 4 Make a list of other similarities between Lower Canada and 16th- and 17th-century Ireland. How may their understanding of the Plantation have affected the attitudes and actions of the British in Canada?
>
> 5 Why it is important for historians to see these links across time and be able to explain how causal factors can influence situations much later in time?

Getting the most from your online ActiveBook

This book comes with three years' access to ActiveBook* – an online, digital version of your textbook. Follow the instructions printed on the inside front cover to start using your ActiveBook.

Your ActiveBook is the perfect way to personalise your learning as you progress through your A Level History course. You can:

- access your content online, anytime, anywhere
- use the inbuilt highlighting and annotation tools to personalise the content and make it really relevant to you.

Highlight tool – use this to pick out key terms or topics so you are ready and prepared for revision.

Annotations tool – use this to add your own notes, for example links to your wider reading, such as websites or other files. Or, make a note to remind yourself about work that you need to do.

*For new purchases only. If the access code has already been revealed, it may no longer be valid. If you have bought this textbook secondhand, the code may already have been used by the first owner of the book.

Introduction
A Level History

WHY HISTORY MATTERS

History is about people and people are complex, fascinating, frustrating and a whole lot of other things besides. This is why history is probably the most comprehensive and certainly one of the most intriguing subjects there is. History can also be inspiring and alarming, heartening and disturbing, a story of progress and civilisation and of catastrophe and inhumanity.

History's importance goes beyond the subject's intrinsic interest and appeal. Our beliefs and actions, our cultures, institutions and ways of living, our languages and means of making sense of ourselves are all shaped by the past. If we want to fully understand ourselves now, and to understand our possible futures, we have no alternative but to think about history.

History is a discipline as well as a subject matter. Making sense of the past develops qualities of mind that are valuable to anyone who wants to seek the truth and think clearly and intelligently about the most interesting and challenging intellectual problem of all: other people. Learning history is learning a powerful way of knowing.

WHAT IS HISTORY?

History is a way of constructing knowledge about the world through research, interpretation, argument and debate.

Building historical knowledge involves identifying the traces of the past that exist in the present – in people's memories, in old documents, photographs and other remains, and in objects and artefacts ranging from bullets and lipsticks, to field systems and cities. Historians interrogate these traces and *ask questions* that transform traces into *sources of evidence* for knowledge claims about the past.

Historians aim to understand what happened in the past by *explaining why* things happened as they did. Explaining why involves trying to understand past people and their beliefs, intentions and actions. It also involves explaining the causes and evaluating the effects of large-scale changes in the past and exploring relationships between what people aimed to do, the contexts that shaped what was possible and the outcomes and consequences of actions.

Historians also aim to *understand change* in the past. People, states of affairs, ideas, movements and civilisations come into being in time, grow, develop, and ultimately decline and disappear. Historians aim to identify and compare change and continuity in the past, to measure the rate at which things change and to identify the types of change that take place. Change can be slow or sudden. It can also be understood as progressive or regressive – leading to the improvement or worsening of a situation or state of affairs. How things change and whether changes are changes for the better are two key issues that historians frequently debate.

Figure 1 Fragment of a black granite statue possibly portraying the Roman politician Mark Antony.

Debate is the essence of history. Historians write arguments to support their knowledge claims and historians argue with each other to test and evaluate interpretations of the past. Historical knowledge itself changes and develops. On the one hand, new sources of knowledge and new methods of research cause *historical interpretations* to change. On the other hand, the questions that historians ask change with time and new questions produce new answers. Although the past is dead and gone, the interpretation of the past has a past, present and future.

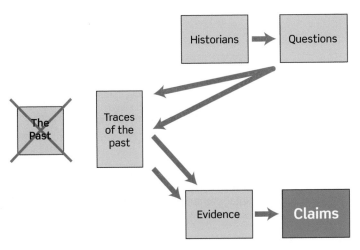

Figure 2 Constructing knowledge about the past.

THE CHALLENGES OF LEARNING HISTORY

Like all other Advanced Level subjects, A Level history is difficult – that is why it is called 'advanced'. Your Advanced Level studies will build on knowledge and understanding of history that you developed at GCSE and at Key Stage 3 – ideas like 'historical sources', 'historical evidence' and 'cause', for example. You will need to do a lot of reading and writing to progress in history. Most importantly, you will need to do a lot of thinking, and thinking about your thinking. This book aims to support you in developing both your knowledge and your understanding.

History is challenging in many ways. On the one hand, it is challenging to build up the range and depth of knowledge that you need to understand the past at an advanced level. Learning

about the past involves mastering new and unfamiliar concepts arising from the past itself (such as the Inquisition, Laudianism, *Volksgemeinschaft*) and building up levels of knowledge that are both detailed and well organised. This book covers the key content of the topics that you are studying for your examination and provides a number of features to help you build and organise what you know – for example, diagrams, timelines and definitions of key terms. You will need to help yourself too, of course, adding to your knowledge through further reading, building on the foundations provided by this book.

Another challenge is to develop understandings of the discipline of history. You will have to learn to think historically about evidence, cause, change and interpretations and also to write historically, in a way that develops clear and supported argument.

Historians think with evidence in ways that differ from how we often think in everyday life. In history, as Figure 2 shows, we cannot go and 'see for ourselves' because the past no longer exists. Neither can we normally rely on 'credible witnesses' to tell us 'the truth' about 'what happened'. People in the past did not write down 'the truth' for our benefit. They often had clear agendas when creating the traces that remain and, as often as not, did not themselves know 'the truth' about complex historical events.

A root of the word 'history' is the Latin word *historia*, one of whose meanings is 'enquiry' or 'finding out'. Learning history means learning to ask questions and interrogate traces, and then to reason about what the new knowledge you have gained means. This book draws on historical scholarship for its narrative and contents. It also draws on research on the nature of historical thinking and on the challenges that learning history can present for students. Throughout the book you will find 'Thinking Historically' activities designed to support the development of your thinking.

You will also find – as you would expect given the nature of history – that the book is full of questions. This book aims to help you build your understandings of the content, contexts and concepts that you will need to advance both your historical knowledge and your historical understanding, and to lay strong foundations for the future development of both.

Dr Arthur Chapman
Institute of Education
University College London

Britain: losing and gaining an empire, 1763–1914

On 19 October 1781, the British surrendered at Yorktown, effectively ending the American War of Independence. Tradition has it that the army of the imperial power marched out to surrender to the strains of the tune, 'The World Turned Upside Down'. The loss of the thirteen colonies was caused by a rebellion against the mercantilist system of trade operated by the British with their first colonies. For Britain, there was no retreat from empire as a result of its defeat by the colonists. Over the next 140 years, Britain acquired the largest territorial empire in world history. In 1914, the British Empire had a population of over 400 million people. The territorial reach of the Empire was such that, during a 24-hour period, some part of the Empire was always experiencing daylight. This was an empire, in the popular phrase, on which the sun never set.

In some ways, the successful growth of Britain's 19th-century empire can be attributed to the lessons learned from the disaster of the American War of Independence. Restrictive trade policies were gradually abandoned in favour of free trade, removing a potential bone of contention between Britain and its colonial possessions. Power over their own affairs was ceded to the white settler colonies from the middle of the 19th century, in absolute contrast to its treatment of the American patriots. The underinvestment which had allowed Britain's navy to deteriorate in strength immediately before the American War of Independence was never allowed to occur again, ensuring naval mastery globally for the British for most of the 19th century. Nevertheless, the lessons of the American Revolution would not have been sufficient on their own to lead to the creation of a second empire. Britain's Industrial Revolution created a market for primary materials from its empire like never before. As the 19th century progressed and Britain's manufacturing industry expanded, territory was acquired:

- to protect established markets, or

- because the territory in question might prove to be a potential market or important source of raw materials, or

- because instability was threatening an existing or potential market for British goods, or

- because the territory in question was perceived to have strategic military potential against other imperial powers, or

- to achieve an imperial vision held by key individuals.

The definition of what the British considered to be its interests proved elastic and covered not only current strategic and trading interests across the globe but also possible future interests.

1776 – 4 July: Declaration of Independence from Britain by the thirteen American colonies following the outbreak of hostilities in April 1775

1776

1788 – 26 January: First Fleet sails into Botany Bay

1788

1807 – 25 March: Abolition of the Slave Trade Act passes in the British parliament, making it illegal to engage in the African slave trade throughout British colonies

1807

1832 – 7 June: Representation of the People Act becomes law in Britain, reforming parliament and widening the franchise

1832

1839 – Durham Report defines and recommends responsible self-government which is eventually adopted in all the settler colonies

1839

1857 – Rebellion breaks out in India, ending the East India Company's rule

1857

1882 – August: Britain occupies Egypt, establishing a 'veiled protectorate' lasting until 1914

1882

1889 – Naval Defence Act formally institutes the 'two power standard' for Britain's navy

1889

1914 – 28 July: First World War begins

1914

1784	**1784** – Pitt's India Act formalises government control over the East India Company's rule of India
1805	**1805** – 21 October: British fleet defeats the combined French and Spanish navies at the Battle of Trafalgar
1815	**1815** – 18 June: Defeat of the French at Waterloo ushers in nearly four decades of peace in Europe
1833	**1833** – 28 August: Slavery is abolished throughout the British colonies except East Indian company possessions and Ceylon
1849	**1849** – Abolition of Navigation Acts formally ends the mercantilist system in favour of free trade
1869	**1869** – November: Suez Canal opens
1884	**1884–85** – Berlin Conference regulates European trade and colonisation in Africa
1898	**1898** – 2 September: Battle of Omdurman – British forces demonstrate the lethal power of technological superiority in the Sudan

The depth studies in this book (Chapters 3–7) highlight the difficulties inherent in the government of an empire spread across such vast distances. In the settlement colonies, like Australia and Canada, Britain moved slowly towards self-government, allowing the white settlers to take charge of executive power themselves and maintaining control of defence only. In Britain's dependent empire, however, a different model was followed. In India, Egypt, Sudan and the rest of Africa, British officials took up the burden of empire in what they claimed was in the best interests of the native populations they ruled over. The Great Rebellion in India was blamed on mistakes in governance by the East India Company and the lesson that many administrators drew from the events of 1857 was that it was the responsibility of administrators to rule fairly and to busy themselves with improving the infrastructure of those colonies with non-white populations, but that at no point in the foreseeable future would these countries be ready for their own self-government. Self-government in the settler colonies was key in cementing the loyalty of these countries to the Empire into the 20th century and through the two world wars. A similar policy in India or Egypt might have prevented the rapid growth of nationalism, which was already apparent in these two countries by 1914.

SOURCE 1

The Devilfish in Egyptian Waters, an American cartoon from 1882 depicting John Bull (England) as the octopus of imperialism grabbing land on every continent.

THE DEVILFISH IN EGYPTIAN WATERS.

3.1

The changing nature and extent of trade

KEY QUESTIONS

- How important was government policy in shaping changes to patterns of trade in the years 1763–1914?

- What was the significance of the evolution of Britain's network of ports, *entrepôts* and trade routes in the years 1763–1914?

INTRODUCTION

Following a decisive victory over France in 1763, the stage seemed set for British military and economic supremacy. However, aggressive trade policy in North America triggered revolt and Britain's European rivals combined during the American War of Independence to successfully challenge the power of the Royal Navy. It was not until 1815 that Britain emerged as the world's superpower, with global dominance of world trade that would not be challenged seriously until the end of the 19th century. Despite the national pride evoked by images of uniformed British soldiers and ever more impressive warships, trade was the lifeblood of the British Empire. Until the industrialisation of emerging powers such as Germany and the USA enabled their businesses to compete commercially with British factories, Britain sat at the centre of a global network of strategic ports and trade routes through which immense wealth flowed into the country and the Exchequer.

HOW IMPORTANT WAS GOVERNMENT POLICY IN SHAPING CHANGES TO PATTERNS OF TRADE IN THE YEARS 1763–1914?

Britain emerged from the Seven Years' War with France victorious but indebted; **government debt** was 157 percent of **gross domestic product (GDP)** in 1763, rising to 260 percent in 1821 as Britain struggled to pay for the American War of Independence, the French Revolutionary Wars and the Napoleonic Wars. Strategies such as repeatedly funding European armies to fight France and maintaining naval squadrons at sea to blockade French ports were effective, but ruinously expensive. The income that Britain generated through trade kept the country solvent throughout this period, but the astronomical cost of maintaining land and sea forces across the globe was a recurring theme behind British economic policy.

KEY TERMS

Government debt
The total amount of money owed by the government expressed as a proportion of GDP, a standard measure of the size of the economy. A higher level of government debt means that the government needs to spend more of its annual income paying the interest on its debt, leaving less for other spending.

Gross domestic product (GDP)
The monetary value of all the services and finished goods produced by a country, usually calculated and expressed over a yearly period.

1763 – Victory over France in Seven Years' War

Britain introduces taxes to raise money from colonies

1779 – Free trade granted to Ireland to prevent civil unrest

1807 – Slave trade is abolished after a 19-year parliamentary campaign

1815 – Victory at Waterloo

Parliament passes Corn Laws to keep grain prices high

1833 – Abolition of slavery in West Indies, compensation paid to slave owners

| 1760 | 1770 | 1780 | 1790 | 1800 | 1810 | 1820 | 1830 |

1775 – American War of Independence begins over 'no taxation without representation'

1805 – Victory at Trafalgar
Royal Navy achieves supremacy at sea

1819 – Founding of Singapore by East India Company shows effectiveness of free trade *entrepôts*

Government policy was initially both **protectionist** and **mercantilist**, designed to obtain advantageous trading relationships with colonies while protecting British producers from competition. These policies stifled trade and alienated colonies; they were a direct cause of the American War of Independence and pushed Ireland towards rebellion. Over time, a policy of **free trade** was adopted, whereby the government aimed to increase the overall volume of trade by reducing taxes on trade, and used diplomacy or coercion to make other countries do the same.

This model was eventually challenged by other European powers seeking increased **geopolitical** influence. Rather than being developed around trading interests, colonies came to be seen as inherently valuable by ideological imperialists in Europe and Britain, leading to a frenzied period of colonisation on the weakest of pretexts, characterised by the **scramble for Africa**. Britain ultimately began to appropriate territory simply to prevent other powers from doing so. In a twist of fate, it was the powers with the smallest colonial empires and infrastructure to maintain that developed fastest during this period, and would eventually overtake Britain in terms of industrial production and military strength: the USA, Germany and Japan.

KEY TERMS

Protectionism
Taxes or prohibitions on imports and exports designed to protect domestic producers. By restricting or prohibiting the sale of foreign goods, governments provide an advantage to their own producers, although the lack of competition can also lead to high prices.

Mercantilism
A policy of government intervention to ensure that the value of exports is more than the value of imports, known as a positive balance of trade. The objective of mercantile systems between the 16th and 18th centuries was to acquire gold or silver bullion through positive balances of trade.

Free trade
An alternative system to mercantilism whereby import and export taxes are minimised to allow merchants to compete across borders. The removal of restrictions favours merchants who can produce the cheapest goods, but risks driving others out of business.

KEY TERMS

Geopolitics
The idea that power derives from territorial dominance of strategic areas. This became increasingly prevalent in imperial thinking, for example the perceived need to control Egypt to safeguard imperial possessions in India.

Scramble for Africa
A period of rapid imperial expansion (1881-1914) during which European powers divided and colonised almost the entire continent of Africa.

This standardisation of trade created in the 19th century suited British merchants perfectly, as they could produce **manufactured goods** that were far cheaper than those of their rivals. By the mid-19th century, British trade dominance extended far beyond Britain's directly managed colonies, into China and South America.

KEY TERM

Manufactured goods
Items that have had value added through some form of processing. Imperial trade often aimed to import raw materials, such as sugar and cotton, from colonies and then export manufactured goods like rum and cloth.

1842 - Victory in First Opium War
Britain forces China to cede Hong Kong and open Shanghai and other ports to Western trade

1849 - Navigation Acts abolished
Free trade supporters dominate parliament

1882 - Britain occupies Egypt to protect interest in Suez Canal

1898 - Britain leases Weihaiwei to counter Russian acquisition of Port Arthur

1840	1850	1860	1870	1880	1890	1900

1846 - Famine in Ireland
Repeal of Corn Laws to lower grain prices splits Conservative Party

1875 - Purchase of Suez Canal shares gives Britain controlling interest in new trade route

1890 - Britain partitions East Africa with Germany, declares Zanzibar a Protectorate

The abolition of the slave trade, 1807

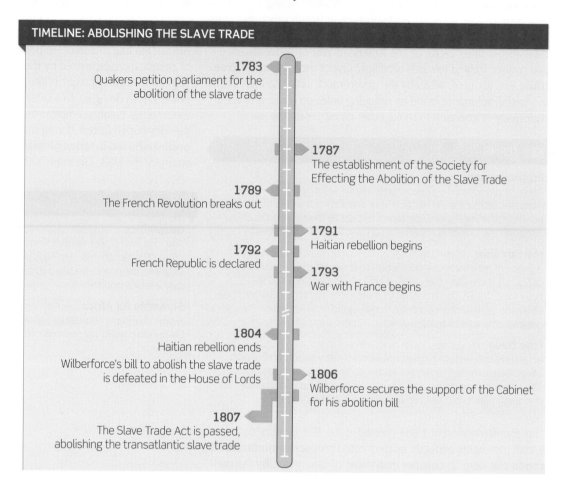

TIMELINE: ABOLISHING THE SLAVE TRADE

1783
Quakers petition parliament for the abolition of the slave trade

1787
The establishment of the Society for Effecting the Abolition of the Slave Trade

1789
The French Revolution breaks out

1791
Haitian rebellion begins

1792
French Republic is declared

1793
War with France begins

1804
Haitian rebellion ends
Wilberforce's bill to abolish the slave trade is defeated in the House of Lords

1806
Wilberforce secures the support of the Cabinet for his abolition bill

1807
The Slave Trade Act is passed, abolishing the transatlantic slave trade

KEY TERMS

Middle Passage
The crossing of the Atlantic between Africa and the West Indies, most frequently used in relation to the slave traders who used this route.

Plantation
A large piece of land where a single crop is cultivated for export and commercial gain, typically using cheap labour.

Triangular trade
A trade route between three regions, the most famous example of which is the slave trade between Europe, West Africa and the Caribbean.

The challenges to abolishing the slave trade

British involvement in the slave trade had begun with the voyages of Elizabethan seafarers in the 16th century, and the fundamental nature of the trade had not significantly changed by the 18th century. Slavers' vessels set sail from English ports and traded goods such as textiles, alcohol and firearms for slaves at West African ports. Using the same winds that carried Columbus, these slaves were then shipped in appalling conditions across the infamous **Middle Passage** to the Americas. Those who survived were mainly destined for the Caribbean, from where they would be resold and shipped to destinations in the West Indies, Spanish America or New England. The slavers then took on a cargo of raw materials such as sugar or cotton, mainly produced on **plantations** by slave labour, and returned to their port of origin.

By the mid-18th century, British ships dominated this **triangular trade**, which was seen as a valuable part of Britain's overseas empire due to the enormous profits to be made. In 1798, the *Lottery* sailed from Liverpool, owned by the millionaire banker Thomas Leyland, three times mayor of Liverpool. It cost £2,307 to outfit the ship and it carried £8,326 of trade goods for Africa. Five months later, its cargo of 453 slaves sold for a total of £22,726 in the West Indies. Excluding any profits made on a return cargo, the *Lottery*'s voyage made a profit of £12,091 – Leyland had doubled his money by selling human lives at an average of £50 per head.

The trade directly enriched not only the slave traders themselves, but the ports they sailed from. Bristol, Liverpool, Glasgow and smaller ports flourished during the slave trade. These cities were full of middlemen: merchants and agents for plantation owners buying and selling ships, trade goods for Africa, supplies for the plantations and sugar imports. The Caribbean island of Nevis, for example, was largely owned by a handful of Bristol families, such as the Pinneys, who also operated a range of business interests in Bristol. By the 1790s, around 120–130 slave ships per year sailed from Liverpool on the triangular trade, the majority of all European ships undertaking slaving voyages.

Much of the capital used by the slave traders to purchase and outfit their ships was provided on credit by English bankers, so by lodging money with these bankers, many of the British gentry were also indirectly investing in and benefiting from the slave trade. The government also benefited through taxes and **tariffs**, using this money to finance the Royal Navy and fight European wars. Additional benefits included creating a large pool of skilled sailors who could be recruited into the Royal Navy during its frequent manpower shortages. In the meantime, conditions on plantations in the Americas were so bad that African men and women were frequently worked to death before they could reproduce, meaning there was never a shortage of demand for new slaves.

This system led to powerful vested interests in Britain that strongly supported the slave trade. *The Gentleman's Magazine* claimed in 1766 that 'upwards of 40' members of parliament were either planters or had business interests in plantations – they could hardly be expected to vote in favour of abolition. William Beckford, twice lord mayor of London, owned thousands of acres in Jamaica and was one of the wealthiest men in Britain. He strengthened his influence by securing parliamentary seats for his two brothers as well. The governor of the Bank of England 1783–85, Sir Richard Neave, also chaired the Society of West Indian Merchants, essentially a pressure group for West Indian planters. Even the Church of England owned the Codrington plantations on Barbados, with some 400 slaves. Given the direct or indirect involvement of so many of the country's ruling class, it is unsurprising that the abolitionist movement in Britain initially made little progress.

The abolition of the slave trade

The **Quakers** organised the first abolitionist movement in Britain, first petitioning parliament in 1783. A major breakthrough was achieved in 1787 when the Quakers joined forces with other non-conformist groups and William Wilberforce was persuaded to lead a parliamentary campaign for abolition. The abolitionists organised an effective **grass-roots campaign**, the first of its kind, to increase pressure on parliament. Abolitionists painstakingly gathered evidence of the horrors of slavery and exposed the public to them via pamphlets, posters, debates and books. Armed with a wealth of evidence and with the support of the prime minister, his close friend William Pitt the Younger, Wilberforce launched the parliamentary campaign in 1789.

KEY TERMS

Tariff
A tax on imports and exports normally charged by customs officers operating at official ports. The purpose of a tariff could either be to generate revenue for the government or to discourage foreign merchants from trading particular goods (a protectionist tariff).

Quaker
A religious minority who translated their Christian faith into progressive political positions, such as the abolition of slavery, opposition to war and charity to the poor.

Grass-roots campaign
A type of political lobbying aimed at winning the support of the public rather than directly influencing politicians. Because so few people could vote at the beginning of the 19th century, this type of campaign was a new phenomenon.

SOURCE

1 A diagram used by abolitionists to demonstrate the conditions of the slave trade, c1750. Some slaves would be sitting, some standing and some lying down.

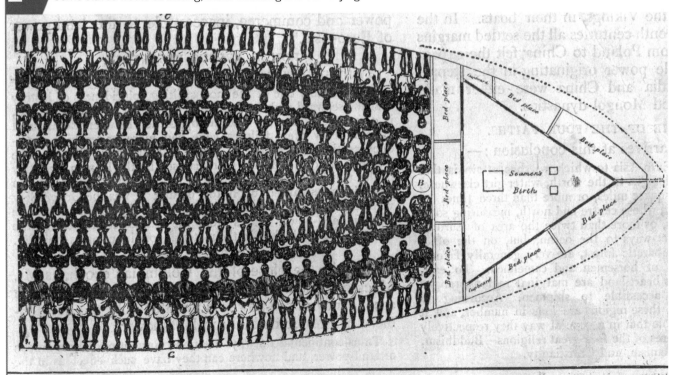

By courtesy of the "Leisure Hour."]

Diagram showing how Slaves were packed.

Events overseas meant that Wilberforce's timing could not have been worse. With the French monarchy driven to bankruptcy by the cost of trying to match British naval power, these economic pressures enhanced an already volatile political environment and France erupted into revolution in 1789, declaring a republic in 1792. This led to renewed hostility with Britain. When a slave rebellion broke out on Saint-Domingue, now Haiti, the French responded by emancipating the slaves, meaning that abolition was now a pro-French position. Britain conspired with the loyalist French plantation owners on Saint-Domingue and invaded the island, hoping to restore the lucrative sugar and coffee slave plantations and seize the colony. In this context, parliament repeatedly voted against Wilberforce's bills.

SOURCE 2

From James Phillips, *Debate on a Motion for the Abolition of the Slave Trade*, published in London 1792. After a lengthy debate, an exhausted Pitt stood before dawn to deliver an impassioned speech in favour of abolition of the slave trade. Despite his eloquence, the motion was defeated by 75 votes. It would be another 15 years before abolition was enacted.

Joining this with all the other considerations, Mr Pitt then pointedly asked, *Can* the decrease of slaves in Jamaica be such – Can the colonies be so destitute of means – so incapable of those improvements which a more prudent management, and a spirit of benevolence must naturally furnish – Can they, at a time when they tell you of new regulations, to the benefit of the Slaves, which, they say, are establishing every day – Can they, under all these circumstances, be permitted to plead that total impossibility of keeping up their number, which they have rested on, as being the only possible pretext for allowing fresh importations from Africa?

... One thing he must touch upon, which was rather a delicate point: the question of emancipating the slaves in the West Indies. A rash emancipation he was clear would be wrong and mischievous: in that unhappy situation to which *our baneful conduct had brought ourselves and them*, it would be no justice on either side to give them liberty. They were as yet incapable of it, but gradually their situation might be mended. They might be relieved from everything harsh and severe, raised from their present degradation, and put under the proper protection of the law: *till then to talk of emancipation was insanity*. But it was the system of fresh importations that interfered with these principles of improvement, and it was the Abolition of the Slave Trade that would furnish the means of effectually regulating the situation of the Slaves in the Islands. This was not a warm idea taken up without due reasoning and reflection, but had its foundation in human nature: Wherever there was the incentive of honour, credit and fair profit, *there* industry would be; and where these labourers should have the natural springs of human actions afforded them, they would then rise to the natural level of human industry; but when degraded into mere machines, they would not even afford you all the benefits of machines, but become more unprofitable, and every way more disadvantageous, than any other instrument of labour whatsoever.

By 1802, the situation had evolved in the abolitionists' favour. British hopes of seizing Saint-Domingue had receded after a huge loss of life due to disease and defeats inflicted by freed slaves. Napoleon had seized power in France and, seeking to restore the revenues from Saint-Domingue, he sent an expedition to restore slavery on the island. The ex-slaves resisted and the British now found themselves supporting them in order to undermine the French. Without changing their position, the abolitionists were now aligned against the French. Public support for their cause revived and, in 1804, Wilberforce successfully passed a bill abolishing the slave trade through the House of Commons, although it was defeated in the House of Lords.

In 1806, the abolitionists capitalised on their anti-French credentials by introducing the Foreign Slave Trade bill, which prohibited any British subjects from supplying slaves to French colonies. Although British ships were already not permitted to trade with French colonies in a time of war, many were doing so by sailing under the American flag. The bill had widespread public support and passed quickly, and the abolitionists carried this momentum into the general election of 1806, where many more abolitionist MPs were elected. Finally, opposition to abolition crumbled and both Houses of Parliament passed the Slave Trade Act by large majorities in 1807, officially ending Britain's role in the slave trade.

The motives for the easy passage of the Act were quite complex, since there was a broad array of influencing factors, of which humanitarianism and anti-French sentiment were only two. Arguably, it was perhaps the changing economic fortunes at the turn of the century that provided the greatest impetus for ending the trade. The dominant lobby of slave traders and plantation owners that had successfully resisted humanitarian pressure for 30 years was weakening by the early 19th century. The economic importance of the slave trade was certainly significant; for example, 40 percent of the income of Bristol's population came from the trade in the 1780s. But losses to foreign privateers during Britain's prolonged wars, together with the threat of disease on tropical voyages and the impact of slave rebellions, created considerable financial uncertainty. One in ten ships during the 18th century would lose its owner profit, and in 1778 merchants in Liverpool lost £700,000. In this context, it was perhaps the worsening economic fortunes of the slave traders that allowed the continued pressure of Wilberforce and the abolitionists to finally gain traction.

Although it had been hoped that slavery would wither away without the trade to sustain it, this did not occur and slavery in the West Indies continued until 1834, when the government emancipated the slaves and effectively bought out the owners of over 700,000 slaves by paying the enormous sum of £20,000,000 in compensation for their 'property', approximately 40 percent of total government expenditure that year.

ACTIVITY
KNOWLEDGE CHECK

The abolition of the slave trade

1 How important was the slave trade to Britain?

2 Why did the movement for abolition become so influential?

3 In your opinion, what was the main reason for abolishing the slave trade in 1807?

THINKING HISTORICALLY   Cause and consequence (7c)

The value of historical explanations

Historical explanations derive from the historian who is investigating the past. Differences in explanations are usually about what the historians think is significant. Historians bring their own attitudes and perspectives to historical questions and see history in the light of these. It is therefore perfectly acceptable to have very different explanations of the same historical phenomenon. The way we judge historical accounts is by looking at how well argued they are and how well evidence had been deployed to support the argument.

Approach A	Approach B	Approach C
Parliament abolished the slave trade because it was morally the right thing to do, even though it was against Britain's commercial interests.	The slave trade was a high-risk investment and was becoming unprofitable, so parliament was reflecting commercial realities in abolishing the trade.	The slave trade was abolished because the French had reintroduced slavery. Parliament wanted to destabilise French colonies and reduce unrest in British ones.

Work in groups of between three and five. (You will need an even number of groups in the class.)

In your groups, devise a brief explanation for the abolition of the slave trade, of between 200 and 300 words, that matches one of the approaches above. Present your explanation to another group who will decide on two things:

1 Which of the approaches is each explanation trying to demonstrate?

2 Considering the structure and the quality of the argument and use of evidence, which is the best of the three explanations?

3 If you choose a 'best' explanation, should you discount the other two? Explain your answer.

The adoption of free trade, 1842–46

Free trade economics

Keen observers, such as aspirant businessmen and commercially minded politicians, had seen how the discovery of huge silver mines in the Americas had allowed the Spanish to finance an empire, but this silver did not remain in Spain; the real beneficiaries were the international merchants, mercenaries and craftsmen who supplied the Spanish with the means of empire. From this observation arose the economic theory of mercantilism, which stated that the secret to prosperity was trade, rather than the possession of gold and silver bullion. Mercantilists argued that wealth was created when a country achieved a **positive balance of trade** by exporting a higher value of goods than were imported. By contrast, countries that had a **negative balance of trade** would be poorer because they would need to spend all their gold and silver to make up the difference. Under this theory, which dominated economic thinking between the 16th and 18th centuries, the aim of government policy should be to obtain positive trade balances wherever possible, and to prevent rival countries from doing the same. The goal was not simply to accumulate vast amounts of treasure, as it was recognised that this would lead to **inflation**. Instead, merchants would use the surplus bullion to invest in more goods overseas, thus becoming even richer.

> **KEY TERMS**
>
> **Positive balance of trade**
> A trade surplus.
>
> **Negative balance of trade**
> A trade deficit.
>
> **Inflation**
> A reduction in value due to oversupply.

SOURCE

3 From Thomas Mun, *England's Treasure by Forraign Trade*, published in 1628. Mun was a director of the East India Company and recognised the importance of a positive balance of trade.

Although a Kingdom may be enriched by gifts received, or by purchase taken from some other Nations, yet these are things uncertain and of small consideration when they happen. The ordinary means therefore to increase our wealth and treasure is by Forraign Trade, wherein wee must ever observe this rule; to sell more to strangers yearly than wee consume of theirs in value. For suppose that when this Kingdom is plentifully served with the Cloth, Lead, Tin, Iron, Fish and other native commodities, we doe yearly export the overplus to forraign Countreys to the value of twenty-two hundred thousand pounds; by which means we are enabled beyond the Seas to buy and bring in forraign wares for our use and Consumptions, to the value of twenty hundred thousand pounds: By this order duly kept in our trading, we may rest assured that the kingdom shall be enriched yearly two hundred thousand pounds, which must be brought to us in so much Treasure; because that part of our stock which is not returned to us in wares must necessarily be brought home in treasure...

... Behold then the true form and worth of forraign trade, which is *The great Revenue of the King, The honour of the Kingdom, The Noble profession of the Merchant, The School of our Arts, The supply of our wants, The employment of our poor, The improvement of our Lands, The Nurcery of our Mariners, The walls of the Kingdoms, The means of our Treasure, The Sinnews of our wars, The terror of our Enemies.* For all which great and weighty reasons, do so many well-governed States highly countenance the profession, and carefully cherish the action, not only with Policy to encrease it, but also with power to protect it from all forraign injuries; because they know it is a Principal in Reason of State to maintain and defend that which doth Support them and their estates.

Leading economic thinkers had begun to question the principles of mercantilism and, in 1776, Adam Smith published *An Inquiry into the Nature and Causes of the Wealth of Nations,* one of the most influential books of all time. In his book, Smith attacked the most fundamental assumptions of the mercantile system. Smith argued that import and export tariffs prevented trade from operating effectively by constraining merchants from finding the best deals. He felt that removing barriers to trade would increase overall wealth, proposing that both parties in a trade benefited, rather than the 'win or lose' position under mercantile theory. Smith published the *Wealth of Nations* the year after the American colonies had resorted to open warfare against Britain over the impact of mercantile policy, although it was still not clear that the colonies had been lost for good.

The adoption of free trade

Despite the popularity of Adam Smith's book, the adoption of free trade as the default government policy was a slow process. Many of the tariffs in place were designed to give British goods, especially agricultural goods, a commercial advantage. Parliament continued to be dominated by wealthy landowners, who often had a direct interest in supporting these measures to protect the incomes from their estates.

SOURCE

4 From Adam Smith, *An Inquiry into the Nature and Causes of the Wealth of Nations*, published in 1776. Smith's radical attack on mercantilism in favour of free trade became highly influential soon after its publication, and by the mid-19th century had become the major economic theory influencing government policy.

That it was the spirit of monopoly which originally both invented and propagated this doctrine [mercantilism], cannot be doubted; and they who first taught it were by no means such fools as they who believed it. In every country it always is and must be the interest of the great body of the people to buy whatever they want of those who sell it cheapest. The proposition is so very manifest, that it seems ridiculous to take any pains to prove it; nor could it ever have been called in question, had not the interested sophistry of merchants and manufacturers confounded the common sense of mankind. Their interest is, in this respect, directly opposite to that of the great body of the people. As it is the interest of the freemen of a corporation to hinder the rest of the inhabitants from employing any workmen but themselves, so it is the interest of the merchants and manufacturers of every country to secure to themselves the monopoly of the home market. Hence in Great Britain, and in most other European countries, the extraordinary duties upon almost all goods imported by alien merchants. Hence the high duties and prohibitions upon all those foreign manufactures which can come into competition with our own. Hence too the extraordinary restraints upon the importation of almost all sorts of goods from those countries with which the balance of trade is supposed to be disadvantageous; that is, from those against whom national animosity happens to be most violently inflamed.

The wealth of a neighbouring nation, however, though dangerous in war and politics, is certainly advantageous in trade. In a state of hostility it may enable our enemies to maintain fleets and armies superior to our own; but in a state of peace and commerce it must likewise enable them to exchange with us to a greater value, and to afford a better market, either for the immediate produce of our own industry, or for whatever is purchased with that produce.

Britain's trade policy had triggered revolution in the Americas, but it also caused the government problems closer to home. Restrictions on the trade of Britain's first colony, Ireland, were nothing new. The mainly agricultural commodities produced by Ireland were similar to those of England, and English landowners had used their influence in parliament from the 17th century to create tariffs and prohibitions to reduce Irish competition.

Despite these restrictions, the Irish economy continued to grow. The combination of large estates, excellent grazing land and cheap labour made Irish agriculture competitive, and Ireland typically profited from the many British wars of the 18th century by selling supplies to the Royal Navy and armies campaigning in Europe or America. After London, Dublin was the second largest and most prosperous city in the British Empire in 1750. In that year, the value of exports from Ireland was £1.9m and imports £1.5m. By 1790, exports reached £4.9m and imports £3.8m, indicating that the Irish economy was growing steadily with a positive balance of trade.

Growth did not prevent trade policy from becoming a major political issue, however. Ireland's wealth was concentrated in a relatively small number of mainly Anglo-Irish Protestant landowners. The Irish Catholic peasants who worked the land remained poor, and the growing middle classes were frustrated by the restrictions on Irish trade. Influenced by calls for 'no taxation without representation' from across the Atlantic, Irish demands for free trade escalated. With Ireland stripped of regular troops to fight in America, societies of armed volunteers were formed to protect the country from a possible French invasion. These large groups of armed men were not controlled by the government and developed a political role, with the lack of free trade normally blamed for any economic difficulties. In 1778, the volunteers protested in Dublin with a cannon, on which was hung a sign reading 'free trade or this!'

In 1779, the government consulted Adam Smith on how to respond to Irish demands for free trade. Smith was sympathetic, pointing out that to protect 'a very slender interest of our own manufacturers' the Irish were unable to export glass or silk anywhere, raw wool anywhere except Britain and woollen cloth anywhere except a few designated British ports. Smith called these restrictions 'unjust and oppressive', and recommended that Ireland should be allowed to trade freely. The government removed trade restrictions on Ireland in 1779.

Granting Ireland free trade was seen as a necessity to avoid conflict, and did not result in a collapse of prices for agricultural goods due to the massive demand for these generated by wars with revolutionary and Napoleonic France. This was a major victory for proponents of free trade, but further change was slow in coming. When war with France ended in 1815, the strength of protectionist interests in parliament can be seen in the passage of the Corn Laws, designed to keep grain prices high by excluding foreign grain from British markets. Wealthy landowners in parliament were typically opposed to any moves towards free trade because lower prices would reduce the profits from their estates. This meant that although successive **Tory** prime ministers, including Pitt, Canning, Liverpool and Huskisson, favoured tariff reductions, they made little progress in achieving this.

The political landscape only changed after the election of the **Whigs** in 1830 on a platform of parliamentary reform and the subsequent passage of the Representation of the People Act 1832. This legislation was a milestone in British politics, as it made constituency boundaries more representative and extended the electorate by around 250,000 people, an increase of 60 percent. After 1832, manufacturers and consumers would have a much larger role in determining trade policy. These groups were typically opposed to protectionist measures, which kept prices high in England, and associated mercantile policies that artificially generated positive trade balances. In 1838, the Anti-Corn Law League was founded by proponents of free trade, and developed into a powerful lobby by holding mass meetings attended by thousands of men where protectionist policies were decried.

KEY TERMS

Tories
A parliamentary grouping of supporting traditional social values. The Tories were not a political party in the modern sense, but a set of individuals characterised by their support of the monarchy and a traditional way of life, and their opposition to enlightenment ideas and French influence. The Tories held power from 1783 to 1830.

Whigs
A parliamentary grouping representing more progressive policies, such as electoral reform, free trade and the abolition of slavery. The Whigs were initially dominated by wealthy landowners influenced by enlightenment ideals, but over time attracted manufacturers and middle-class support.

This changing political landscape was exemplified by Sir Robert Peel, the son of a textile manufacturer. Peel was a strong believer in free trade, and founded the Conservative Party in 1834 in line with these values. Peel's Conservatives comprised an uneasy coalition of 'Old Tories', who were opposed to free trade, and 'Peelites', who supported it. In opposition, Peel managed to keep these factions united and made significant in-roads on the Whig majority in parliament in the 1835 and 1837 elections. In the 1841 election, the Conservatives secured a majority and Peel became prime minister. Under Peel's leadership, supported by progressive Whigs and Liberals if not all of his own party, laws supporting mercantilism and protectionism were definitively dismantled. Over 1,200 import tariffs were abolished between the years 1842–46.

ACTIVITY
KNOWLEDGE CHECK

Free trade
Using the material you have read and your own knowledge, write a 200-word explanation of why free trade was adopted. This explanation should include a brief definition of what free trade actually means.

The repeal of the Navigation Acts 1849
The Navigation Acts
Under mercantilism, colonies were seen as dependent trading partners, intended to support a negative balance of trade so that the colonising country could achieve a positive balance of trade. Mercantilism went hand-in-hand with protectionism, whereby governments used taxes, tariffs, quotas and prohibitions to discourage foreign involvement in trade, and to encourage their own merchants to trade only with their colonies. In Britain, the most important expressions of mercantilism were the Navigation Acts, passed between 1651 and 1673 to protect British interests and govern trade. These laws were the basis of the mercantilist economic relationship between Britain and its colonies, and reflected a belief that colonies existed to supply the mother country with raw materials and to provide employment for its shipping fleet. The Navigation Acts meant that:

- colonial goods produced for export could only be carried on English-built and owned ships

- certain goods (including sugar, cotton, indigo, dyewoods, ginger and tobacco) had to be shipped to an English port even if they were to be exported to another European destination

- European imports to British colonies also needed to land at an English port and then be reshipped onwards.

These laws can be interpreted as preventing the development of more sophisticated colonial economies. In practice, they were not too onerous for colonies in the Americas, partly due to the fact that these largely produced raw materials anyway and therefore the mercantilist system suited their economic model. More important to the smooth pattern of relations between Britain and its colonies was the soft-touch approach Britain took towards enforcement of the mercantilist system. **Salutary neglect** meant that Britain tended not to enforce the trade regulations too tightly and smuggling was rife, especially in the Americas. Typically, customs officials were British and were based in Britain. They deputised the collection of taxes to local deputies who did not enforce collection and turned a blind eye to smuggling.

KEY TERM

Salutary neglect
The 'light-touch' approach by the British to American government and tax collection until the 1760s. Under this system, the Navigation Acts were not too strictly enforced and the local management and setting of local taxes rested in the hands of governors and local assemblies.

This soft-touch approach to the collection of duties changed in 1763, when the British government decided to create a large standing army in North America, to deter France from further conflict there. Given that the government was already heavily indebted due to the costs of the Seven Years' War, a series of laws were passed to generate enough revenue to pay for this army. The government's stated aim was to make the North American colonies pay for their own protection. In addition, the overwhelming force of the Royal Navy was used to strictly enforce the Navigation Acts, which they did far more effectively than customs officials. The Royal Navy began to seize ships and their cargos, often impressing their crews to serve on naval ships. This policy was anathema to the merchants of New England who depended heavily on trade in the Caribbean and now found previously profitable trade routes either closed or highly disadvantageous to their business. Although the government scaled back some of the most extreme measures, the policy of extracting revenue from North American trade remained and was a major cause of the American War of Independence in 1775.

SOURCE 5

Reasons against the Renewal of the Sugar Act, a pamphlet written by Massachusetts' merchants in 1764 to explain their opposition to the government's protectionist tariffs. American colonists were not represented in parliament, and when pamphlets and lobbying such as this had no impact on government policy, they rallied around a position of 'No taxation without representation'.

As the act, commonly called the sugar act, has been passed upwards of thirty years, without any benefit to the crown, the duties arising from it having never been appropriated by parliament to any particular use; and as this act will soon expire, the following considerations are offered as reasons why it should not be renewed.

First, it is apprehended that the trade is so far from being able to bear the high duty imposed by this act, on sugar and molasses, that it will not bear any duty at all. As the price of molasses now is, it will barely answer to distill it into rum for exportation: Should this duty be added, it would have the effect of an absolute prohibition on the importation of molasses and sugar from the foreign islands, and consequently the same effect on the exportation of fish, lumber and other commodities from hence to those islands, as the French, Dutch and other foreigners, whom we supply with those articles, will not permit us to bring away their money; so that unless we can take their ordinary sugars and molasses in return, this trade will be lost.

Repealing of the Navigation Acts 1849

Peel was well-versed in economic theory and was a committed free trader. After becoming prime minister in 1841, he put many of his ideas into practice in his landmark budget of 1842. This included the abolition of hundreds of protectionist tariffs, compensating for the lost income through the reintroduction of income tax. Two major protectionist laws remained however: the sugar duties and the Corn Laws.

The sugar duties, which ensured preferential rates for sugar producers in the British West Indies, were seen as essential for plantation owners in these colonies, because after the abolition of slave ownership in 1833 they were uncompetitive compared to slave colonies like Cuba and Brazil. The Corn Laws, despite intense lobbying by the Anti-Corn Law League, had acquired symbolic importance for many landowners.

Peel finally abolished these tariffs in 1846. From 1845 onwards the potato crop failed in Ireland, causing severe food shortages, and Peel argued that the solution was to repeal the Corn Laws in order to lower grain prices. Although this was deeply unpopular with most of his own party, he pushed the Importation Act 1846 through parliament with Whig support, simultaneously abolishing the sugar duties and the Corn Laws. This was seen as a great betrayal of both the West Indian plantation owners and the landowners in the Conservative Party. The party split and Peel was forced to resign.

EXTEND YOUR KNOWLEDGE

Disputed laws of the 1760s

The residence of customs officials in America after 1763
From 1763, customs officials were obliged to live in America. Previously, British men had held the position (and benefited from some of the income) while living in Britain and delegating their duties to poorly paid local deputies, who had little or no interest in the efficient collection of duties. Americans were fearful that this would introduce a class of 'placemen' who were loyal to their paymasters in London and would result in an extension of unjust power by the executive. Likewise, trials of smugglers were not to be held in local colonial courts (whose jurors were very lenient to smugglers) but by a naval court in Halifax, Nova Scotia, and cases were to be held under judges alone rather than by jury trial. This appeared to be an extension of military power over civilians and an attack on the principle of trial by jury.

The Sugar Act 1764
George Grenville, prime minister during 1763–65, next passed the Sugar Act in 1764. The Sugar Act 1733 had set a duty of 6d per gallon on molasses and sugar imported from non-British Caribbean colonies and had yielded only £21,652 in over 30 years. The new Sugar Act actually lowered the duty set on sugar from 6d to 3d, but the expectation was that this would now be collected rather than avoided. As approximately 1d of duty was being paid on every gallon imported, this represented an actual rise of 2d. British officials estimated that the new rate, properly enforced, would raise £78,000 annually. Nine colonial assemblies sent messages to London arguing that London had abused its power by raising the tax. They accepted the British parliament's right to regulate trade, but not its right to tax and raise revenue in America. The tax was resented by the merchants and affected the cost of alcohol, but its impact was limited to a small group of people and its collection was relatively successful.

The Mutiny Act 1765
The Mutiny (or Quartering) Act 1765 required colonial assemblies to make provision for providing accommodation and supplying British troops stationed in each colony. Most colonies accepted this grudgingly (they saw no need for the quantity of troops that the British deemed necessary), but the New York Assembly refused because the headquarters of the army was based in New York and their burden was greater than that of other colonies. The British responded by passing the New York Restraining Act in 1767, which prevented the New York Assembly from taking any legislative action until they complied with the Quartering Act.

The Stamp Act 1765
The introduction of the Stamp Act in 1765 had been announced a full year beforehand, giving the Americans ample time to build themselves up into a fury. This Act required stamps to be fixed on almost all formal documents and was a much broader tax. It was widely and vigorously opposed by the colonial assemblies who now petitioned London for repeal and passed resolutions condemning the Act and denying parliament's right to pass such a law. An inter-colonial congress with deputies from nine colonies (the first such assembly) met and condemned the Act. Leaders of the protests, such as Sam Adams, did not confine themselves to petitions and protests but the Sons of Liberty organised mob activity in Boston. There was also formal and informal boycotting of British goods. In 1766, the Stamp Act was repealed. However British resolve was hardening and the repeal of the Stamp Act was accompanied with the Declaratory Act, which stated that 'the colonies were subordinate to the Crown and parliament of Great Britain' and that the British parliament had full authority to make laws for the Americans 'in all cases whatsoever'.

The abolition of the sugar duties led to economic decline in the West Indies as plantation owners lost business to slave-grown foreign sugar. Ultimately, the repeal of the Corn Laws did not improve the situation for the poor of Ireland, who by 1846 had no money to buy grain at any price; over one million people died in Ireland between 1845 and 1852 and another million were forced to emigrate.

After Peel's resignation, the Whig prime minister Lord Russell continued to expand the government's free trade policy. With the support of Peelite Conservatives, the Whigs could command a majority in parliament on free trade issues for the first time, which enabled them to dismantle virtually all remaining tariffs.

The dominance of the free-trade movement can be shown in the repeal of the Navigation Acts, which had been the basis of Britain's defence policy for the last 200 years. In addition to embedding mercantilist economic policy, a major aim of the Navigation Acts was to increase the number of British ships, on the basis that this would provide a larger pool of manpower for the navy to draw on in time of war. By dismantling the Acts, Russell and his supporters were effectively prioritising free trade over national defence. Even Adam Smith had supported the Navigation Acts because he felt that the needs of the navy should come before the needs of merchants. By 1849, however, free trade dominated government thinking to the point where these concerns could be overruled.

SOURCE

From Adam Smith's *An Inquiry into the Nature and Causes of the Wealth of Nations*, published in 1776. Smith supported the Navigation Acts on grounds of national security.

There seem, however, to be two cases in which it will generally be advantageous to lay some burden upon foreign for the encouragement of domestic industry.

The first is, when some particular sort of industry is necessary for the defence of the country. The defence of Great Britain, for example, depends very much upon the number of its sailors and shipping. The act of navigation, therefore, very properly endeavours to give the sailors and shipping of Great Britain the monopoly of the trade of their own country in some cases by absolute prohibitions and in others by heavy burdens upon the shipping of foreign countries... As defence, however, is of much more importance than opulence, the act of navigation is, perhaps, the wisest of all the commercial regulations of England.

The Navigation Acts were duly repealed by the Whig government, supported by the Peelites but opposed by the 'old Tory' remainder of the Conservative Party.

SOURCE

From a speech made by William Gladstone in the House of Commons on 12 March 1849. Gladstone would be a hugely influential figure in late 19th-century politics. This shows how the debates on free trade in the 1840s would set a new economic orthodoxy for the rest of the century.

Sir, I shall not dwell upon the argument (admitted, I think, on all hands), that if the question of the navigation laws is to be dealt with at all by Parliament, it ought to be done at this moment, rather than at any future period. We never can again give so vast a stimulus to the import trade as was recently given by the great and fundamental alterations that took place in our customs laws. With respect to the most bulky articles of freight, and therefore those that give most employment to the shipping, if I had no other fact to stand upon than this—that lately you took the duty off corn, that you greatly reduced the duties on sugar, that you removed the cotton, the wool, the hides, the oils, the silk, and the hemp duties, and in fact the duties upon every bulky commodity of import—I say, and I appeal to the House to acknowledge the justice of what I say, that this, and no other than this, is the period at which we ought to consider whether the navigation law itself ought to be maintained, and if it should, upon what basis it ought to be founded. There is another consideration, the menaces—if they can be called the menaces—of foreign Powers, and the excitement beginning to prevail in many of our colonies upon this question, all of which I regard as enhancing the force of the argument that now is the proper time for dealing with these laws. But even independently of these considerations, upon commercial grounds alone, I am quite sure that this is the season when our duty binds us to approach and definitively settle the whole question. Well, then, if a change is to be made, and now to be made, I come next to the manner in which such change ought to be carried into effect. And here I differ not materially from many of those who have thus far accompanied me in what I have already stated. And at the same time I freely admit that I differ from them without the least substantial hope of conciliating those who are friendly to the existing laws; because my doctrine is, that we should walk in the path of experience—that we should continue to apply more extensively the principles that we have already applied—that, adhering to those rules of action which Mr. Huskisson and others adopted, we may safely part with the navigation laws under the conditions, and in the manner, in which they indicated their readiness, if not altogether to abolish, at least to relax them.

A Level Exam-Style Question Section C

How far can the repeal of the Navigation Acts in 1849 be regarded as a key turning point in the changing patterns of trade in the years 1763–1914? (20 marks)

Tip

When answering this question, you should compare the nature of trade before and after 1849. Did it substantially change and, if so, was this down solely to the repeal of the Acts?

Mercantilism

1 Explain the intended benefits of mercantilism.

2 What were the failures of mercantilism in the Americas?

3 Why did it take so long for free-trade policies to be adopted by parliament?

WHAT WAS THE SIGNIFICANCE OF THE EVOLUTION OF BRITAIN'S NETWORK OF PORTS, *ENTREPÔTS* AND TRADE ROUTES IN THE YEARS 1763–1914?

TIMELINE: GROWING BRITISH TRADE ROUTES

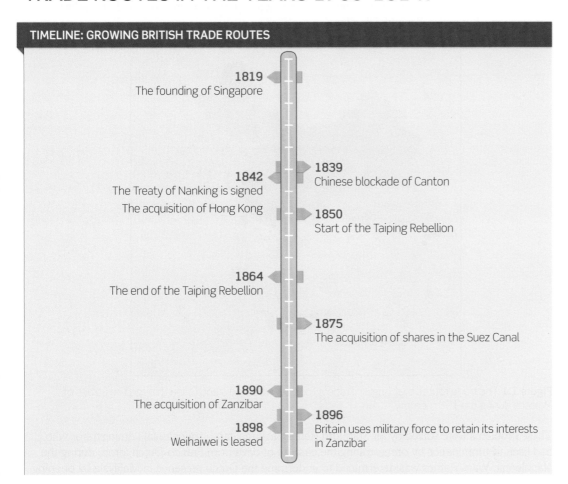

1819
The founding of Singapore

1839
Chinese blockade of Canton

1842
The Treaty of Nanking is signed
The acquisition of Hong Kong

1850
Start of the Taiping Rebellion

1864
The end of the Taiping Rebellion

1875
The acquisition of shares in the Suez Canal

1890
The acquisition of Zanzibar

1896
Britain uses military force to retain its interests in Zanzibar

1898
Weihaiwei is leased

In the 19th century, the infrastructure of trade was continuously evolving, and the impact of changes during this period can be seen in the location and nature of Britain's colonial acquisitions. The government had paid a high price for trying to enforce colonial rule on the North American colonies, and was initially reluctant to engage in further territorial expansion. At first, British merchants led the way, motivated by profit rather than conquest. An imperial ideology based on free trade and naval supremacy was emerging however, and by the 1840s the government was willing to dispatch warships and acquire naval bases in the Far East to protect its merchants. By the late 19th century, the government was increasingly driven by the need to protect its valuable possessions, even at the cost of colonising parts of the world that had little to offer commercially.

KEY TERM

East India Company
A private trading company that had exclusive rights to trade with India after receiving a royal charter from Elizabeth I.

The acquisition of Singapore, 1819

By the 1800s, the trade routes on which Britain relied were becoming increasingly extended. The **East India Company** was seeking to expand its trade with China. The company had lost its monopoly in India under the Charter Act 1813, but retained a monopoly on trade with China until 1833, which it was keen to exploit. There was a good and growing market in England for a range of Chinese goods such as tea, silk and porcelain.

However, conditions for trade in China were less than ideal. Foreign trade was heavily regulated by the Chinese authorities. Europeans were not permitted to leave their trading base at Canton, were only licensed to deal with a guild of merchants known as the 'Hongs' and were heavily taxed by the local governor. In addition, the only way to reach Canton from the East India Company's base in Calcutta was to pass through the Straits of Malacca. This area had already been colonised by the Dutch, who had established a monopoly over the spices that the region exported. Operating under a protectionist policy, the Dutch either refused British ships entry to their ports or charged high tariffs for the privilege. The straits were also known for piracy, so the trade route to China from India was not only long, but expensive and dangerous.

Figure 1.1 The trade routes that English traders took between India and China through the Straits of Malacca during the 19th century.

These problems were solved by Sir Stamford Raffles, a Jamaican-born colonial administrator who had risen to prominence by orchestrating the capture of Java from Franco-Dutch forces during the Napoleonic Wars. Raffles was determined to undermine the Dutch presence in Malaysia by opening up the trade route to China, and obtained permission from his superiors in the East India Company to seek a British base in the region. Having located the sparsely inhabited port of Singapore in 1819, he arranged a treaty with the local rulers and established a trading post there. The legal grounds for this were shaky; the British parliament and the government were initially unaware of the new settlement, the extent to which the local rulers had ceded sovereignty was unclear under the treaty, and the Dutch were angered by the encroachment on territory they regarded as theirs.

The settlement was added to the issues being negotiated in an Anglo-Dutch treaty to agree territorial rights in the area, and the Dutch were initially adamant that the British withdraw from Singapore. The future of British Singapore was only secured by its rapid growth. In its founding year of 1819, trade worth 400,000 Spanish dollars passed through Singapore. By the time the Anglo-Dutch treaty was finalised in 1824, this volume had increased over 2,700 percent to 11 million Spanish dollars, surpassing the settlement of Penang that was founded 30 years earlier. This was noted by government negotiators, who refused to relinquish Singapore and instead gave up Bencoolen and Sumatra to the Dutch.

The growth of Singapore

The secret to Singapore's explosive growth was its status as an *entrepôt*, where ships of all nationalities could dock without incurring taxes or tariffs. This was a deliberate choice by Raffles, who had intended to create a staging post for the India–China trade route. The tax-free status of Singapore quickly drew merchants from the Malay Archipelago and further afield, and goods from all over South-East Asia flooded into the city. A key aspect of Singapore's growth was that individual ships no longer needed to complete the whole journey to the destination port of their goods. Ships with goods from China destined for Britain could offload these at Singapore in exchange for textiles, guns and opium. Ships bound for Europe could take on the Chinese goods without needing to visit China, as well as acquiring spices from the Malay Archipelago without visiting expensive Dutch ports. This trade led to the creation of merchant houses with their own docks for loading and unloading cargo, and warehouses for storing it. By 1846, the city boasted 20 British merchant houses, with others owned by European countries. Multiple Jewish, Chinese and Arab merchant houses also flourished. As the city continued to grow rapidly, the merchants were supported by a network of chandlers, banks and auction houses.

Singapore's status as an *entrepôt* was not exactly unprecedented. Amsterdam and Antwerp had grown into global commerce hubs in the 16th and 17th centuries using a similar model. Even within the British Empire, the ports of the West Indies were often only clearing houses for slaves to be shipped to Spanish colonies or where North American goods could be loaded onto slave ships for their return journey to ports like Bristol or Liverpool. However, the explosive growth of the colony, due to its strategic location on some of the world's most valuable trade routes, signalled a new era in imperial trade. The commercial growth of Singapore rapidly outpaced established Dutch and English colonies in the region that imposed taxes and tariffs on shipping. The success of the city demonstrated to young, ambitious and thoughtful British politicians like Robert Peel the possibilities of an empire run on free trade.

EXTEND YOUR KNOWLEDGE

Informal empire in South America

By destroying the Spanish navy along with the French at the Battle of Trafalgar in 1805, Britain effectively isolated Spanish South America from Spain. It seemed like a golden opportunity to seize strategic colonies on the Rio de la Plata, an immense navigable river that allowed ships to sail and trade deep into the interior the South American continent. The British occupied Buenos Aires twice, but on both occasions the Spanish colonists rallied and the British were bloodily ejected.

With Spain itself a key battleground in the Napoleonic Wars and the Royal Navy unchallenged in the Atlantic, the Spanish Empire in South America imploded, with a number of civil wars between loyalists and separatists during which the separatists eventually prevailed. Many of the new countries emerging from these wars, and especially Argentina, became valuable trading partners for Britain. In exchange for British textiles and manufactured goods, Argentina provided cheap salt meat, wool and cow hides from its almost limitless expanses of good grazing land. In the context of this emerging trade, Britain occupied the Falkland Islands to ensure a naval presence in the South Atlantic. The islands were in a strategic location for supplying and refitting whalers, sealers and ships sailing around Cape Horn, although their importance diminished with the opening of the Panama Canal and the age of reliable steam travel.

With Argentina and other South American economies heavily dependent on British trade, Britain had achieved what is often known as an 'informal empire' in this region. Britain was highly influential in determining foreign and trade policy in these countries, but did not intervene in domestic politics. This model appealed to the government because there were none of the administrative costs or political risks that frequently arose with directly managed colonies. The success of trade with South America and the growth of the international *entrepôt* at Singapore showed that it was not necessary to rule a territory in order to profit from it.

The acquisition of Hong Kong, 1842

The establishment of Singapore as a free-trade city had proved to be a winning formula, but did not resolve all of the issues with the India–China trade. Strict enforcement of Chinese trade laws meant that British merchants remained confined to a small area at Canton, and could not travel up China's large river network to negotiate directly with producers. Ambassadors had been sent to the Chinese court in 1792 and 1816 in an attempt to negotiate better terms for British merchants, but these had returned empty-handed. In addition, pirates sailing from the Philippines and North Borneo continued to plague the seas between Singapore and Canton. Up to 100 small but heavily armed pirate vessels operated on this stage of the trade route, capable of attacking large European sailing ships. The few ships provided by the East India Company to patrol the route were often less well armed and inadequate to the task.

SOURCE

8 An engraving by G.W. Terry c1841 of the East India steamer *Nemesis* and other boats destroying Chinese war junks in Anson's Bay, 7 January 1841.

This was concerning to the East India Company because trade with China had become integral to their operations and profits. In the 18th century, British wool and Indian cotton had been traded at modest returns for tea, porcelain and silk, but Chinese demand for these textiles was limited and did not match the ever-growing British market for Chinese goods. The East India Company found itself with a negative balance of trade, forced to use silver bullion to purchase goods in China. Their solution was to switch to opium, which could be grown cheaply in India. The addictive properties of opium were well known and, although the drug had been made illegal in China by imperial edict as early as 1729, Chinese coastal merchants were willing to smuggle opium to supply a growing number of Chinese opium users.

With the East India Company improving its opium supplies in India, dealing directly with producers rather than Indian middlemen from 1797, and Singapore opening for business in 1819, the opium trade accelerated. Despite an imperial ban, China imported 75 tons of opium in 1775, 200 tons in 1800 and 347 tons in 1822 – all through small coastal traders who were able to smuggle in the banned good without much difficulty – and usually with the connivance of corrupt local officials. Other British merchants were initially prohibited from entering the trade by the East India Company's **monopoly**, but when this expired in 1833 the market expanded dramatically. By 1839, Chinese opium imports reached 2,553 tons, and it is estimated that between four and 12 million Chinese men and women were regular users by the mid-19th century. The balance of trade was reversed and silver bullion flooded out of China.

The Chinese blockade, 1839

In 1839, the Chinese government acted decisively to address the problem. Chinese troops blockaded the settlement at Canton, effectively holding the merchants there hostage, and demanded that they surrender their goods. Ships waiting in international waters for Chinese coastal smugglers to offload their opium were boarded and searched. Over 1,000 tons of opium were burned. When news of the crackdown reached Britain, the government acted equally decisively, dispatching an expedition to China with an ultimatum without waiting to discuss the matter in parliament.

SOURCE
9

From H.B. Morse *International Relations of the Chinese Empire*, published in 1910. Palmerston's ultimatum to the emperor of China, 20 February 1840. Palmerston went to war for the right of British merchants to sell opium.

The British Government demands security for the future, that British Subjects resorting to China for purposes of trade, in conformity with the long-established understanding between the two Governments; shall not again be exposed to violence and injustice while engaged in their lawful pursuits of Commerce. For this purpose, and in order that British Merchants trading to China may not be subject to the arbitrary caprice either of the Government at Peking, or its local Authorities at the Sea-Ports of the Empire, the British Government demands that one or more sufficiently large and properly situated Islands on the Coast of China, to be fixed upon by the British Plenipotentiaries, shall be permanently given up to the British Government as a place of residence and of commerce for British Subjects; where their persons may be safe from molestation, and where their Property may be secure.

... The British Government therefore has determined at once to send out a Naval and Military Force to the Coast of China to act in support of these demands, and in order to convince the imperial Government that the British Government attaches the utmost importance to this matter, and that the affair is one which will not admit of delay.

And further, for the purpose of impressing still more strongly upon the Government of Peking the importance which the British Government attaches to this matter, and the urgent necessity which exists for an immediate as well as a satisfactory settlement thereof, the Commander of the Expedition has received orders that, immediately upon his arrival upon the Chinese Coast, he shall proceed to blockade the principal Chinese ports, that he shall intercept and detain and hold in deposit all Chinese Vessels which he may meet with, and that he shall take possession of some convenient part of the Chinese territory, to be held and occupied by the British Forces until everything shall be concluded and executed to the satisfaction of the British Government.

... The Undersigned has further to state, that the necessity for sending this Expedition to the Coast of China having been occasioned by the violent and unjustifiable acts of the Chinese Authorities, the British Government expects and demands that the expenses incurred thereby shall be repaid to Great Britain by the Government of China.

The decision to defend the opium traders by force was taken by Lord Palmerston, the foreign secretary. A wealthy aristocrat with large estates in Ireland, Palmerston was a believer in both Britain's imperial destiny and free trade. As foreign secretary for a total of 15 years under successive governments between the years 1830 and 1851, and then prime minister 1855–58 and 1859–65, he was one of the greatest influences on Britain's foreign policy during the 19th century. He was known for his willingness to use the might of the Royal Navy to settle disputes with other powers, which came to be known as '**gunboat diplomacy**'. The war with China that came to be known as the First Opium War was no exception.

The British Naval squadron, including the first British ocean-going steam-powered warship *Nemesis,* easily defeated the antiquated Chinese ships that opposed them, relieving Canton and putting themselves in a position to dictate terms to the Chinese emperor. In accordance with Palmerston's instructions to occupy a 'convenient part of the Chinese territory', the navy seized the island of Hong Kong in 1841, sparsely populated but blessed with one of the best deep-water harbours in the world.

Hong Kong was at first little more than a staging post for the Royal Navy, but was established as an *entrepôt* along similar lines as Singapore. The establishment of Hong Kong coincided with the Chinese government being forced to open new ports to foreign trade in addition to Canton. Hong Kong provided an ideal and secure location for large ocean-going vessels to offload their cargo without paying import tariffs. The goods could then be transferred to coastal and river traders for distribution to these ports. From around 15,000 in 1841, the population of Hong Kong grew to almost 300,000 in 1900. As the city grew, the British government pressured the Chinese government to allow the expansion of the settlement into Kowloon and then the New Territories through successive treaties.

KEY TERM

Gunboat diplomacy
A means of conducting foreign policy by deliberately displaying naval power as a means of intimidation.

The opening up of Shanghai to trade, 1842

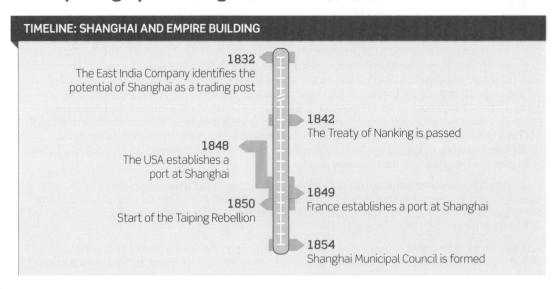

TIMELINE: SHANGHAI AND EMPIRE BUILDING

1832 The East India Company identifies the potential of Shanghai as a trading post

1842 The Treaty of Nanking is passed

1848 The USA establishes a port at Shanghai

1849 France establishes a port at Shanghai

1850 Start of the Taiping Rebellion

1854 Shanghai Municipal Council is formed

The Treaty of Nanking was signed in 1842, and was known by the Chinese as the first of the **'unequal treaties'** due to Britain's overwhelming display of naval strength. In the treaty, the Chinese government agreed to:

- pay 6 million silver dollars in compensation for the destroyed opium, 3 million in debts to British merchants in Canton, and 12 million in reparations to cover the cost of the war. The fine was to be paid within three years with interest of 5 percent annually applied to any late payments.

- cede the island of Hong Kong to the British in perpetuity.

- open the ports of Amoy, Foochow, Ningpo and Shanghai to foreign traders, in addition to lifting the restrictions in place at Canton. Import tariffs at these ports were to be standardised at the low rate of 5 percent.

- grant British citizens legal protections in China.

Of the new ports opened to trade, Shanghai was by far the most important. The city is situated at the mouth of China's largest river, the Yangtze, a navigable waterway of over 1,000 miles for ocean-going ships and further for river craft. Shanghai was already a principal trading port for China, and the British East India Company had identified it as a promising trading centre in 1832, but had been refused permission to trade there by the Chinese authorities. Under the terms of the Treaty of Nanking, British merchants were not only allowed to trade at Shanghai, but could now trade with anyone rather than a Hong monopoly, and could access the length of the Yangtze. The treaty did far more than just allowing more coastal trade, it opened up the interior of China. Shanghai was the gateway to this previously inaccessible territory.

Although Shanghai was technically still Chinese sovereign territory under Chinese law, the British established a settlement there that was effectively self-governing. Other powers soon followed, as the Chinese government's inability to resist the demands of foreign powers became clear. The Americans established a settlement in 1848 and the French in 1849. In 1854, businessmen from these settlements formed the Shanghai Municipal Council to co-ordinate services like road maintenance and waste disposal. The council, on which Chinese were not allowed to sit, grew in importance and, by the 1860s, it was effectively governing the city. This was a new development – a colonial city that was neither answerable to the country on whose territory it stood, nor under the control of an imperial power. Shanghai became known as an international city, governed by businessmen whose main preoccupation was trade.

Under this model, the opium trade boomed. Opium imports grew steadily, reaching an incredible 6,500 tons of opium in 1880. Although British merchants could now travel up the Yangtze to trade, it was generally easier to sell the opium to Chinese middlemen at Shanghai. This was partly because the authority of the Chinese emperor had been fatally undermined, and violence broke out in 1850 with the **Taiping Rebellion**. This quickly escalated into a full-scale civil war that lasted until 1864, during which time 20–30 million Chinese are estimated to have died. The international community at Shanghai was never seriously threatened by the warfare sweeping the Chinese countryside, due to the protection of modern gunboats and other weapons provided by Britain to safeguard their interests. Indeed, Shanghai businessmen benefited from the war, especially through arms sales to the embattled Chinese emperor. In addition, the British persuaded the Chinese government to outsource the collection of customs tariffs to them, a profitable enterprise that employed 3,000 people by the end of the 19th century.

KEY TERM

Taiping Rebellion
A political and religious uprising that lasted for 14 years in China.

EXTEND YOUR KNOWLEDGE

Taiping Rebellion, 1850–64
This was a 14-year-long political upheaval that took place in China and left over 20 million people dead. It was begun by a disaffected civil service candidate by the name of Hong Xiuquan, who believed himself to be the son of God and brother to Jesus Christ sent to reform the politically conservative Chinese state. The movement he established was known as the 'God Worshipper's Society' and its principles of shared property and wealth attracted thousands of impoverished farmers. In 1851, after a successful rebellion in Guangxi Province, Hong pronounced a new dynasty – 'Taiping Tianguo' ('Heavenly Kingdom of Great Peace'). In the years that followed, the movement spread through China but alienated the landowning classes who rallied behind the government and, along with British support, helped to defeat the rebellion by 1864.

ACTIVITY
KNOWLEDGE CHECK

Growing British trade routes
  1 a) Create a list of Britain's acquisitions between 1763 and 1875.

   b) Explain how you feel they were useful to the British Empire.

  2 Why did the government consider it vital that British merchants continued to sell opium in China, despite the opposition of the Chinese government?

  3 Explain the rapid growth of *entrepôts* in the 19th century and their advantages over more traditional ports.

The purchase of Suez Canal shares, 1875

The narrow **isthmus** of Suez separating the Red Sea from the Mediterranean Sea had been of strategic military interest for some time. In 1798, Napoleon had invaded Egypt with the specific objective of attacking British commerce and threatening the trade routes to India and the East Indies. He considered the idea of building a canal, but was forced to abandon it when his surveyors informed him that the difference in sea level between the two seas made it impractical. In 1846, a French-led group of experts proved definitively that the difference in sea levels was in fact negligible, reviving interest in a canal as a commercial venture. In 1854, a French entrepreneur named Ferdinand de Lesseps obtained a concession from the Khedive of Egypt to construct a canal in return for a 99-year lease on its operation. Lesseps had been keen to attract international investment, but bankers in Britain, Germany and the USA would not commit large sums to the project. So a majority of the stock was sold in France, while the Khedive also invested heavily, purchasing 44 percent of shares in the company to ensure construction progressed.

KEY TERM

Isthmus
A narrow strip of land with sea either side that acts like a bridge and links two larger pieces of land together.

Construction of the Suez Canal

Construction of the Suez Canal took ten years, from 1859 to 1869; it was excavated mostly by hand by tens of thousands of forced labourers. Financially, the Suez Canal was initially in a precarious position. Construction costs had been estimated at 200 million francs but had escalated due to disease and technical problems, and the canal was finally completed for 433 million francs. The commercial value of the canal was uncertain, as the Red Sea–Mediterranean route was only suitable for steamships – sail or sail-assisted steamers would not have the prevailing winds in their favour for much of the journey. In addition, political uncertainty in Egypt made investing in the canal a risky venture. When the canal opened, shipping passing through it was initially lower than expected at 436,000 tons in 1870, and its financial future was doubtful.

SOURCE 10   A high-angle view of dredges at work on the Suez Canal, Egypt, in the 1860s.

Over time, however, the canal had a major impact on long-distance trade routes, especially to India. More powerful and reliable steamships had been replacing sailing ships on short-distance routes for decades, but sailing ships continued to dominate long-distance trade around the Cape of Good Hope because of the costly volumes of coal that long-distance steamers consumed on these routes. In 1868, only 2 percent of 1.1 million tons of shipping entering Britain from Asia was on steamships, compared to 60 percent of 7.5 million tons entering from Europe, North America and the Mediterranean. Because the canal was not practical for sailing ships, its opening meant that steamships became competitive on Asian trade routes for the first time. With the most industrialised dockyards, British shipping was the major beneficiary of this. Between 1868 and 1874, the steam tonnage entering British ports from Asia increased 178 percent and, by 1874, three-quarters of the tonnage passing through the canal was British.

The growing commercial benefit of the canal was matched by political concerns over the lack of British influence over its operation. With the canal rapidly becoming an indispensable lifeline to India and traditional sailing trade around Africa diminishing, the government faced the prospect of relying on French infrastructure to access India and other Asian colonies. There was no evidence of any actual restrictions on British shipping, but the potential for this to occur in future, fuelled by memories of Napoleon, was deeply worrying.

An opportunity to acquire influence in the canal arose in 1875 when the heavily indebted Khedive was forced to sell his stock in the canal to meet the demands of his creditors. When the well-connected British prime minister, Disraeli, heard of this, he acted immediately to procure the shares on behalf of the British nation by borrowing money from **Rothschilds** at short notice. In this way, he was able to acquire the Khedive's shares for £4,000,000 without issuing government bonds or informing parliament. This proved to be a canny investment, as dividends on the shares gradually increased from 4.7 percent in the first five years to 33 percent in 1911, when tonnage passing through the canal reached 18,324,000 tons. Although it was ostensibly a financial transaction, Disraeli did not see the purchase of Suez Canal shares as a commercial investment. He explained it to parliament and the public as a way to secure a 'great hold' over Egypt and to secure 'a highway to our Indian empire'. In a marked departure from earlier rationalisations of colonial expansion in the 19th century, Disraeli openly admitted that his intention was to advance Britain's geopolitical interests rather than deliberately provide the nation with financial gains; in the case of the Suez Canal, its acquisition was more strategic rather than exploitative.

This development of imperial policy was not uncontested. Both the fact that Disraeli had purchased shares for the British nation and the manner in which he had done so were controversial. The prime minister had acted without the approval of parliament to borrow a large sum of money from a private bank, and Disraeli was criticised in the House of Commons by Gladstone and others for acting unconstitutionally. Gladstone also warned that Britain now risked being drawn into political intrigues and military adventures in Egypt to protect the investment. This is precisely what happened when, with Gladstone as prime minister, Britain occupied Egypt to protect British interests in 1882. In 1875, however, Disraeli was able to brush off such warnings and with the queen and the public firmly behind him, he emerged from the episode triumphant.

SOURCE

11 From a speech by Benjamin Disraeli to the House of Commons Supply Committee. It relates to the British purchase of shares in the Suez Canal. Disraeli's government had already purchased the shares in 1875 by borrowing money from Rothschild's bank without parliamentary approval. Less than six years after this debate, Britain invaded and occupied Egypt in defence of British interests.

The noble **Lord** himself has expressed great dissatisfaction, because I have not told him what the conduct of the Government would be with regard to the Canal in a time of war. I must say that on this subject I wish to retain my reserve. I cannot conceive anything more imprudent than a discussion in this House at the present time as to the conduct of England with regard to the Suez Canal in time of war, and I shall therefore decline to enter upon any discussion on the subject.

... What we have to do to-night is to agree to the Vote for the purchase of these shares. I have never recommended, and I do not now recommend this purchase as a financial investment. If it gave us 10 per cent of interest and a security as good as the **Consols**, I do not think an English Minister would be justified in making such an investment; still less if he is obliged to borrow the money for the occasion. I do not recommend it either as a commercial speculation, although I believe that many of those who have looked upon it with little favour will probably be surprised with the pecuniary results of the purchase. I have always, and do now recommend it to the country as a political transaction, and one which I believe is calculated to strengthen the Empire. That is the spirit in which it has been accepted by the country, which understands it though the two right hon. critics may not. They are really seasick of the **'Silver Streak'**. They want the Empire to be maintained, to be strengthened; they will not be alarmed even it be increased. Because they think we are obtaining a great hold and interest in this important portion of Africa—because they believe that it secures to us a highway to our Indian Empire and our other dependencies, the people of England have from the first recognized the propriety and the wisdom of the step which we shall sanction tonight.

The acquisition of Zanzibar, 1890

The city of Zanzibar had developed an *entrepôt* model well before British involvement. As a possession of the Sultanate of Oman, Zanzibar became a hub where goods were bought from coastal traders and then loaded onto ocean-going ships for transport to the Middle East and India. The trade relied mainly on slaves and ivory, and Zanzibar's influence extended deep into East Africa with a network of trade routes channelling these towards the coast. In the 1830s, the sultans moved their capital to Zanzibar and created the Sultanate of Zanzibar, an indication that the city had grown in wealth and importance.

KEY TERM

Rothschilds
A banking family that began operations in Frankfurt in the 1760s. By the 19th century, the Rothschilds had branches across Europe and were the wealthiest family in the world. The English branch of Rothschilds profited hugely by lending money to the British government throughout the Napoleonic Wars, and later financed imperialist projects like the Suez Canal share purchase (1875) and the foundation of the British South Africa Company (1889).

A Level Exam-Style Question Section C

To what extent was the acquisition of the Suez Canal a new departure for British trading policy in the years 1763–1914? (20 marks)

Tip
Consider the motivations for acquiring the canal and identify whether you feel these motivations were any different from earlier actions. Did the canal offer anything different at all?

KEY TERMS

Lord
Lord Hartington, the eldest son of the Duke of Devonshire and so sat in the House of Commons, where he was Leader of the Liberal Opposition at this time.

Consols
Short for 'consolidated annuities', British government bonds issued by the Bank of England. With interest rates guaranteed by the British government, they are extremely secure investments.

'Silver Streak'
The English Channel. Disraeli is speaking pejoratively about politicians who opposed overseas interventions and advocated staying behind the Channel.

British influence in the region began to increase after 1815, but was not territorial in nature. The main British concerns were initially limited to safeguarding the trade route around the Cape to India and suppressing the slave trade. This was achieved through the diplomatic efforts of consular officials at key ports, backed by the Royal Navy where necessary. Royal Navy squadrons were fairly ineffective at intercepting slavers in the vast Indian Ocean, but their intimidating presence allowed the British to influence local rulers. This pressure was applied to Zanzibar, where approximately 50,000 slaves were traded annually. In 1822, the British persuaded the sultan to ban the export of slaves from Zanzibar, although slaves could still be imported from Africa and put to work on plantations. A total ban on slavery would not be achieved until 1873, again due to British pressure. Through their efforts to abolish the slave trade, British diplomats were drawn into Zanzibar's domestic politics, supporting candidates for sultan who were favourable to British interests and blocking those who were not.

The loss of the slave trade decreased the traditional importance of Zanzibar as a slave port for the Arabian peninsula and, in 1861, the sultan lost control of Oman through a British-adjudicated settlement, which split his territory and granted Oman to his brother. By contrast, Zanzibar increased its status as a valuable *entrepôt* on the route between India and Europe where merchants could acquire African ivory and rubber, or cloves and other spices grown on Zanzibar's plantations. Between 1859 and 1879, the volume of European and American shipping docking at Zanzibar grew from 65 ships and 18,877 tons to 96 ships and 95,403 tons. Most of this shipping was British, an indication of the dominance of British merchants in the Indian Ocean. Influenced by European powers, the sultan kept tariffs low and, in 1844, signed a treaty fixing import duties at a reasonable 5 percent. It appeared that as a useful port where European merchants were welcome, Zanzibar would retain its independence as an Islamic state, albeit under British influence.

East Africa, where the sultan exercised a limited trade-based authority over local rulers, was not particularly attractive for European investors or governments. Without a large river system, railways would be required to transport goods to the coast, and that would require significant capital investment. Investors in Europe were unwilling to provide much funding to speculative projects, and their governments refused to either take on the concessions as colonies (which would incur the costs of administering them) or to fund the development of railways to make the region profitable.

German expansion and the British East Africa Association

A new type of imperialist was emerging however, driven more by status and patriotism than by commercial gain. Several of these imperialist entrepreneurs had managed to negotiate trade concessions in East Africa, but these ventures failed due to lack of capital. This position changed with a German initiative headed by Karl Peters in 1884, which again obtained trading concessions on the mainland. Peters had only managed to secure £8,750 start-up capital for his intended East German Trading Company, mostly from small investors with imperial dreams; big investors and banks stayed well clear. It is likely that the company would have folded but, unlike previous ventures, Peters was successful in obtaining government support. The German chancellor Bismarck had previously been reluctant to involve Germany in colonial expansion. In 1885, he reversed this policy and published a declaration that Peters was under imperial protection. Peters used this to attract a little more funding, but the company's future remained uncertain until 1887 when Bismarck persuaded the Kaiser to invest £25,000 of his personal fortune; other investors were quick to follow. It would be some time before there was any real money made however, as it was not until 1904 that the government sponsored the construction of a railway into the interior.

German expansion changed the British position in East Africa. William Mackinnon, the wealthy owner of the Zanzibar–Aden steamship service, had tried to set up a trading company there in 1878; he negotiated an exclusive trade concession with the sultan in return for a 20 percent share of profits, but did not progress with the venture as he could not secure government support. Once the Germans were establishing themselves, he was encouraged to have another go. Mackinnon obtained another concession and raised £250,000 for a 'British East Africa Association', although as with the German company this funding was not from big commercial investors. The biggest investor in the association was Mackinnon himself with £25,000; the remainder came mainly from ardent imperialists and evangelical or anti-slavery philanthropists.

The association never made money; by 1892 its expenditure was £85,000 and income only £35,000. What it did achieve was to secure a foothold for British interests in East Africa, a region that was becoming increasingly important to the government's imperial strategy. The idea of establishing colonies in Africa's interior was becoming attractive in order to safeguard the upper reaches of the Nile and, therefore, Britain's increasingly permanent-looking occupation of Egypt. In retrospect, it seems highly unlikely that any other powers could have used this region in any way to force the British out of Egypt, but at the time theories about the potential to divert the Nile to starve Egypt were taken seriously. Despite the dire financial position of the association, the government established a series of East African protectorates in 1895 and funded a railway from Mombasa to Uganda in 1896. In this period, the 'scramble for Africa' colonisation had acquired its own logic that went far beyond the largely commercial interests of earlier imperialists.

As Britain and Germany vied for a strategic advantage on the mainland, the sultan's rights to territory there were effectively ignored, despite controlling the area for 200 years. Britain and Germany carved up the region in an 1890 treaty, where Germany gave up any rights in Zanzibar in exchange for a small island in the North Sea. In the same treaty, the British established a protectorate in Zanzibar. The Zanzibaris were not involved in these negotiations, despite this effectively ending the independence of the Sultanate. The British prime minister, Lord Salisbury, patronisingly stated that **protectorate** status was 'more acceptable for the half civilised races and more suitable for them' than a full colonial status, as well as being cheaper. However, there was no doubt as to who was in charge. In 1896, the pro-British sultan died and his cousin seized power. The British had preferred another candidate and bombarded the city. There were 500 Zanzibari casualties and one British sailor was injured; the encounter lasted 38 minutes and is known as the shortest war in history.

KEY TERM

Protectorate
A relationship status between two countries that allows the smaller power in the relationship a degree of autonomy while being under the protection and general control of the stronger one. Under this relationship, often the protecting power also has significant influence over the decisions made by the smaller one.

SOURCE

12 Rear Admiral H.H. Rawson, who was in charge of the Royal Navy during the Anglo-Zanzibar War in 1896, known as the shortest war in history.

The lease of Weihaiwei, 1898

The casual acquisition of Zanzibar had shown that the concerns or status of traditional rulers were increasingly unimportant in British government policy considerations. The power imbalance between industrialised countries and the rest of the world by the end of the 19th century was huge, with machine guns, artillery and ironclad warships enabling small numbers of men to easily defeat traditional military forces. Local rulers without industrial production systems scrambled to purchase modern weapons, but these were expensive and quickly became obsolete.

By contrast, Britain's advantage as the first industrialised country was rapidly eroding, as the technological innovations of the Industrial Revolution spread. France, Germany, the USA and Japan were quickly developing as major powers able to challenge British supremacy. The Russian Empire was slow to industrialise and had very low productivity compared to these countries, but was still regarded as a Great Power due to the sheer size of its territory and army. The Russian and British Empires were strategic opponents for most of the 19th century, although the Crimean War (1853–56) was the only major conflict between them. Of particular concern to Britain was Russia's expansion in central Asia, well away from the oceans dominated by the Royal Navy. Russia was the only power capable of threatening British India by land, and the two powers engaged in an economic and political struggle known as **the 'Great Game'** in which rulers of countries like Afghanistan and Persia were the pieces. After a succession of diplomatic crises in Afghanistan, a border agreement between the two empires was reached in principle in 1893 and finalised in 1895.

Russian interests

Simultaneously, the tsar was seeking to expand the Russian Empire in the East, where the lack of a warm-water port had prevented much Russian involvement in the opening up of China through the opium trade. Russia made some territorial advances in Chinese Turkistan, but abandoned these when threatened with war by China in 1881. Previously powerless to resist incursions, the Chinese government had embarked on a military modernisation programme, buying hundreds of thousands of modern rifles and other military equipment from Germany. In the 1880s, China also commissioned German engineers to build a coastal fortress at Port Arthur to control the Yellow Sea, which soon became a focal point for international tension. Japan, which had itself rapidly industrialised and was seeking to expand its influence, captured the port in 1894 after decisively defeating Chinese forces based in Korea.

The Russian Empire saw this as an opportunity to obtain the strategic port it desperately needed. Russia persuaded France and Germany to support an intervention to force Japan to withdraw from the area. Both powers agreed in return for promises of Russian support for their own interests in China. Together, the three powers had 38 ships totalling 95,000 tons in the region, compared to Japan's navy of 31 ships totalling 57,000 tons. This time it was Japan that backed down, evacuating Port Arthur in December 1895. Legally the port was now returned to China, but the Chinese were unable to protect it effectively, and they were persuaded to lease it to Russia from 1898 rather than risk a Japanese return.

These developments were of extreme concern to the British government, which had stayed neutral when Japan was being forced out of Port Arthur. Already in possession of a strategic port at Hong Kong to the south, Britain was reluctant to get involved in a power struggle between China, Japan and Russia for Port Arthur. On the other hand, Russia's success in securing the port raised prospects of a new 'Great Game' to protect British interests in China. The British government's response was to demand another port from the Chinese government from which the Royal Navy could oversee developments in Port Arthur. This was secured in 1898 through the lease of Weihaiwei.

The lease of Weihaiwei is significant because it demonstrates how far British colonial interests had come from their commercial beginnings. Although the lease was ostensibly for 'the better protection of British commerce', the port had no commercial value and British shipping was far better served by the Royal Navy squadron at Hong Kong. The true function of the lease is revealed by its duration: 'for so long a period as Port Arthur shall remain in the occupation of Russia'. In East Africa, the British had established unprofitable British protectorates to prevent the expansion of unprofitable German ones. At Weihaiwei, Britain seized the nearest harbour it could find to Port Arthur just in case it turned out to be useful in countering Russian development.

SOURCE

From the convention for the lease of Weihaiwei, 1898. The agreement was signed at Peking on 1 July 1898 and ratified in London on 5 October 1898.

In order to provide Great Britain with a suitable naval harbour in North China, and for the better protection of British commerce in the neighbouring seas, the Government of His Majesty the Emperor of China agrees to lease to the Government of Her Majesty the Queen of Great Britain and Ireland Weihaiwei in the province of Shantung and the adjacent waters, for so long a period as Port Arthur shall remain in the occupation of Russia.

The territory leased shall comprise the island of Liu Kung and all other islands in the Bay of Weihaiwei, and a belt of land ten English miles wide along the entire coast line of the Bay of Weihaiwei. Within the above mentioned territory leased Great Britain shall have sole jurisdiction.

Great Britain shall have in addition the right to erect fortifications, station troops, or take any other measures necessary for defensive purposes, at any points on or near the coast of the region east of the meridian one hundred and twenty-one degrees, forty minutes east of Greenwich, and to acquire on equitable compensation within that territory such sites as may be necessary for water supply, communications and hospitals. Within that zone Chinese administration shall not be interfered with, but no troops other than Chinese or British shall be allowed therein.

EXTRACT

From Ronald Hyam, *Britain's Imperial Century, 1815–1914: A study of empire and expansion*, written in 2002.

Britain controlled Europe's access to much of the outside world, and during the eighteenth century wars locked its rivals up in Europe and out-ran them in the extra-European race. Moreover, being outside the continent, Britain was not tempted as were continental states to associate power or security with subduing Europe to its hegemonic authority. Initially involved in seaborne commercial expansion, the British became by a most extraordinary achievement the ruler of India (or much of it), and thus an Asian land-based empire, rather than an uncomplicated thalassocratic [maritime] one. This transition brought the imperial system, in the North-West frontier of India, hard up against one of the world's other fundamental and unyielding geopolitical facts, Russian dominance of the Eurasian 'heartland'. This rivalry, the 'Great Game', was something which 'provided a world role for the British empire'. The possession and defence of India, the need to ensure communications with it, and the fear of the French which followed from this, were quintessential concerns of the British Empire. A 'geopolitical template' was drawn during the Napoleonic Wars. It continued to govern British official thinking about the Middle East and the Mediterranean right through to the Suez fiasco of 1956.

At the height of late-nineteenth-century geopolitical nervousness, Lord Salisbury came to the conclusion that 'the constant study of maps is apt to disturb men's reasoning powers'. Strategists, he commented ruefully, 'would like to annex the moon in order to prevent it being appropriated by the planet Mars'.

A Level Exam-Style Question Section C

To what extent did economic interests govern the expansion of the British Empire during the years 1763–1914? (20 marks)

Tip

When answering this question, you should consider the manner in which the British Empire developed. Did motivations for its expansion change over the period and under what context did this expansion take place?

THINKING HISTORICALLY Change (7a)

Convergence and divergence

Technological progress, 1763–1914				
1781	**1820**	**1830**	**1833**	**1869**
Cotton mill: James Watt files patent for steam engine to drive cotton machines.	Medicine: Quinine isolated as active ingredient for malarial treatment.	Railways: First inter-city route from Liverpool to Manchester opened.	Ocean-going steamships: SS *Savannah* makes first Atlantic crossing largely under steam power.	Suez Canal: Franco-Egyptian construction project completed.

Territorial growth, 1763–1914				
1819	**1833**	**1858**	**1882**	**1890**
Singapore: Colonised despite Dutch protests.	Falkland Islands: Disputed but peaceful acquisition.	India: Formal acquisition from East India Company.	Egypt: Occupied after Anglo-Egyptian War.	East Africa: Partition with Germany agreed.

1 Draw a timeline across the middle of a landscape piece of A3 paper. Cut out ten small rectangular cards and write the above changes on them. Then place them on the timeline with technological changes above the line and territorial changes below. Make sure there is a lot of space between the changes and the line.

2 Draw a line and write a link between each change within each strand, so that you have five links that join up the changes in the technological part of the timeline and five that join the territorial changes. You will then have two strands of change: technological and territorial.

3 Now make as many links as possible across the timeline between technological change and territorial change. Think about how they are affected by one another and think about how things can link across long periods of time.

You should end up with something like this:

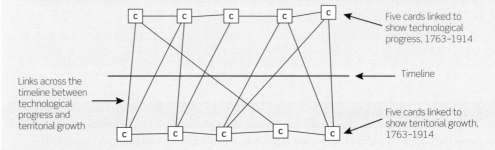

Five cards linked to show technological progress, 1763–1914

Timeline

Links across the timeline between technological progress and territorial growth

Five cards linked to show territorial growth, 1763–1914

Answer the following:

4 How far do different strands of history interact with one another? Illustrate your answer with two well-explained examples.

5 At what point do the two strands of development converge (i.e. when do the changes have the biggest impact on one another)?

6 How useful are the strands in understanding the evolution of trade routes during the 18th and 19th centuries?

ACTIVITY
KNOWLEDGE CHECK

Colonial acquisitions

1 Why did the government attach progressively less importance to the sovereignty of non-developed countries?

2 Why did Britain begin to acquire colonies that had no immediate economic benefit?

ACTIVITY
SUMMARY

Trade and empire

1 Summarise the role of trade in losing and gaining colonies between the years 1763 and 1914.

2 a) How did Britain's colonial acquisitions between 1819 and 1898 reflect changes in the attitude of British leaders towards the Empire?

 b) In your opinion, what was the cause of this changing attitude?

WIDER READING

Collins, B. *War and Empire: The Expansion of Britain, 1790–1830*, Routledge (2010)

Ferguson, N. *Empire: The Rise and Demise of the British World Order and Lessons for Global Power*, Basic Books (2004)

Hyam, R. *Britain's Imperial Century 1815–1914: A Study of Empire and Expansion*, Palgrave (2002)

James, L. *The Rise and Fall of the British Empire*, St Martin's Griffin (1997)

Johnson, R. *The British Empire: Pomp, Power and Postcolonialism*, Humanities-Ebooks (2010)

Lloyd, T.O. *The British Empire 1558–1995*, Oxford University Press (1997)

Robinson, H. *The Development of the British Empire*, CreateSpace Independent Publishing Platform (2015)

3.2 The changing nature of the Royal Navy

KEY QUESTIONS

- How did the role of the Royal Navy evolve in the years 1763–1914?
- What were the reasons for the acquisition of key naval bases and how did these change in the years 1763–1914?

INTRODUCTION

KEY TERMS

Age of Sail
The period between the 16th and mid-19th centuries when trade and naval warfare were dominated by sailing vessels.

Geopolitical game
Referring to the influence of geography upon international relations and politics.

From the destruction of the Spanish Armada in 1588 to the development of effective steam warships in the mid-19th century, naval warfare was dominated by cannon-firing sailing ships, a period that became known as the **Age of Sail**. By 1763, the Royal Navy had achieved supremacy over its great enemies of the previous two centuries: the French, Dutch and Spanish fleets. However, it was not until the destruction of the Franco-Spanish fleet at Trafalgar in 1805 that this supremacy was unchallengeable by other European powers, even by combining their forces. Driven by government policy and supported by growing revenues from imperial trade, the Royal Navy maintained this hegemonic position (see page 40) until the early 20th century, well into the 'Age of Steam'. While the basic ships and tactics of the navy in 1763 would have been instantly recognisable to Elizabethan seafarers like Drake and Hawkins, by 1914 the pace of technological change had changed the nature of war at sea.

The period 1763–1914 was, therefore, a time of immense change for the Royal Navy, driven initially by the need to decisively destroy European rivals. Once this was achieved, the Navy played a central role in trade, diplomacy and exploration, transforming Britain from a European to a truly global power at the centre of the largest empire the world has ever seen. This evolution can be evidenced by the navy's key naval bases across the world, from the military necessity of retaining Gibraltar in 1783 to the diplomatic acquisition of Cyprus in 1878 as a piece in a **geopolitical game** with the Russian Empire.

1803-15 – War with Napoleonic France

Naval expenditure increases from £2.4 million in 1793 to £22.8 million in 1815

Naval supremacy achieved at Trafalgar in 1805

1763-69 – Budget cuts to the war-winning, but expensive, Royal Navy; naval expenditure falls from £7 million in 1762 to £1.5 million in 1769

1778-83 – Royal Navy outnumbered and outgunned after France, Spain and the Netherlands enter American revolutionary war against Britain

1789 – France, virtually bankrupted by naval costs, falls into revolution

1833 – Britain acquires Falkland Islands to protect sealing fleet

| 1760 | 1770 | 1780 | 1790 | 1800 | 1810 | 1820 | 1830 |

1768-71 – Captain Cook explores South Pacific for Royal Navy, the first of many voyages of exploration

1781 – American colonies effectively are lost after the Royal Navy is driven off Chesapeake Bay

1793-1802 – Wars with revolutionary France

1815 – Treaty of Paris after final defeat of Napoleon at Waterloo

Britain acquires Ceylon, the Cape and Malta

HOW DID THE ROLE OF THE ROYAL NAVY EVOLVE IN THE YEARS 1763–1914?

The significance of changing ship types

The Royal Navy in 1763 was the culmination of nearly two centuries of tactical and technological developments in sailing ship warfare between European powers. It was designed to destroy a similar fleet in pitched naval battles, and had recently demonstrated its proficiency through decisive victories against the French at Lagos and Quiberon Bay.

Naval tactics during the Age of Sail differed considerably from those in medieval or earlier periods, where the main objective had been to ram or pull alongside the enemy vessel so that soldiers carried on the deck could board it. Instead, sailing ships carried rows of cannon mounted in their sides, and sunk or disabled their enemies by discharging these simultaneously in a devastating **broadside**. Victorious ships were those that had more and bigger guns, could fire their guns faster and more accurately and could manoeuvre during battle to avoid an enemy's broadside while firing their own. The most important factors in manoeuvring were the speed of the ship's hull and the skill of the sailors in manipulating its sails. Success in battle, therefore, depended on well-constructed ships that combined speed and powerful guns, sailed by well-drilled crews who were proficient at gunnery and sailing.

Naval tactics

In battles, fleets approached the enemy in a long line, which had the following advantages.

- It enabled sustained bombardment, with each ship able to fire a broadside as the line passed an enemy.

- It avoided friendly ships firing on each other, as none of their broadsides would be facing each other.

- It reduced the exposure of vulnerable bows and sterns to enemy fire, as only the bow of the leading ship and the stern of the last ship were exposed.

- It improved the speed and effectiveness of signalling by flags between the admiral's ship and the rest of the fleet.

KEY TERM

Broadside
The simultaneous discharge of large guns mounted along on the side of a warship. The rapid firing of broadsides was the main battle tactic in the Age of Sail. With up to 60 cannon on each side of a warship, a single well-aimed broadside could completely disable or sink an enemy vessel. At very close range, guns could be loaded with two or even three cannonballs for increased damage.

1839 – Britain acquires Aden to facilitate steam mail route to India

1878 – Britain acquires Cyprus from declining Ottoman Empire to counter Russian expansion

1914 – Beginning of First World War signals end of a century of relative peace upheld by Royal Navy known as *Pax Britannica*

| 1840 | 1850 | 1860 | 1870 | 1880 | 1890 | 1900 | 1910 |

1850 – France re-emerges as a naval power and signals end of the Age of Sail with the launch of the *Napoleon*

1889 – Naval Defence Act commits government to spend as much on navy as next two largest powers combined

1906 – HMS *Dreadnought* launched, triggering new arms race

Battles were often indecisive if neither fleet could gain a positional advantage, with fleets sailing in parallel lines firing broadsides at each other. By contrast, if a fleet could sail across the enemy line, it could concentrate fire at the point of intersection, while receiving only limited fire in return. To a far greater extent than other navies, British captains and admirals were trained and encouraged to adopt hyper-aggressive tactics, frequently seeking to break the enemy line and engage at close range. This tactic could result in decisive victories, as at the Battle of Trafalgar in 1805.

SOURCE

Nelson 'crossing the T' at Trafalgar. By sailing his smaller fleet in two perpendicular lines straight towards the enemy line, Nelson obtained superiority in firepower at the points of intersection. The Franco-Spanish fleet lost 22 ships and over 13,000 men, compared to no ships and under 2,000 men lost by the British.

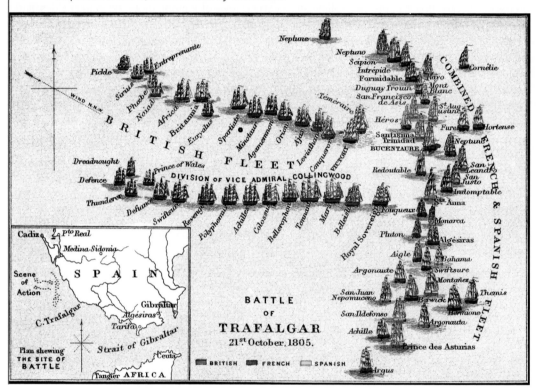

Ship types used by the Royal Navy

Ship types reflected the needs of this model of warfare. The main ship involved in pitched battles was the **ship of the line**, and until the end of the Age of Sail, naval strength was primarily expressed in terms of numbers of ships of the line. These ships were built to be long, to allow a large number of cannon to be mounted on each side, and narrow, to maximise speed. They had deep hulls to cut through the water, powered by huge sails from three masts.

In the Royal Navy, a rating system was used whereby ships of the line were classed as first, second, third or fourth rate, depending on their number of guns and manpower. First and second rate ships of the line had three gun decks and anywhere from 80 to 120 cannon. Admirals often used these as their flagships, such as Nelson's 100-gun *Victory*, but the extra firepower made them top heavy and less manoeuvrable so relatively few were built. Fourth rate ships of the line, with less than 64 cannon, were phased out from the late 18th century because they lacked sufficient firepower. The backbone of the fleet was, therefore, the third rate ships of the line with between 64 and 80 cannon on two gun decks and a crew of around 500 men; these made up 76 percent of all Royal Navy ships of the line in 1794 and 80 percent in 1814. The most common type was a French design from the 1730s adopted by the British and other navies, with a 52-metre hull with 74 guns mounted on two gun decks.

Between 1763 and 1805, the Royal Navy engaged in a life or death struggle with other European navies, characterised by pitched battles between fleets. Despite some major setbacks, most notably during the American War of Independence, the Royal Navy progressively outpaced its rivals during this period. This culminated in the Battle of Trafalgar in 1805, where the Royal Navy decisively defeated a Franco-Spanish fleet and achieved a lasting naval supremacy.

KEY TERM

Ship of the line
A ship deemed strong enough to take its place in the line of battle. A line that included slow or weak ships could be easily broken, so a ship needed the right balance of speed and firepower to merit inclusion in the line.

Despite the concentrated power of ships of the line, they were less effective outside of fleet-to-fleet pitched battles. Their firepower and extra gun decks were achieved by sacrificing manoeuvrability as well as speed. This made them dangerous to sail near the shore, and they were often unable to catch more lightly armed warships or merchantmen. In addition, admirals needed to keep their firepower assembled in one place to be decisive, so ships of the line were rarely used for duties like patrolling, destroying enemy trade and escorting friendly shipping.

These roles were filled by fifth and sixth rate ships known as frigates. Frigates were only slightly shorter than ships of the line but typically had a single gun deck, so were faster and more manoeuvrable, as well as able to sail closer to shore. This made them more suitable for operating independently or in small squadrons well away from the main battle fleets in Europe. While ships of the line were often tied up on blockade duties, frigates roamed the world's oceans looking for enemy shipping. This made them appealing to ambitious young captains, and there were fortunes to be made in **prize money** on a successful frigate. On the frigate *Speedy*, for example, Captain Cochrane captured or destroyed a total of 53 French ships over a period of 13 months in 1800–01. Despite the growing superiority of Britain's fleet in European waters, other nations used frigates successfully against British shipping, in particular French and American forces. The French built 59 fast frigates between 1777 and 1790, and many of these continued to raid British shipping well after the Battle of Trafalgar. The highest British merchant losses of the Napoleonic Wars were 619 ships lost in 1810, when French frigates attacked the Baltic trade despite France being unable to challenge the supremacy of the main British fleet after Trafalgar.

KEY TERM

Prize money
Under the Cruisers and Convoys Act 1708, a captain and his crew were entitled to shares of the value of a captured ship and its cargo. A single capture could mean more than a year's pay, so successful captains could become rich in the course of a battle or a campaign.

The development of steam power

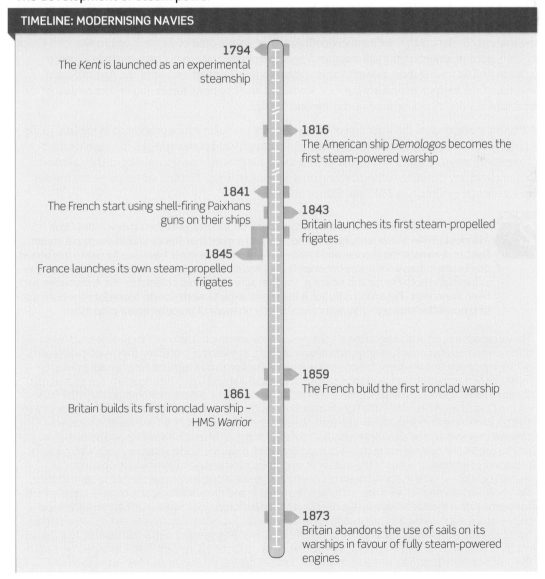

TIMELINE: MODERNISING NAVIES

1794
The *Kent* is launched as an experimental steamship

1816
The American ship *Demologos* becomes the first steam-powered warship

1841
The French start using shell-firing Paixhans guns on their ships

1843
Britain launches its first steam-propelled frigates

1845
France launches its own steam-propelled frigates

1859
The French build the first ironclad warship

1861
Britain builds its first ironclad warship – HMS *Warrior*

1873
Britain abandons the use of sails on its warships in favour of fully steam-powered engines

The Royal Navy finished the Napoleonic Wars in 1815 with 214 ships of the line and 792 frigates, which was rapidly reduced to 100 ships of the line and 162 frigates. After further reductions during a prolonged period of peace, the navy had only 58 operational ships of the line in 1835. However, during this period, the navy retained the ability to rebuild quickly and was able to retain supremacy over the world's oceans with this skeleton force because no other powers embarked on a major shipbuilding programme.

The position of naval **hegemony** meant that there was often little desire within the Admiralty to experiment with new ship types. While wooden sailing ships armed with cannon were the most powerful warships, the Royal Navy could maintain its dominance because it had more of these ships and was able to produce them more quickly than any other power. There was, therefore, no incentive for the Admiralty to develop ships which could upset this beneficial situation, and many naval innovations during the 19th century were first developed by rival powers, and then quickly adopted by the Royal Navy to avoid its fleet becoming obsolete.

Despite trials of steam propulsion as early as the experimental *Kent* in 1794, steam had little impact on the dominance of ships of the line and frigates in naval warfare for decades. Early steam engines were unreliable, slow, and consumed a large volume of coal for the power they produced. Propulsion was based on paddle-wheels, which were unsuitable for heavy seas, difficult to protect from cannon fire and took up valuable broadside space that could otherwise be used for guns. In 1816, the American *Demologos* became the first steam warship, but was little more than a floating gun battery inside New York harbour and was never used in action.

Steamships first became effective in areas where sailing ships did not have room to navigate using the wind – in particular, river systems. Hybrid ships were produced with sails for ocean travel and steam paddles for river navigation. These were initially simply used to tow British warships up rivers, from the Irrawady in Burma to the Piraná in South America. By the time of Britain's opium war with China in 1840, guns mounted on the sail-steamer *Nemesis* were adequate to dispatch multiple Chinese junks as well as towing more powerful sailships far upriver. The first impact of the Age of Steam was, therefore, to open previously inaccessible inland areas to naval forces, rather than to disrupt the established order of sailing ships of the line and frigates.

A major innovation was the invention of more powerful propeller screw propulsion in the late 1830s, which made ocean-going steam travel practical. Although wind power was still the main method of transport, steam engines could be used in a battle for greater manoeuvrability, as they allowed movement in any direction without relying on a favourable wind. The first steam-propelled frigates were launched by Britain in 1843 and France in 1845.

SOURCE

2

From a British response to a pamphlet by Admiral de Joinville, published in *Revue des Deux Mondes* in 1844. In the pamphlet, the Admiral had argued that France should develop a steam fleet to dominate the channel and Mediterranean while the Royal Navy was forced to rely on sail due to the massive distances between Britain and its empire. De Joinville's pamphlet was highly influential in both France and America. The first screw-powered steamship, the *Archimedes*, had been launched in Britain in 1838, but British naval experts were slow to appreciate the potential of this new technology – this author was clearly unaware of propeller screw propulsion.

The young admiral, after dilating on the advantages of a steam-navy as the only effective means by which an offensive and defensive warfare may be carried on- as the only means of protecting the French coasts and of carrying on operations against the coast of an enemy, goes on to advise his countrymen not to keep up munitions and accoutrements, and ships' provisions in docks and arsenals, but to equip at once an available steam fleet. In other words he says 'Burn all your old vessels, sell your old marine stores- and with the money equip a fleet of war-steamers'. If the French were to follow this silly sailor's advice, they could not do anything that could be more favourable to our interests. Steam vessels may, no doubt, be employed as excellent convoys, they may also be advantageously distributed as the guardships of roadsteads and ports- they may be used in the conveyance of troops to short distances, they may render subsidiary services to vessels becalmed, or lead out of action or the wake of an enemy disabled vessels- they may act as a species of guerrilla or tirailleur force to a great fleet- or in laying a large ship alongside an enemy: - but to say that they can wholly supersede all other ships – till fuel can be compressed into a smaller space, or some improvement has been made in the paddlewheels that has not yet been invented, - is to maintain a theory irrational and preposterous. It is possible that half a century hence, war galleys propelled by steam may be used in warfare, but till we have actual experience of their great efficiency in an engagement with an old seventy-four, we will not theorise on a subject on which data are wanting. If any nation on earth might make the experiment which the Prince de Joinville advises his countrymen, it would be England, yet how foolish it would be to do so.

KEY TERM

Hegemony
Influence or authority over others.

The French realised the potential of steam-powered battleships more quickly than the British and launched the 90-gun *Napoleon* in 1850, capable of reaching 14 knots (26 km/hour) without wind. This signalled the end of 35 years of low-cost naval supremacy for the Royal Navy and the beginning of a naval arms race between major powers that would continue until the outbreak of the First World War in 1914. Both Britain and France poured money into equipping their fleets with steam in the 1850s; France built ten new steam battleships and converted 28, and Britain built 18 new battleships and converted 41.

New technology

Steam power was not the only new technology. The Napoleonic Wars had been won at sea by ships with cannon firing solid round shot. Artillery on land had been using explosive shells for many years, but these weapons had high trajectories and were used for bombarding towns and fortifications. Shell-firing guns with the flat trajectory needed to hit an enemy ship at sea were not produced until the 1820s by the French engineer Henri-Joseph Paixhans. When the French began to fit these Paixhans guns to warships from 1841, the Royal Navy and others quickly did the same. The new guns could easily destroy wooden ships, and there was great concern among naval strategists over the destruction that would occur in the event of a major battle.

To counter the deadly new guns, it did not take long for iron plates to be fitted as armour to wooden ships, taking advantage of advances in metallurgy and the increasing availability of iron. This technology made the fleets of wooden steamships produced by Britain and France in the 1850s obsolete without having been used in a major battle. The first of these 'ironclads' was the French warship *La Gloire* in 1859. Again, the Royal Navy was slow to innovate but quick to imitate; the Admiralty quickly decided that all new ships commissioned would be ironclads, beginning with HMS *Warrior* in 1861. By 1862, the use of ironclads in the American Civil War had demonstrated their power against wooden ships and all major navies abandoned the production of unarmoured wooden warships.

The *Victory* was launched in 1765 and retired from active service in 1824 after almost 60 years as one of Britain's most powerful warships. By the late 19th century, however, revolutionary warships such as *La Gloire* and the *Warrior* themselves became obsolete within a decade as technological developments gathered pace. Rapid improvements were made in each of the three new technologies: steam engines, armour plating and naval guns. The result was that new battleships became progressively bigger, heavier and more reliant on their engines. Sails were finally abandoned with the launch of HMS *Devastation* in 1873, which was 87 metres long and was armed with two 35-ton guns and protected by hull armour 250–300 mm thick. This vessel was perhaps one of the most significant to be created for the Royal Navy since it was not only a powerful ship in its own right, but it symbolised a turning point in maritime history whereby traditional sailing techniques were now a thing of the past as Britain fully embraced the benefits of industrialisation in the pursuit of continued naval dominance.

For Britain, the end of the Age of Sail had major implications for the network of ports acquired as supply stations across the world, in particular those on the trade routes to India and the East Indies. Previously, these ports had been important stopping points for sailing ships, but they were vital for steamers. The *Devastation* alone carried 1,350 tons of coal and had no other means of movement, so without friendly deep-water ports at which to stock up on coal, it would not be possible for it to undertake lengthy sea voyages. The same was true for all of the new warships, and a fleet of coal-transporting merchant ships began to sail between the Empire's main ports to ensure a continuous supply was available. This was a greater challenge for the British than for other nations because of the huge extent of Britain's empire.

The end of the Age of Sail also eliminated one of the Royal Navy's traditional advantages – the superior seamanship of British sailors. With the largest number of experienced sailors and by far the biggest merchant fleet from which to draw replacements, the Royal Navy had prided itself on the ability of its crews to sail their ships better than any of their rivals. This advantage had often proved decisive in the days of Nelson, but was negated by the Age of Steam, where the technical superiority of the ship was far more important than the skill of the crew. From the 1870s onwards, naval strength was derived from the number and quality of ships that a country could produce rather than differences in seamanship. This development allowed powers with a limited maritime tradition but an advanced industrialised economy, in particular Germany and Japan, to produce strong fleets capable of rivalling established naval powers.

KEY TERM

Two power standard
The idea that the Royal Navy should be as strong as the next two largest navies combined. This had originated as an idea in the late 18th century, but was not official policy until the Naval Defence Act 1889, which required the government to match the naval expenditure of the next two most powerful countries combined.

The desire to maintain naval supremacy

In light of the growing industrial output of rival powers, Britain sought to retain its position as a pre-eminent naval power and maintain the **two power standard**. It was argued by the Admiralty that by rapidly expanding the navy and enshrining a commitment to maintain naval supremacy in law, Britain's position would become so unassailable that other powers would be deterred from further naval expenditure. In the Naval Defence Act 1889, Britain committed to ten battleships, 42 cruisers and 18 torpedo gunships by 1893–94, at a total cost of £21.5 million. Thus Britain would actually save money in the future by expanding the fleet now. This argument was immediately proved wrong when France and Russia increased their joint production to 12 battleships in the same period, two more than Britain's increased production. Germany and the USA both accelerated their naval construction as well.

John Fisher became first sea lord of the Admiralty in 1904 and introduced a huge modernisation programme. He immediately scrapped 154 older warships and restructured Britain's fleets across the world so that the largest and most modern ships were concentrated in Europe. His intention was to end the arms race by producing warships that were so technologically advanced no other navy could challenge them. His ideas culminated in HMS *Dreadnought* in 1906, a ship so powerful that it instantly made all existing battleships obsolete.

SOURCE

At a cost of £1,783,883, the 160-metre long HMS *Dreadnought* was easily the most powerful ship afloat. With a top speed of 21 knots (39 km/hour), its main armament was five huge guns, each capable of firing a 385 kg shell over 22 km.

However, Fisher's aim of ending the arms race through deterrence was no more successful than the Naval Defence Act had been. Powers like Germany, the USA and Japan immediately started to produce their own dreadnoughts, although less industrialised maritime powers like France and Russia could not keep pace. As the world moved towards the First World War, the Royal Navy was still by far the most powerful military force in the world, but it did not enjoy the same global dominance as it had in 1815.

ACTIVITY
KNOWLEDGE CHECK

Evolving a navy
Using the material you have read and your own knowledge, construct a list of factors that influenced the expansion and development of the Royal Navy. You should then number these in order of importance and briefly justify your reasoning alongside the list you have created.

THINKING HISTORICALLY Change (8a, b & c) (I)

Imposing realities

Look at the image above and answer the following questions.

1 Explain why the conversation in the cartoon above would not have happened.

The shape of history is imposed by people looking back. People who lived through the 'history' did not always perceive the patterns that later historians identify. For example, some people living through the Industrial Revolution may have understood that great change was taking place, but they would not have been able to understand the massive economic, social and political consequences of industrialisation.

2 Consider the first steamships.

   a) Who would have made the decision that the Age of Sail was over?

   b) Could anybody have challenged this decision?

   c) Explain why someone living in the 19th century would have been unable to make a judgement about the beginning of a new era.

3 Who living at the present time might regard the beginning of the 'Age of Steam' as an important event?

4 What does this cartoon tell us about the structure of history as we understand it?

The growing role of commerce protection

The Royal Navy had a close association with trade in the 18th century, founded upon the Navy's continual need for skilled sailors. Life for ordinary seamen in the navy was notoriously tough, with cramped living conditions and harsh discipline, including flogging for relatively minor offences. Pay was modest; an able seaman's wage in 1794 was only £14 per year – the same as that of a male servant working in a landowner's home in Durham in the same year. Together with the high chance

KEY TERM

Impressment
The forcible recruitment of sailors into the navy. To supply the navy with men, press gangs roamed British ports offering gold, getting sailors drunk or simply kidnapping them. The majority of impressments happened at sea, where the navy had the power to stop a civilian ship and take some of the men aboard.

of injury or death in naval service, it is hardly surprising that the navy struggled to attract volunteers to man its ships and therefore had to rely upon the liberal use of **impressment**, which was often very unpopular.

The burden of impressment was felt less if the navy was drawing its manpower from a very large number of civilian ships, so a large merchant navy was encouraged. The British government had adopted this 'blue water' policy from the 17th century, under which the merchant fleet and the Royal Navy were seen as mutually sustainable. The navy protected the seas for the merchantmen, as well as capturing foreign merchantmen during wars. This made trade routes safe for English merchants and dangerous for their foreign competitors; the Royal Navy captured 1,165 French merchant ships in the Seven Years' War, totally disrupting French trade to the considerable advantage of English merchants. By contrast, British merchant shipping was expected to provide tens of thousands of skilled sailors to the Royal Navy, and trade profits also increased revenue to the Exchequer, indirectly funding the expansion of the navy.

Government policy was to support this relationship, mainly through the Navigation Acts of the 1660s, which mandated that trade between Britain and its colonies must be carried in British ships. In addition, the Royal Navy was empowered to press civilian sailors into service against their will, ensuring a continuous flow of men from the merchant fleet onto naval ships.

Over time, the role of the Royal Navy developed from a mutually beneficial exchange of protection for manpower with British merchant ships to the ultimate guarantor of Britain's free-trade Empire. With far lower manpower requirements once scurvy had been abolished, the French threat eliminated and impressment was stopped, Royal Navy ships sailed the world's oceans to support Britain's commercial empire. From the suppression of slavery to forcing unfriendly powers to trade and maintaining a network of naval supply bases, the Royal Navy played a pivotal role in developing Britain's commercial interests.

The slave trade: protection and suppression

Slavery and the slave trade

By the late 18th century, the slave trade was the biggest and most lucrative trade route for British shipping, with over 150 ocean-going ships leaving British ports annually on the long triangular voyage between Europe, West Africa and the West Indies. The slave economies of the West Indies were an important source of income for Britain, at a time when the Exchequer was badly in need of money from the colonies in order to finance wars with France. In each of the four major wars that Britain fought with France between 1756 and 1815, fleets were dispatched to the West Indies as France and Britain invaded each other's colonial possessions. These actions came at a high cost; Britain lost thousands of men to combat and disease in trying to defend plantation colonies in the West Indies.

Supporters of slavery had argued that the slave trade was the 'nursery of the Royal Navy' due to the number of experienced sailors recruited by the Royal Navy from slaving ships, but this argument was less persuasive when the Admiralty was losing thousands of men defending West Indian slave economies. The abolitionist Thomas Clarkson produced figures in 1788 showing that of the 5,000 men leaving Britain on slaving voyages in 1785, only 2,329 returned. Sailing between tropical regions of West Africa and the West Indies with no medicine for diseases found in those regions, slave crews suffered high mortality rates, effectively depriving Britain of skilled manpower. The perception that the Royal Navy and the slave trade were mutually dependent was gradually undermined and, when the abolitionists finally succeeded in passing legislation to abolish the slave trade in 1807, the Royal Navy became the enemy of the slavers.

Early efforts to disrupt the slave trade

Given the other challenges faced by the Royal Navy during the Napoleonic Wars, few resources could initially be spared to enforce the new legislation. A new squadron was created in 1808 to stop the transatlantic slave trade, but only two ships were dispatched to patrol 5,000 km of West African coastline. Even after peace in Europe freed up resources, enforcement was not a priority for the Admiralty; by 1821, there were six ships in the squadron and in 1831 this had only risen to seven. The estimated annual number of slaves shipped across the Atlantic actually increased from 80,000 in 1800 to 135,000 in 1830. Slavery, but not the slave trade, was still legal in the British colonies of the West Indies and many of these slaves were smuggled into British plantations.

The West Africa squadron was one of the least desirable postings for a naval officer during this period. With long periods at sea, no welcoming cities, mosquitoes and constant equatorial heat, the work was hard and unglamorous. It was also dangerous; tropical disease took a terrible toll on the West Africa squadron, with 204 of the 792 men on the squadron dying in 1829 alone. In addition, the squadron's effectiveness was severely limited by its terms of engagement. During the Napoleonic Wars, Royal Navy ships were able to board and seize enemy ships at will, but once there was peace in Europe, engagements with foreign ships were strictly regulated. Slavers could often operate with impunity by carrying papers and flying the flag of nations that Royal Navy ships were not permitted to seize. The *Presidenté*, for example, was captured in 1828 after flying a Buenos Aires flag and then a French flag – its crew spoke English and had anglicised names like Brown, Williams, Oxford and Rogers.

Some of these challenges were overcome over time. The squadron eventually grew to 32 warships in 1847. Through a process of often tortuous negotiations, successive foreign secretaries used Britain's strong diplomatic position to create a series of treaties which allowed the Royal Navy to board and seize foreign slaving ships. These allowed a little more leeway but were still restrictive; typically the navy could only act if slaves were actually being carried – no action could be taken against ships merely equipped as slavers lingering along the coast. Sometimes, this led to horrible scenes, such as the Spanish slavers *Regulo* and *Rapido* throwing 150 chained slaves overboard in 1831 while being chased by the Royal Navy. Under instructions from abolitionist foreign secretaries like Lord Palmerston, the Royal Navy was sometimes permitted to act unilaterally against ships from weaker countries like Portugal in 1839 and Brazil in 1845, but treaties had to be strictly followed with American and French ships.

SOURCE

From the report of His Majesty's Commissioner in Sierra Leone to the Earl of Aberdeen, 23 March 1829. Actions like the *Black Joke*'s victory over the *Almirante* captured the public imagination, but the Royal Navy squadron was often outsailed and outgunned by the slavers, or stymied by complex rules over boarding foreign vessels. The Earl of Aberdeen was the new and inexperienced foreign secretary, and the commissioner at Sierra Leone took advantage of this successful action to appraise him of the realities of the situation.

Although, perhaps, not strictly within our immediate province, the circumstances of this Case, (all the Officers on board the Almirante having been killed, with the exception of the third Mate,) combine, with the extraordinary skill and gallantry displayed on this occasion, to induce us to call on your Lordship's attention to the particulars of this Capture.

The Almirante had been boarded repeatedly by different Vessels of His Majesty's Squadron, and, among the rest, by the Black Joke, only a few days previous to the engagement, so that both vessels were perfectly well acquainted with each other.

The Spaniard was armed with 4 nine-pounders, and 10 eighteen pounders, and had a crew of 80 men; the black joke had only 2 guns and about 40 men; yet with this astonishing disparity, she forced her antagonist to strike, after an action of 2 hours, with the loss only, we are happy to say, of one man wounded (since dead) on board the Tender.

This event furnishes, at the same time, another proof, of how very necessary it is, that the powers of the capturing Squadron should be enlarged in the case of Spanish Vessels, and of the determination, which is becoming more daring every day, to persist in these speculations at all hazards; in fact, the trade is assuming a new character, and the Vessels now employed are of such a class, as not only to lessen the chance of capture by superiority of sailing, but also to enable them to make a very formidable resistance, in the event of their being boarded after the actual shipment of Slaves; and this inhuman traffic is, at this moment, carrying on by the Subjects of Spain, to a most lamentable extent, with, we regret to be obliged to add, very great success, and with facilities, afforded by the want of the Additional Article relative to the equipment, greater even, in some respects, than existed before the professed abolition of it by that Power.

The Royal Navy and the end of the slave trade

Anti-slave trade operations in West Africa led to technological developments on both sides. In the 1840s, the Royal Navy began using paddle steamers which could follow slaving ships into river systems inaccessible by ocean-going warships. The paddle steamer HMS *Hydra* captured four slave ships between 1844 and 1846. By contrast, the slavers began to use clipper ships, small ships of around 200 tons with large sails designed solely for speed. Clippers were first built in America specifically to break British blockades and were fast enough to outrun Royal Navy ships of the line and frigates. Their use by slavers put the West Africa squadron at a disadvantage until some were eventually captured and added to the squadron, including the famous *Black Joke*, which captured 11 slavers in a single year.

Between 1810 and 1860, the Royal Navy captured and freed around 150,000 slaves. Most of these were put ashore at the Royal Navy base at Freetown, an old slaving port that became the capital of Sierra Leone, Britain's main colony in West Africa. While this was a major achievement, the Navy was not successful in stopping the Atlantic slave trade, and the freed slaves only represented about ten percent of the total number shipped to the Americas during this period. The slave trade was only ended when slave ownership was made illegal in the Americas, beginning with the British West Indies in 1833. When the American Civil War eliminated the market for slaves in the southern states of America in 1865, the transatlantic slave trade was effectively ended.

The slave trade still continued on Africa's east coast, although the Royal Navy was able to apply pressure on the **sultan** of Zanzibar to end his lucrative slave markets. There was never a concerted effort to end slavery in the Red Sea or Indian Ocean, but the Royal Navy operated infrequent slave patrols there until the early 20th century. As with the transatlantic trade, the reduction in demand for slaves was more important in achieving abolition than efforts to target the trade at sea.

Suppressing piracy and defending British commerce

In the early 19th century, the trade route linking China, the East Indies, India and England became a major source of income for Britain, and the Royal Navy devoted significant resources to protecting this route. The suppression of piracy in the Indian Ocean was a major task. French **privateers** operating out of Isle de France wreaked havoc on British shipping in this area during the Napoleonic Wars. The Royal Navy blockaded Isle de France, but this had limited effect due to the fast ships used by the privateers. Robert Surcouf, the most renowned French privateer, captured over 40 prizes in a profitable career, including 16 in a single expedition in 1807–08. The French threat was only eliminated when the British gathered sufficient forces to capture Isle de France in 1810; the island was renamed Mauritius and became a naval base.

Arab pirates continued to threaten shipping from the Red Sea to Bombay, however, and the Royal Navy increased its operations in the region in response. To facilitate future operations, Royal Navy surveyors charted the Red Sea area between 1800 and 1809. Treaties were signed with the Imam of Mocha and the sultan of Aden for the protection of British commerce as early as 1802. In 1820, Mocha was bombarded until the Imam accepted a commercial treaty. Berbera was blockaded from 1827 to 1832, until compensation was obtained for an attack on British shipping.

SOURCE

From the Anglo-Dutch Treaty, signed in London on 17 March 1824. The treaty resolved territorial disputes in the East Indies between the British and the Dutch, and formalised responsibilities for the supression of piracy. After the treaty, Britain took responsibility for patrolling the territories outlined in Article X, while the Netherlands did the same for the territories in Article IX. The demarcation line in this treaty became the modern border of Indonesia and Malaysia.

Article V

Their Britannick and Netherland Majesties, in like manner, engage to concur affectually in repressing Piracy in those Seas; They do not grant either asylum or protection to Vessels engaged in Piracy, and They will, in no case, permit the Ships or merchandise captured by such Vessels, to be introduced, deposited, or sold, in any of their Possessions.

Article IX

The Factory of Fort Marlborough and all the English Possessions on the Island of Sumatra, are herby ceded to His Netherland Majesty; and His Britannick Majesty further engages that no British Settlement shall be formed on that island, nor any Treaty concluded by British Authority, with any Native Prince, Chief, or State therein.

Article X

The Town and Fort of Malacca, and its Dependencies, are herby ceded to His Britannick Majesty; and His Netherland Majesty engage, for Himself and his subjects, never to Form any Establishments on any part of the Peninsular of Malacca, or to conclude any Treaty with any Native Press, or State therein.

The Straits of Malacca, a narrow channel linking China to India, was a hotbed of piracy. A large fleet of up to 100 pirate ships operated in this area from bases in the Philippines and South-East Asia, able to capture even large European merchantmen. As opium sales to China increased steadily throughout the 19th century, suppression of piracy in this area became a priority for the British East India Company (see page 26). In 1824, the company agreed with the Dutch to divide the area and introduce naval patrols. The introduction of a naval squadron, based at the new settlement of Singapore, helped reduce piracy levels but could not eliminate them completely.

ACTIVITY
KNOWLEDGE CHECK

The Royal Navy and British commercial interest

1 How significant was the Royal Navy for protecting British commerce?

2 How important was the slave trade to British interests?

3 Did the abolition of the slave trade result in significant changes to the role of the Royal Navy?

4 In your opinion, was the evolution of the Royal Navy mainly motivated by the need to protect commercial interests or as a tool for enhancing British political power?

The attack on Algiers, 1816

SOURCE

The bombardment of Algiers August 27, 1816 under Admiral Pellew, resulting in surrender of over 1000 European [i.e. Christian] *hostages including the British consul*, painted by Thomas Whitcombe (c1752–1824), a British maritime painter of the Napoleonic Wars.

Pirates and slavers had operated out of Algiers and other North African ports like Tunis and Tripoli, known collectively as the 'Barbary States', since at least the 16th century. They were well armed and organised enough to capture shipping as well as undertaking large-scale coastal raids, capturing an estimated 1–1.25 million Europeans between the 16th and 19th centuries. Prisoners were ransomed or enslaved, and the rulers of the Barbary States, known as the Beys, grew rich from a ten percent share.

The Royal Navy had been strong enough to intimidate the Beys into leaving British shipping alone since the 17th century, when Royal Navy fleets had secured treaties after bombarding Tripoli in 1675 and Algiers in 1682. Similarly, France bombarded Algiers three times and Tripoli once in the 1680s to secure French shipping. However, smaller powers without great fleets were still vulnerable: the American government paid $1 million in ransom to the Barbary States in 1795 and 900 Sardinians were taken as slaves in a single raid in 1798.

The Royal Navy had sourced supplies from the Barbary States during the wars with France, but by 1815 it was both the dominant force in the Mediterranean and able to resupply from a peaceful Europe. It was, therefore, well placed to tackle the Barbary States and in 1816, following criticism that Britain was more interested in suppressing the slave trade in Africa than Europe, an expedition under Admiral Pellew, Lord Exmouth, was sent to North Africa. Backed by a naval squadron, he secured treaties with the Beys of Tunis, Tripoli and Algiers. However, before he returned to England, 200 captured Corsicans, Sardinians and Sicilians were massacred on the Algerian island of Bona. Exmouth returned with a larger fleet the same year and bombarded Algiers, firing over 50,000 cannonballs and sinking over 40 vessels. Not knowing that the British were virtually out of ammunition, the Bey of Algiers capitulated the next day, repaying over £80,000 in ransom money and freeing 3,000 slaves.

SOURCE

7 From a letter from Lord Exmouth to the Admiralty, published in the *London Gazette*, 15 September 1816. Lucky to be given a second chance after his diplomatic failure, Exmouth heaped praise upon his superiors. The references to 'adequate' and 'proportionate' resources reflect criticism that his fleet of five ships of the line and ten frigates and bomb-ships was insufficient to subdue Algiers.

Sir,

In all the vicissitudes of a long life of public service, no circumstance has ever produced on my mind such impressions of gratitude and joy as the event of yesterday. To have been one of the humble instruments, in the hands of Divine Providence, for bringing to reason a ferocious Government, and destroying forever the insufferable and horrid system of Christian slavery, can never cease to be a source of delight and heartfelt comfort to every individual happy enough to be employed in it. I may, I hope, be permitted, under such impressions, to offer my sincere congratulations to their Lordships on the complete success which attended his majesties fleet in their attack upon Algiers yesterday: and the happy result produced from it on this day by the signature of peace....

My thanks are jointly due for the honour and confidence His Majesty's Ministers have been pleased to repose on my zeal, on this highly important occasion. The means were by them made adequate to my own wishes, and the rapidity of their measures speak for themselves. Not more than 100 days since, I left Algiers with the British fleet, unsuspicious and ignorant of the atrocities which had been committed at Bona; that fleet on its arrival in England was necessarily disbanded, and another, with proportionate resources, created and equipped; and although impeded in its progress by calms and adverse winds, has poured the vengeance of an insulted nation, in chastising the cruelties of a ferocious Government, with a promptitude beyond example, and highly honourable to the national character, eager to resent oppression or cruelty, whenever practised upon those under their protection.

The bombardment of Algiers in 1816 was not entirely effective. As the Beys were heavily reliant on piracy for their wealth, sporadic raiding continued; Britain again bombarded Algiers in 1820 and piracy was not eliminated until France conquered Algiers in 1830. It was nonetheless a significant moment in world affairs, showing that Britain was willing to use the might of the Royal Navy to protect foreigners under British protection. The Royal Navy had assumed the role of the world's police force, a role it would keep until 1914 in a period that became known as the **Pax Britannica**.

KEY TERM

Pax Britannica
A Latin term for 'British peace' that referred to the period 1814–1914 when there was reasonable stability in Europe.

The work of exploration and mapping

The Seven Years' War (1756–63) was the world's first truly global conflict, with battles between French and British forces taking place from India to Europe to North America. The reliance on ships of the line to fight major engagements created a problem in such a long-distance conflict, as the deep keels and long sides of these ships meant they were not well equipped to sail in unknown coastal waters. Even in home waters, accurate charts and good navigational skills could be the difference between victory and disaster at sea. The Royal Navy was still haunted by the Scilly naval disaster of 1707, when four warships and 1,550 men were lost due to a navigation error. Admiral Hawke had won a major victory by following a French fleet into Quiberon Bay during a severe gale in 1759, but in his account of the battle he made clear the danger of being 'on a part of the coast, among islands and shoals, of which we were totally ignorant'. Between 1803 and 1815, 223 of the 317 Royal Navy ships lost ran aground on dangerous coastline or sank at sea; wind and rocks were more dangerous than enemy guns.

It was clear that global operations required accurate knowledge of the world's oceans, and the Admiralty gave a high priority to voyages of exploration and mapping.

EXTEND YOUR KNOWLEDGE

The importance of longitude

To be able to calculate a position at sea, it is necessary to know both latitude (distance north or south from the equator) and longitude (location east or west). Mariners had been able to calculate latitude for centuries by measuring the altitude of the sun or specific stars above the horizon, but until the 18th century there was no way of measuring longitude at sea. Captains could only estimate their position by guessing the distance they had already travelled east or west, a method known as 'dead reckoning', which was unreliable due to variations in wind and currents. The usual solution was to sail to the right latitude, then head east or west for as long as it took to reach the destination. This could be dangerous, however, and was not practical for the co-ordination of large fleets.

More importantly, with ships never able to determine their precise position, it was not possible to produce accurate charts, so many cartographers used inaccurate information based on dead reckoning.

Any navy able to calculate longitude at sea would, therefore, have a significant advantage, and the government passed the Longitude Act in 1714 to provide 'a Publick Reward for such Person or Persons as shall Discover the Longitude at Sea'. While some researchers concentrated on a complex set of calculations based on lunar observations, others tried to produce a clock that would keep time at sea.

This puzzle was finally solved by a clockmaker, John Harrison, in 1759. Using a number of innovative techniques and the most precise craftsmanship in the world at the time, Harrison produced a watch that could keep time at sea. The Admiralty tested the watch on a trip to the West Indies, and it was found to have lost only five seconds on the 81-day voyage, allowing accurate calculations to within one nautical mile. The problem of longitude, and therefore of accurate chart-making, had been solved. Although some at the Admiralty remained sceptical, Harrison claimed his reward after petitioning parliament and the king directly.

Captain Cook's exploration of the South Seas, 1768–71

Given the growing importance of increasing the Royal Navy's knowledge of the world's oceans, the Admiralty was receptive to a proposal in 1768 by the Royal Society for a scientific expedition to the Pacific. The Royal Society was interested in using the transit of Venus in front of the sun to measure the distance between the earth and the sun, while the Admiralty wanted to lay claim to new lands and chart potential anchorages for warships. The scientifically minded Captain James Cook was appointed to lead the mission and was successful in completing a **circumnavigation** of the globe between the years 1768 and 1771.

KEY TERM

Circumnavigation
To sail all the way around the globe.

SOURCE

From Captain Cook's log, Wednesday, 22 August 1770. Cook discovered that New Guinea was not linked to the Australian continent as had previously been thought. He went ashore on an island he named Possession Island and claimed the whole eastern coastline of Australia for the king. Having described the traditional owners of the land in one paragraph, he relates depriving them of their land in the next.

Before and after we Anchor'd we saw a Number of People upon this Island, Arm'd in the same manner as all the others we have seen, Except one man, who had a bow and a bundle of Arrows, the first we have seen upon this Coast. From the appearance of the people we expected they would have opposed our landing; but as we approached the shore they all made off, and left us in peaceable possession of as much of the Island as served our purpose. After landing I went upon the highest hill, which, however, was of no great height, yet no less than twice or thrice the height of the Ship's Mastheads; but I could see from it no land between South-West and West-South-West, so that I did not doubt but there was a passage. I could see plainly that the lands laying to the North-West of this passage were compos'd of a number of Islands of Various extent, both for height and Circuit, ranged one behind another as far to the Northward and Westward as I could see, which could not be less than 12 or 14 Leagues.

Having satisfied myself of the great Probability of a passage, thro' which I intend going with the Ship, and therefore may land no more upon this Eastern coast of New Holland, and on the Western side I can make no new discovery, the honour of which belongs to the Dutch Navigators, but the Eastern Coast from the Latitude of 38 degrees South down to this place, I am confident, was never seen or Visited by any European before us; and notwithstanding I had in the Name of his Majesty taken possession of several places upon this Coast, I now once More hoisted English Colours, and in the Name of His Majesty King George the Third took possession of the whole Eastern coast from the above Latitude down to this place by the Name of New Wales together with all the Bays, Harbours, Rivers, and Islands, situated upon the said Coast; after which we fired 3 Volleys of small Arms, which were answer'd by the like number from the Ship.

Cook was unable to take accurate measurements of the transit of Venus due to the limitations of his instruments, but his voyage was important for several reasons.

- It showed that it was possible for an expedition to stay at sea for three years without losing an unacceptable number of men to disease, if cleanliness and access to fresh food were maintained.

- It proved the effectiveness of new technology for making accurate charts. Cook was a dedicated **cartographer** and, using a duplicate of Harrison's watch, the charts he produced of the Pacific remained in use until the 20th century.

- It established a British claim to new lands in Australia, New Zealand and the Pacific.

Cook's first voyage forestalled new territorial acquisitions by Britain's European rivals, notably France, and was the basis for future colonial expansion, including the establishment of a penal colony in New South Wales (see Chapter 4). He undertook two more voyages for the Admiralty before being killed on the island of Hawaii in 1779.

After Cook, voyages of exploration became more common, and Royal Navy captains were often required to undertake mapping of uncharted waters. Exploration became more systematic after 1795, when the Admiralty established a Hydrographic Office to collate reliable charts, with a focus on unfamiliar waters where the Royal Navy was beginning to operate. The first Admiralty chart was published in 1801.

> **KEY TERM**
>
> Cartographer
> A person who draws maps.

> **A Level Exam-Style Question Section C**
>
> How far do you agree that the role of the Royal Navy did not substantially change in the years 1763–1914? (20 marks)
>
> **Tip**
> *When answering this question, you should consider the whole timeframe carefully and think about the context of the changing world. What is the primary role of the Royal Navy and does this change over the period?*

> **ACTIVITY**
> **KNOWLEDGE CHECK**
>
> **Mapping the world**
> 1 Read Source 8 and write down what you feel it says about the motivations for British exploration.
>
> 2 How might the source support the suggestion that exploration helped to enhance Britain's standing in the world?
>
> 3 Why was exploration so important to the development of the Royal Navy?

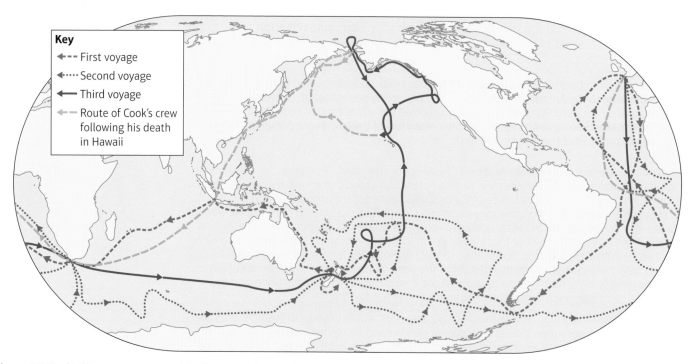

Figure 2.1 Cook's three voyages completed huge sections of the world map for the Admiralty. On his second voyage, he disproved the existence of a vast southern continent, known since antiquity as the mythical Terra Australis. On his last voyage, he showed that there was no practical northern sea route from the Pacific to Europe.

WHAT WERE THE REASONS FOR THE ACQUISITION OF KEY NAVAL BASES AND HOW DID THESE CHANGE IN THE YEARS 1763–1914?

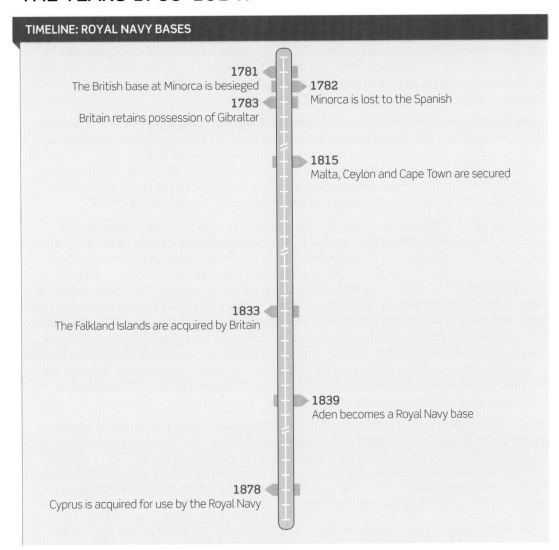

TIMELINE: ROYAL NAVY BASES

1781
The British base at Minorca is besieged

1782
Minorca is lost to the Spanish

1783
Britain retains possession of Gibraltar

1815
Malta, Ceylon and Cape Town are secured

1833
The Falkland Islands are acquired by Britain

1839
Aden becomes a Royal Navy base

1878
Cyprus is acquired for use by the Royal Navy

The importance of the acquisition and retention of key strategic bases around the globe, 1763–1914

Between 1763 and 1815, the Royal Navy's main aim was the destruction of France and its allies. During wars with France, previously remote and unimportant ports became vital assets as French and British fleets pursued each other around the globe. With the final defeat of Napoleon, the navy seized the most valuable of these ports to act as bases in the event of future aggression. However, territorial expansion was limited due to the reduced size of the navy and of naval expenditure in the peace that followed 1815. During this period, the promotion of free trade and limited intervention characterised the government's approach to the Empire. In the absence of major rivals in Europe, the navy's main task was to ensure that the world's sea lanes were secure for the merchant shipping that flowed to and from Britain from across the globe.

By the middle of the century, the resurgence of European powers and technological advances meant that the supremacy of the navy was no longer guaranteed. Politicians and colonial officials began to link Britain's dominant position in world affairs to control of key territories, supported by an unassailable navy. Under this approach, cost and profit were no longer the primary considerations in acquiring new territories, but were subordinate to extending British naval power across the globe and obtaining a strategic advantage over Britain's rivals.

The retention of Gibraltar, 1783

Whereas the 17th century was characterised by the Anglo-Dutch struggle for naval supremacy over the English Channel and the trade routes of the Atlantic, by the 18th century the two greatest maritime powers were Britain and France, which made control of Gibraltar vital. Situated where the sea between Europe and Africa is only 13 kilometres wide, the port was the gateway for British ships to enter the Mediterranean. Equally importantly, it separated the French Atlantic and Mediterranean coastlines, creating a major obstacle to France's ability to move warships and supplies between its main ports. Together with Minorca, which had one of the best ports in the Mediterranean and was well positioned to supply ships attacking or blockading France's main Mediterranean port at Toulon, Gibraltar was considered a key strategic asset by the Admiralty.

Britain had captured Gibraltar in 1704 and Minorca in 1708 from Spain during the War of Spanish Succession, and Spain had formally ceded these territories in 1713 to secure Britain's withdrawal from the war. However, both territories were precariously held; Spain had tried to recapture Gibraltar in 1727, while France occupied Minorca for a period during the Seven Years' War. The importance with which the Admiralty viewed the retention of these ports can be judged by the execution of Admiral Byng in 1757 when he decided not to attack the French fleet at Minorca.

Recovering territory from Britain remained a major priority for both France and Spain, and the American War of Independence presented an ideal opportunity. Funding for the Royal Navy had been progressively cut over the 12 years between the Seven Years' War and the American War of Independence, and many of its ships of the line were poorly built and suffered from rot. In 1778, it was rapidly rebuilding, but its forces were spread across the world, including the Atlantic Ocean, West Indies, Indian Ocean, East Indies and English Channel. In that year, France entered the war against Britain with the goal of regaining West Indian colonies lost during the Seven Years' War. Soon after diplomatic relations broke down in March, the French fleet at Toulon slipped through the Strait of Gibraltar before war was declared. Together with a fleet at Brest and supported by a growing number of American privateers raiding British merchant shipping, the French were now able to match the Royal Navy in the Atlantic. By failing to close the Strait of Gibraltar in time, the Royal Navy had fatally undermined its position in America.

Britain's position deteriorated further when France secured Spain's entry into the war in return for supporting the Spanish reconquest of Minorca and Gibraltar under the Treaty of Aranjuez in 1779. Together, the combined navies of France and Spain had 121 ships of the line in 1779, compared to 90 for the Royal Navy. These numbers changed to 137 and 94 respectively when the Dutch joined the coalition against Britain in 1781. The Royal Navy was outnumbered and outgunned across the world, even losing control of the English Channel.

In this situation, it seemed inevitable that both Gibraltar and Minorca would be lost, shutting the Royal Navy out of the Mediterranean. Gibraltar was blockaded by sea and surrounded by land in 1779, leading to a food shortage among the 5,000-strong garrison and civilians in the town. A Franco-Spanish fleet also landed an army to besiege the British base on Minorca in 1781. Despite its other challenges, the Admiralty made supplying Gibraltar a priority, sending supply convoys escorted by warships in 1780, 1781 and 1782. The Spanish fleet blockading Gibraltar was unable to prevent its resupply due to the poor sailing skills of its inexperienced crews and adverse winds blowing them out of position. For the same reasons, the garrisons at Gibraltar and Minorca were initially able to stay in contact through the use of small fast ships, which evaded the blockade. Letters sent by the governor of Minorca on 12 and 13 November were delivered to England by 4 December 1781.

The British garrison at Minorca had barricaded itself within the fortress of St Philip's Castle as soon as the Franco-Spanish force landed and was initially successful at repelling assaults. However, the lack of fresh food in the castle led to the development of scurvy among the soldiers, and General Murray surrendered his garrison after a five-month siege in February 1782. By contrast, at Gibraltar there were just enough gardens behind British lines to prevent many fatalities from scurvy, although the disease broke out repeatedly during the siege. In September 1782, the Franco-Spanish forces mounted a major assault on Gibraltar, with over 5,000 men on 'floating batteries' supported by 18 ships of the line and other vessels. However, the attack failed when accurate cannon fire from the British garrison sank three of the batteries and damaged the others. The garrison was able to hold out until the end of the war in 1783.

Scurvy and its cure

Scurvy is a disease resulting from a lack of vitamin C in the diet. Typical symptoms progress from tiredness, spots on the skin and bleeding membranes to loss of teeth and suppurating wounds. Although a rapid recovery is normal if vitamin C is reintroduced into the diet, scurvy can be fatal if left untreated.

Scurvy was a major cause of death in the Royal Navy throughout the 18th century. It inevitably broke out when ships were at sea for long periods of time, which often made blockade strategies fatal even when there were no battles. In the Seven Years' War, over 130,000 sailors out of the 184,000 recruited were lost to disease, a combination of scurvy and the tropical diseases present on West Indian campaigns. Even though there had been several instances of men being cured by eating fresh fruit or vegetables, doctors were misled by a theory that scurvy was a digestive problem. Most treatments produced were potions designed to affect the digestion, made of ingredients like vinegar, malt and wort, or even sulphuric acid, which had no impact on scurvy.

One of Captain Cook's objectives on his first voyage in 1768 was to test different scurvy remedies. He did not lose a single man to the disease, which was almost unheard of at the time. On Magellan's expedition of a similar length in 1520, 208 men out of 230 were lost. Cook thought that an infusion of malt and wort was the most effective in preventing scurvy, even though this would have had no effect. His journals show that he took on fresh food wherever he landed, and used strict discipline to force his officers and men to eat unfamiliar fruits, vegetables and animals. This saved his crew from the disease, although he did not know it.

Anecdotal evidence from the siege of Gibraltar and other situations suggested that citrus fruits prevented scurvy, but it was only in 1794 that this was proved when HMS *Suffolk* sailed to India in four months without a trace of scurvy by using lemon juice. The Admiralty quickly moved to supply other ships with lemons or limes and scurvy was quickly eliminated, a key development which allowed the Royal Navy to blockade French ports for years at a time.

The retention of Gibraltar showed the importance of such a strategically placed port for the Royal Navy. Had the opportunity to close the Strait been taken in 1798, it may have affected the outcome of the American War of Independence. When Britain was in peril, Gibraltar had provided a line of defence which the enemy had failed to subdue, tying up large numbers of Franco-Spanish naval and ground forces which could otherwise have been concentrated against Britain. When the Royal Navy returned to the ascendency in the wars between 1792 and 1815, it provided a vital staging post for British fleets in the Mediterranean, for example by resupplying Nelson's fleet before the critical battle of Trafalgar.

The acquisition of Malta, Ceylon and Cape Town in 1815

As a Dutch colony, Ceylon initially belonged to one of Britain's allies in the French revolutionary wars. After multiple wars with the Portuguese, French and the native Kingdom of Kandy, the Dutch had occupied the coastal region. The interior remained under the control of the independent Kingdom of Kandy, which was effectively cut off from the outside world after 1765 by the ring of Dutch territory around the coast. With its trading ports of Trincomalee and Colombo, the colony was one of the only sources of cinnamon in the world. This spice was extremely valuable, and the British East India Company began to cultivate it in India from 1767, but Ceylon remained the main producer until the end of the 18th century.

When the Netherlands were conquered by France in 1794, the Dutch royal family fled to England, where they were pressured into ordering Dutch colonies to surrender to British forces for 'protection'. A ship of the line, HMS *Suffolk*, was duly dispatched with an accompanying frigate to capture Ceylon. Simultaneously, the French set up a puppet government in the Netherlands which ordered the colonies to ally with France. This left the Dutch governor of Ceylon in a difficult position, a position that quickly became untenable once the *Suffolk* arrived, supported by British East India Company troops. The Dutch settlements quickly surrendered and a British governor was installed, while the commercial side of the colony was left to the British East India Company. The capture of Ceylon immediately yielded around £300,000 of money in goods, as well as the acquisition of the cinnamon plantations, making this a profitable venture.

As a strategically located naval base that could pay for itself, Britain regarded Ceylon as a valuable asset and, unlike other Dutch colonies, Ceylon was retained in the Treaty of Amiens in 1802. The Kingdom of Kandy in the mountainous interior of the island hoped that the British would restore some of the coastline to them in order to conduct overseas trade, but this was not the case and sporadic warfare broke out. Already stretched by the war with France, the British government had no appetite for a potentially expensive war in a far-flung colony and instructed its governors to make peace with Kandy without conceding any coastal territory. A fragile peace was established until Governor Brownrigg, an ex-soldier with imperial ambitions, took advantage of dissension within the Kandyan court and supported a group of nobles against the king in 1815; Kandy was occupied and the king was captured. Brownrigg imposed the Kandyan Convention, under which Kandy became a self-governing protectorate with a requirement to pay tribute to the British coastal colony. A rebellion against this arrangement in 1817–18 was brutally suppressed by Brownrigg, who authorised the confiscation of land, burning of villages and destruction of rice paddies. The whole of Ceylon was then annexed as a British Crown colony, with successive governors concentrating on establishing a road and rail network to open up the interior to plantation farming and tighten military control.

The Dutch colony at Cape Town held no economic significance except as a stopping point for shipping between Europe and the East Indies. This position made it strategically valuable as a naval fleet there could prevent enemy shipping from sailing between the Indian and Atlantic oceans, cutting a major trade route. The Royal Navy had attempted to capture the colony during the American War of Independence in 1781, but were prevented from doing so by a French fleet which arrived first and fortified the colony. By 1795, the Royal Navy was again in the ascendancy and took advantage of this by seizing strategic colonies which other European powers were unable to defend. As with Ceylon, soon after France had conquered the Netherlands, a British fleet under Sir George Elphinstone arrived demanding that the colony surrender itself to the British for 'safekeeping'. After brief Dutch resistance, Britain occupied the colony until the Peace of Amiens in 1802, when it was returned to the Dutch. After war again broke out with France, Britain reoccupied the Cape to prevent French troops being landed there in 1806, and this time maintained a permanent presence, which was formalised by a treaty with the Dutch in 1814.

Napoleon had captured Malta from the **Knights Hospitaller** in 1798 after they refused to supply his fleet on the way to Egypt. The local population soon rebelled against the French garrison and asked the British for help. Nelson blockaded Valletta in 1799 and the French surrendered in 1800. The Royal Navy did not initially regard the island as strategically important, preferring Gibraltar and Minorca. Britain agreed to leave Malta in the temporary peace of 1802, but maintained a presence there when war recommenced in 1803. By 1815, the deep-water port and welcoming local population meant that Malta was sufficiently useful to be retained, but the port did not become a major naval base until the opening of the Suez Canal placed it on Britain's main seaway to India.

KEY TERM

Knights Hospitaller
A religious and military order whose full title was Knights of the Order of the Hospital of St John of Jerusalem, which was founded in the 11th century to protect pilgrims to the Holy Land and to tend to the sick.

The acquisition of the Falklands in 1833

Britain had established a settlement on the Falkland Islands in 1766, but abandoned this ten years later during the American War of Independence when the overstretched Royal Navy could no longer defend it. The islands continued to be used by South Atlantic sealing ships until the ex-Spanish colonies in South America, known as the United Provinces, authorised a European merchant called Luis Vernet to found a colony there in 1828.

With both the British and United Provinces claiming sovereignty over the islands, Vernet was in a difficult position diplomatically and also struggled to make the settlement a financial success. The only valuable commodity on the islands was the seal colonies, but these were rapidly being depleted by British and American sealers. Britain had over 70 sealing ships in the South Atlantic in the early 19th century. Vernet wanted to preserve the seals for his own use and confiscated three American sealing ships in 1831, taking their captains for trial in Buenos Aires. Britain considered this a dangerous development for British trade prospects and sent a single ship to reassert British sovereignty over the Falklands in 1833. Without the support of his men, many of whom were themselves British, Vernet surrendered without a fight.

EXTRACT

From *The Empire Project: The Rise and Fall of the British World System: 1830–1970* by John Darwin (2009). The acquisition of the Falklands can be seen as a response to a local threat to the important sealing trade, or as Darwin argues, part of a wider trend of territorial expansion designed to cement Britain's dominance of the world's oceans and the trade carried upon them.

The collapse of Spain, and the client status of Portugal, had now opened the South Atlantic coast to British maritime influence in Brazil and La Plata and (with the occupation of the Falkland Islands in 1833) gave them a guard-post that commanded Cape Horn. In themselves, the territories that the British acquired were not of great value and had small or poor populations. But their geostrategic meaning was huge. Their capture by Britain signalled the end of the mercantilist order that had partitioned Europe's seaborne trade with the Americas and Asia between the closed economic empires of Spain, Portugal, the Netherlands, France and Britain. The age of 'free' trade was about to begin.

SOURCE

9

Hunting party on Penguin Island in the Falkland Islands, c1822 from the *Histoire du voyage* by Louis Isidore Duperrey. Although the remote island group was inhospitable – Charles Darwin called it 'desolate and wretched' when he visited in 1833 – its seal colonies were valuable and it was well located to guard the passage to Cape Horn and maintain a naval force close to growing British trade interests in South America.

The acquisition of Aden in 1839

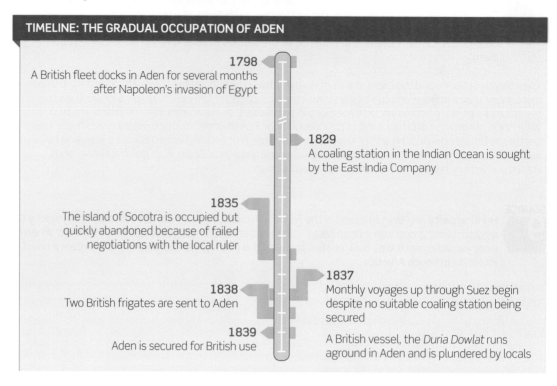

TIMELINE: THE GRADUAL OCCUPATION OF ADEN

1798
A British fleet docks in Aden for several months after Napoleon's invasion of Egypt

1829
A coaling station in the Indian Ocean is sought by the East India Company

1835
The island of Socotra is occupied but quickly abandoned because of failed negotiations with the local ruler

1837
Monthly voyages up through Suez begin despite no suitable coaling station being secured

1838
Two British frigates are sent to Aden

A British vessel, the *Duria Dowlat* runs aground in Aden and is plundered by locals

1839
Aden is secured for British use

The port of Aden (now in Yemen) had been an important trading *entrepôt* during the Middle Ages for bringing pepper and spices from India and the East Indies to the markets of Egypt and Arabia; it had then become prosperous as a major coffee producer in the Early Modern Period. By the 18th century, European sailing ships around the Cape dominated East Indian trade and Arabian coffee was supplanted by cheaper coffee from slave plantations in the Dutch East Indies and French West Indies. Portuguese engravings of Aden from 1513 show a large city with strong walls and many fine stone buildings, but by 1800 fewer than 1,000 people lived at the port, governed by a sultanate that exercised a precarious independence from Egypt and the **Ottoman Empire**. British interests in Aden began in 1798 with Napoleon's invasion of Egypt, after which a British fleet docked at Aden for several months at the invitation of the sultan. The French were defeated in Egypt in 1801 and their privateers tracked down over the subsequent decade. As there was little British trade in the Red Sea, most British politicians until the 1830s had no further interest in the area beyond the suppression of piracy. However, a small number of government ministers and East India Company officials thought that a British base in the area was necessary to prevent another French advance through Egypt or Russian expansion through Persia. The emergence of Mehmet Ali Pasha as a strong local ruler in Egypt only increased their concerns. The governor of Bombay from 1834 to 1838, Sir Robert Grant, was one of those who believed that India could only be protected by pre-emptively seizing 'places of strength' to protect the Indian Ocean.

KEY TERM

Ottoman Empire
An empire founded in 1299 by the Turkish leader Osman I. By the 17th century, it encompassed much of south-eastern Europe, western Asia and North Africa and had its capital at Constantinople. It declined in the 19th century as industrialised European powers began to gain military advantage.

The growing importance of Aden

The Red Sea increased in importance after the steamship *Hugh Lindsay* sailed from Bombay to the Suez isthmus in 1829, stopping at Aden with the sultan's consent to resupply with coal. Although cargo was still carried around the Cape in sailing ships, a steam route to Suez could provide a much quicker option for transporting officials and important communications. Grant felt that armed ships steaming regularly between Bombay and Suez would help secure British interests in the region and did all he could to progress this vision. After lengthy negotiations due to the cost involved in investing in the new technology, the government agreed to pay half of the costs for six voyages per year and the East India Company board approved the purchase of two steamers in 1837. Grant immediately announced that monthly voyages to Suez would take place, despite the fact that no secure coaling station had been found.

The search for a coaling station had started in 1829 with intensive surveying of the Arabian coast, but the governor general of India, Lord Auckland, ordered that any East India Company involvement should be peaceful and negotiated with local rulers. Under Grant's instructions, East India Company troops had occupied the island of Socotra in 1835, but abandoned it when negotiations with the local ruler collapsed and illness broke out among the troops. The failed negotiations at Socotra were led by Commander Stafford Haines, who then suggested to Grant that Aden should be occupied on the basis that the sultan was little better than a pirate, citing incidents of the sultan's interference with British shipping. Grant agreed with Haines and, when the sultan's forces plundered the merchantman *Duria Dowlat* after it ran aground, he pressured Lord Auckland to allow Haines to act. This aggressive attitude was familiar in Britain during the 19th century and was arguably born not just from an imperialistic and racial sense of superiority towards other ethnic and racial groups, but also from a determination to make examples of those who challenged British dominance. Given the growth of rival powers, this particular motivation perhaps bears greater urgency since it, in the first instance, presented a direct insult to the British government and also afforded that government an opportunity to demonstrate its power and thereby remind the world of the country's naval capacity.

Haines arrived in Aden in 1837 with a mandate to secure satisfaction for the 'outrage' of the *Duria Dowlat* and to negotiate use of a coal depot, but in negotiations with the sultan he demanded much more: full British occupation of the port. During negotiations, Haines secured a letter from the sultan stating 'you can then make houses or forts or do what you like; the town will then be yours', although the context of the letter suggests that the sultan was only setting out a negotiating position. When negotiations broke down amid rumours that the sultan's son was planning to kidnap Haines, the letter was used by Haines to claim that a treaty for occupation had been agreed.

As negotiations deteriorated, a series of letters were sent between Bombay, Calcutta and London as Grant sought approval for an armed intervention. Lord Auckland remained reluctant to fight a war for a port with no commercial value, but Grant's arguments were more persuasive in London. The president of the India Board, John Hobhouse, and the foreign secretary, Lord Palmerston, both encouraged Grant to take action and seize Aden. Grant died in 1838, so the decision to send troops to assist Haines was taken by his deputy, Farish. Without the approval of either the government in London or the governor general in Calcutta, but guided by private letters of support from Hobhouse, he sent two frigates and 700 men to Aden. Haines quickly captured the port and presented with a *fait accompli* supported by the foreign secretary, there was little the East India Company could do but accept their new territory.

KEY TERM

Fait accompli
Something that has already happened before those affected by it are made aware.

EXTRACT

2 From R.J. Gavin, *Aden under British rule, 1839–1967* (1975). Gavin examined the correspondence between key players in the acquisition of Aden and concluded that a few individuals acting decisively on their imperial vision had successfully subverted normal decision-making processes.

> The Prime Minister was kept informed of what was happening but that was all. There is no record of a Cabinet meeting being held to discuss the matter.... Aden was of course occupied by the East India Company, and after occupation formed part of that organisation's possessions. The Company was in control and the decision to occupy was nominally theirs. But that was as far as it went. In reality the crucial decisions were not taken by the Company. Had the Court of Directors been consulted there is little doubt that they would have pronounced a veto. Three years after the occupation they refused to take any responsibility for what had been done....
>
> The decision to take Aden had been the work of a few energetic men – Grant, Hobhouse, Palmerston and Farish – with Haines acting as the initiator and executor. This was to have an important bearing on the early history of the settlement. One by one, those men were replaced by others who had quite different ideas about Aden's importance. Grant died in July 1838. In June 1839 Farish handed over to Carnac who, from the moment of his arrival until the Autumn of 1840, regarded the new possession as a waste of money and did his best to prevent its being put on a permanent footing. In the Summer of 1841 the main architects of the whole new policy in the Indian Ocean – Hobhouse and Palmerston – went out of office.

With the death of Grant and the change of cabinet in London, Haines was left without political allies in charge of a remote port which was valued by neither the government nor the East India Company. He ran the new acquisition on a shoestring budget, using bribes to keep the peace locally and working tirelessly for 15 years without a holiday to turn the settlement into a major depot. Unlike successful new *entrepôts* at Singapore and Hong Kong, however, Aden did not sit on a crossroads of trade routes or have the presence of a Royal Navy squadron to boost business. The coaling of mail steamers simply did not produce enough income to meet expenses, and Haines ran up a deficit of £28,000 before being recalled to Bombay and tried for fraud and embezzlement in 1854. He was acquitted, but spent six years in debtor's jail in Bombay as the new governor held him personally responsible for the colony's debts. The future of Aden remained uncertain until the opening of the Suez Canal made it a boom town, now perfectly situated on the main shipping route from India to Europe.

ACTIVITY
KNOWLEDGE CHECK

Early expansion

Using the material you have read and your own knowledge, write a 200-word explanation for the expansion of British naval ports during the late 18th and early 19th centuries.

In your explanation, you should include the following:

- motivation for such expansion
- significant ports that were acquired.

The acquisition of Cyprus in 1878

Extending British influence

The seizure of Aden was the logical extension of the acquisition of naval bases begun during the French wars and formalised in 1815. Whereas the British Empire, and in particular the East India Company, had primarily been a profit-making enterprise, the new bases had little to offer economically. A new way of thinking was beginning to emerge, whereby the seizure of territory was justified by the need to protect existing territory rather than to seek additional profit. In this sense, the motivation for acquisition was arguably becoming more strategic as nations' empires were growing at a considerable rate and, in order to maintain a dominant position in the shrinking world, Britain was careful to secure and advance its existing possessions.

By the 1870s, Palmerston's brand of imperialism, which asserted British values and interests, had become mainstream in the Conservative Party. It was characterised by prime ministers like Disraeli and then Lord Salisbury, who were imbued with a sense of imperial destiny and supported both increased naval power and territorial expansion. These politicians thought primarily in terms of geopolitics rather than economics and were willing to spend heavily in order to achieve strategic advantages over rival powers. The Russian Empire was considered Britain's greatest rival, largely because it was out of reach of Royal Navy warships and expanding rapidly into central Asia with the conquest of Tashkent (1865), Samarkand (1868) and Bukhara (1868).

EXTEND YOUR KNOWLEDGE

Benjamin Disraeli (1804–81)

Benjamin Disraeli was a novelist and politician who became prime minister in 1868 and 1874. He is credited with the creation of the modern Conservative Party, having set out his vision of 'one-nation conservatism', which accepted a greater degree of paternalism when designing policy, and especially the adoption of more pragmatic actions in the light of the extended electorate which Britain enjoyed after first 1832 and then 1867, when the vote was extended to the middle classes and some more skilled members of the working class.

As a politician, Disraeli was both ambitious and considered in his actions – especially when confronting his political rival William Gladstone, with whom he had a bitter rivalry. In his second term of office after 1874, Disraeli became preoccupied with the Eastern Question – the decline of the Ottoman Empire – and was able to secure significant territorial and economic interests for Britain from that empire: in 1875 he purchased shares in the Suez Canal and, during the Congress of Berlin in 1878, he was able to limit the influence of the Russian Empire by pushing for the recognition of sovereign principalities for Romania, Serbia and Montenegro.

By contrast, the Liberal Party under Gladstone (prime minister four times between 1868 and 1894) remained committed to less government expenditure and minimal overseas involvement. Gladstone achieved a lasting peace with the USA in the Washington Treaty (1871), but to achieve this he made concessions on disputed fisheries and agreed to pay damages for American shipping sunk by confederate privateers sailing from British ports during the American Civil War. Although Gladstone's liberals received 189,000 more votes, the better-organised Conservatives won a majority of seats in the 1874 general election, bringing Disraeli to power.

Disraeli and expansion

Disraeli soon extended Britain's interests overseas by purchasing shares in the Suez Canal in 1875, a move that was widely popular with the public. In 1876, he passed legislation giving Queen Victoria the title 'Empress of India' to give her the same rank as the Russian emperor, Tsar Alexander II. Disraeli aimed to limit Russian expansion by supporting powers bordering Russia, including Afghanistan in the East and the bankrupt Ottoman Empire in the West. In 1876 he ignored Gladstone's demands from opposition to intervene against the Ottoman Empire's massacres of Balkan Nationalists, and instead sent Lord Salisbury to Constantinople to negotiate support for the Ottomans. As Russia prepared for war against the Ottoman Empire, Disraeli tried unsuccessfully to persuade his cabinet to occupy parts of the Balkans.

When the Russo-Turkish War broke out in 1877, the Russian army quickly defeated the Ottoman army and threatened to take Constantinople. This would have given Russia open access to the Mediterranean, as well as the ability to close the Black Sea to British shipping. In Britain, imperial **jingoism** was widespread and there was strong support for immediate war with Russia. Disraeli persuaded parliament to approve £6 million to prepare the navy and army for war; Gladstone voted against the measure but half of the Liberal Party supported Disraeli.

SOURCE 10
The Opening of the Suez Canal on 17 November 1869 by French engraver Edouard Riou. In addition to his own engravings, Riou also provided illustrations for the author Jules Verne.

KEY TERM

Jingoism
An extreme type of nationalism which favours war and aggressive foreign policy to secure national interests. The term originates from the chorus of a music-hall song that was popular during the Russo-Turkish War:

We don't want to fight but by Jingo if we do
We've got the ships, we've got the men, we've got the money too
We've fought the Bear before, and while we're Britons true
The Russians shall not have Constantinople.

Gaining territories from the Ottoman Empire

The Ottoman Empire surrendered in 1878, signing a peace treaty that directly or indirectly ceded most of the Balkans to Russia. This was unacceptable to Disraeli, who convened a congress at Berlin to apply pressure on Russia. At the talks, Disraeli allied with the German chancellor, Bismarck, to force the Russians to abandon some of their territorial gains or face war with both Britain and Germany. The Dardanelles remained under Ottoman control, but Russia retained some of their conquered territory.

Disraeli also secured Cyprus for Britain as a suitable base in the eastern Mediterranean from which the Royal Navy could monitor and counter any further Russian expansion. The island also provided another link in the chain of British ports on the route to India and a base from which Britain could intervene in Egypt if necessary to protect the stake Disraeli had purchased in the Suez Canal.

Cyprus was previously held by the Ottoman Empire, but the Ottomans had no choice but to accept Disraeli's demand for the island as they were relying on British support to reclaim at least some of their territory from Russia. Under the Cyprus Convention, the island was technically leased to Britain by the Ottoman Empire for £92,799 annually. This money was raised by taxing the inhabitants of the island, but was never paid to the Ottomans; instead, Disraeli insisted that it was sent to London to pay debts from the Crimean War 25 years earlier that the Ottoman Empire had defaulted on.

The acquisition of Cyprus was an important milestone for the development of the Empire. It showed that British imperial policy was no longer determined by liberal economics and trade routes. Britain was now willing to acquire colonies simply to constrain the territorial ambitions of other powers. The growing power gap between the major European imperial powers and other countries was also clear; the Ottoman Empire was helpless to prevent Britain and Russia acquiring large tracts of its territory. No thought was given to what the Cypriots might have wanted – a majority of them favoured unification with Greece.

Disraeli's bloodless acquisition of Cyprus was widely seen as a diplomatic coup. He followed this success with annexation of the Transvaal in 1877, the invasion of Afghanistan in 1878 and the conquest of Zululand in 1879. Although Britain was ultimately successful in these wars, they were costly in both money and lives. At the Battle of Isandlwana, the Zulus had defeated the British army, killing over 1,300 British and colonial troops. In his famous **Mid-Lothian campaign**, Gladstone undermined Disraeli's popularity and consequently the Conservatives were defeated in the 1880 election.

KEY TERM

Mid-Lothian campaign
A series of four speeches by Gladstone attacking Disraeli's foreign policy, in which he argued that Disraeli's government was financially incompetent and had abused Britain's position of strength to engage in unnecessary and unjustifiable wars.

A Level Exam-Style Question Section C

To what extent is it reasonable to suggest that the expansion of the Royal Navy in the years 1763–1914 was the result of political imperatives? (20 marks)

Tip
When answering this question, you should consider different motivations for the expansion of the Royal Navy and judge them against the role played by politics – are the other motivations linked to politics in any way?

Growing support for further expansion

TIMELINE: PUBLIC SUPPORT FOR THE ROYAL NAVY

1884
Gladstone is criticised for reducing government spending on the Royal Navy

1885
Gladstone is forced to resign after British failure in the Sudan

The Conservative leader, Lord Salisbury, supports greater investment in the Royal Navy

1889
High spending on the Royal Navy is commonplace

Gladstone attempted to reduce Britain's overseas involvement, but was drawn into conflict in Egypt to protect the interest in the Suez Canal that Disraeli had acquired. At a time when most European powers were entering an expansionist phase, Gladstone tried to scale back naval expenditure, which left him vulnerable to criticism. In 1884, media articles suggesting that the Royal Navy was underfunded caused a public furore.

Failure to appease an increasingly militaristic and imperialist public damaged Gladstone's popularity, and he was forced to resign after the defeat of British forces in the Sudan in 1885. Lord Salisbury, leading the Conservative Party after Disraeli's death, again pursued an imperialist policy, notably by expanding British territories in Africa. By 1889, huge spending increases on the Royal Navy had become common as the Conservative Party capitalised on the popularity of an expansionist imperial policy.

SOURCE 11

From W.T. Stead, 'What is the truth about the Navy?' published in *The Pall Mall Gazette*, 15 September 1884. Stead wrote a series of articles demanding more funding for the Royal Navy, based on conversations with an anonymous source widely believed to be John Fisher. The articles created public pressure on Gladstone to drastically increase funding to the navy; in 1884 alone, Gladstone spent an additional £3.1 million on warships and £2.4 million on naval bases and ordnance.

The [Liberal] party now in power is the party of Free Trade, and Free Trade without command of the seas is death. That is to say, a system by which two-thirds of all the bread eaten in England has come to be grown over the sea can only be defended on the assumption that the ocean highway is as secure as the Great Northern railway. The maintenance of an undisputed and indisputable ascendency on every sea is the indispensible corollary to the abolition of the Corn Laws. This was clearly realised by Mr. Cobden, whose antipathy to expenditure on the Services was notorious. In a well-known passage, which Mr. Morley quotes with undisguised admiration, Mr Cobden assured Lord John Russell in 1860 that; so far from wishing to place his country at the mercy of France, "I would, if necessary, spend one hundred millions sterling to maintain an irresistible superiority over France at sea". It is, therefore, an axiom of the Liberal free traders that our superiority at sea must be "absolutely irresistible", and that our hundred millions sterling must, if needs be, be spent cheerfully rather than that our irresistible superiority should be challenged by any possible combination of hostile Powers. It is the fashion to speak of Mr. Gladstone as an obstacle to the execution of the policy so courageously defined by Mr. Cobden. There is no doubt that the Prime Minister would shrink with natural horror from any proposal to increase the Estimates. But those who are perpetually taunting him with his Midlothian orations might at least remember that nothing figured more prominently in that famous campaign than declarations of a determination to maintain our supremacy by sea. Lord Beaconsfield had seized Cyprus to guard our road to India. Mr Gladstone denounced that act with vehemence, and propounded, as the alternative policy, the maintenance of our naval supremacy. With withering scorn he denounced the utter folly of keeping out of view this supremacy at sea, which he declared was the true mode of guarding the road to India, in opposition to the multiplication of garrisons and military posts. Mr Gladstone's policy, therefore, is that of naval supremacy as distinguished from that of military conquest, and on Midlothian principles he could not for a moment hesitate to demand even the hundred millions named by Mr. Cobden if it were clearly demonstrated that our naval supremacy was not absolutely irresistible.

SOURCE 12

From the second reading of the Naval Defence bill in 1889. Henry Labouchere was an ally of Gladstone's who had been blocked from a cabinet position by the intervention of Queen Victoria. His arguments were unsuccessful and the Admiralty got their money. Unable to resist popular demands for massive increases in naval expenditure, Gladstone himself was forced to resign in 1894 after refusing to introduce inheritance tax to fund yet another request by Lord Hamilton.

MR. LABOUCHERE (Northampton): The first Lord of the Admiralty [Lord George Hamilton] told the House that the new standard of the Fleet was that it should be equal to any two navies in the world. I was shocked when I heard a Minister of the Crown make such a declaration. I have no doubt the hon. and gallant Admiral (Admiral Field) would have supported the First Lord of the Admiralty if he had asked for double the amount. [Admiral FIELD: Hear, hear!] I thought so, but I am not a quarterdeck politician, and therefore I was shocked. This was really a gauntlet thrown down to Europe, threatening, in effect, that "whatever you spend we will spend double." Perhaps some hon. Gentlemen opposite are acquainted with the game of poker. Great Britain is playing a game of poker with all Europe, ships of war being the stakes. It is perfectly avowed that we are throwing down the gauntlet. Lord Armstrong is an authority on this subject. Two or three days ago I was reading an article in the Nineteenth Century, written by Lord Armstrong, in which he suggests that, in order to frighten the world and show them what thorough devils we are, we should spend £20,000,000 instead of £10,000,000. Is it not reasonable to suppose that foreign nations are likely to accept our challenge?... THE CIVIL LORD OF THE ADMIRALTY (Mr. ASHMEAD BARTLETT): Why have the Government submitted this programme to the country? They have done so, in the first place, to ensure the maritime supremacy of England, which the hon. Gentleman the Member for Northampton has ridiculed. We on this side of the House do not hold with the hon. Gentleman. We believe in the maritime supremacy of the country as necessary, not only for its greatness, but also the magnificence of the Empire, its commerce, and, indeed, for the national existence of our people. Our object has been to make the Naval Power of Great Britain equal, and indeed, superior to the combined forces of any two great Naval Powers. Why, it is asked, is the Naval supremacy of this country essential? I answer that it is needed, first, to secure the safety and prosperity of the people at home; secondly, to maintain the strength of our world-wide Empire; thirdly, to defend the commerce of the country, is the value of which is almost immeasurable; and, fourthly, to protect the food supply of the people, which means our national existence.

Increased naval expenditure and colonial expansion went hand in hand, and the debates over the Naval Defence bill vividly demonstrated how the Royal Navy had evolved from the war-winning machine built up from 1763 to 1815. The acquisition of Malta, Ceylon and the Cape in 1815 was essentially a reaction to the threats France had posed; these ports gave the navy the ability to blockade France in the Mediterranean while safeguarding the main route to India. The long peace that followed 1815 was characterised by reduced naval expenditure and limited colonial expansion; the Royal Navy typically intervened where trade was threatened, for example in the Falklands in 1833. By the reign of Queen Victoria, however, some politicians and colonial officials were thinking in geopolitical rather than economic terms, as shown by the acquisition of Aden in 1839. By the 1870s, this thinking had become mainstream and imperial expansion and heavy naval expenditure were seen as expressions of Britain's rightful place at the top of the world order, despite the efforts of statesmen like William Gladstone to limit overseas interventions. By the time Cyprus was seized in 1878 after war with Russia was narrowly averted, public opinion favoured aggressive colonial expansion underpinned by an ever more powerful Royal Navy. In the context of this popularity, therefore, the stage was set for the partition of the African continent and a subsequent arms race among the Great Powers that would continue until the First World War.

ACTIVITY
KNOWLEDGE CHECK

Naval acquisitions

1 On a blank map of the world, label and date the ports and bases that Britain acquired during the years 1763–1914 and write a brief comment about the importance of each one to Britain.

2 Using your annotated map, identify any trends that you think were influential to the growth of Britain's naval acquisitions. This might include things such as geopolitical or economic interests.

EXTRACT

 From Stephen Conway in *Empire, the Sea and Global History: Britain's Maritime World, c1760–c1840*, David Cannadine (ed.), (2007).

After all, the main area of imperial growth between 1763 and 1833, at least in terms of population under British control, was India, where the grant of the *diwani* by a Mughal emperor in 1765 transformed the British East India Company from a trading and financial concern into a territorial power, and Lord Wellesley's conquests of 1798 to 1805 completely changed the political map. This expansion owed very little in any direct sense to the Royal Navy...

EXTRACT

 From Ronald Hyam, *Britain's Imperial Century, 1815–1914: A Study of Empire and Expansion* (2002).

Owing to the fact that it had in effect nothing to do, the prestige of the royal navy was low and its development as a fighting service was heavily circumscribed financially. There was continual reduction of naval force in the 1830s and 1840s, largely because there was no serious military or commercial competition. It was possible to have naval supremacy on the cheap.

EXTRACT

 From Ben Wilson, *Empire of the Deep: The Rise and Fall of the British Navy* (2013).

This represented an awesome power. The Royal Navy was Britain's instrument in re-ordering the world in her interests. Sometimes this could be overt, as at Algiers, Navarino and Acre. More often it was subtle. During Latin America's struggle for liberation from Spain and Portugal the Royal Navy's South America Squadron was a potent force. It did not actively intervene but it prevented Spanish and Portuguese ships from operating freely.

EXTRACT

 From Paul Kennedy, *Rise and Fall of British Naval Mastery* (2001).

The Navy's decisive victories in the eighteenth century had given its merchants the lion's share in maritime trade, which itself had stimulated the industrial revolution; yet this in turn was to provide the foundations for the country's continuing and increasing growth, making it into a new sort of state – the only real world power at that time. Industrialization not only furthered the British ascendency in commerce and finance and shipping, it also underpinned its own naval supremacy with a previously unheard-of economic potential.

THINKING HISTORICALLY Change (8a, b & c) (II)

Judgements about change

If two professionals were asked to track a patient's health over time, one might approach this task by measuring heart rate, weight and cholesterol, while the other professional might assess the patient's mental wellbeing, relationships and ability to achieve their goals. Both are valid approaches, but result in different reports. What is true in this medical case is true in historical cases. Measuring change in something requires: (a) a concept of what that something is (e.g. 'What is "health"?' 'What is an "economy"?'); (b) judgements about how this thing should be measured; and (c) judgements about what relevant 'markers of change' are (how we distinguish a change from a temporary and insignificant fluctuation).

Historians have differed in their accounts of the Royal Navy in the 18th and 19th centuries and debated the importance of its role in the development of Britain's empire during this period.

Look at Extracts 3–6 about the Royal Navy and answer the following questions.

1 Do all four accounts agree that the Royal Navy achieved supremacy in the 18th and 19th centuries?

2 Do all four accounts agree in the chronology of change (do they see it happening in the same time periods and at the same pace)?

3 Do all four accounts agree in characterising change in the role of the Royal Navy as (a) rapid, (b) dramatic and (c) impacting Britain's position as a whole?

4 Do the historians all think of the Royal Navy in the same way (for example, do they all focus on naval power as a way to increase trade interests)?

5 Generalising from these examples, to what extent do historians' judgements about change depend upon what historians decide to look at and how they decide to measure change?

ACTIVITY
SUMMARY

The changing face of the Royal Navy

1 Create a mind-map about how the Royal Navy developed between the years 1763 and 1914.

2 Using this map, plan an answer to the following question: 'How far did the Royal Navy evolve as a result of exploration between the years 1763 and 1914?' Your plan should include a full introduction and conclusion and an outline for each paragraph in the body of your answer.

 WIDER READING

Cannadine, D. *Empire, the Sea and Global History: Britain's Maritime World, 1763–1840*, Palgrave (2007)

Grove, E. *The Royal Navy Since 1815: A Short History*, Palgrave (2005)

Kennedy, P. *Rise and Fall of British Naval Mastery*, Scribner (1976)

Leyland, J. *The Royal Navy: Its Influence in English History and the Growth of Empire*, Cambridge University Press (2012)

Robson, M. *A History of the Royal Navy: Seven Years War*, IB Tauris (2015)

Spence, D.O. *A History of the Royal Navy: Empire and Imperialism*, IB Tauris (2015)

Wilson, B. *Empire of the Deep: The Rise and Fall of the British Navy*, Weidenfeld & Nicolson (2013)

3.3 The loss of the American colonies, 1770–83

KEY QUESTIONS

- Why did tensions between the colonists and the British reach a point of no return between 1770 and 1775?
- Why did clashes between the colonists and the British develop into a struggle for independence?
- Why did Britain lose the American colonies?

INTRODUCTION

The loss of Britain's thirteen American colonies, or what has been called the 'first British empire', had its cause firmly rooted in Britain's conflict with France. The ongoing struggle throughout the 18th century to limit the territorial expansion of France, both within Europe and globally, drove British policy. Britain's need to fund a conflict with France was foremost in its policy choices regarding the thirteen colonies during the 1770s. For the colonials, descended from those who had largely left Britain to seek a new life and religious freedom and used to self-government under a system of salutary neglect (see page 18), the introduction and nature of British taxation proved wholly unacceptable.

In the 1760s and 1770s, the British attempted to alter the terms of the economic relationship which existed between the American colonies and Britain. The new terms were dictated to the colonists and they seemed necessary and self-evidently sensible to the British. However, the result was the development of a new American identity and a breakdown in the relationship between the countries.

Boston in 1770

In 1770, Boston, one of the largest cities in the colonies, was in chaos as the colonists rioted against British duties on imports to the colonies. Tensions ran high, the British had stationed 600 troops in the city from September 1768 to preserve the peace and enforce the law, and this only inflamed the mood of the city further. Baiting troops and avoiding taxes were patriotic duties according to the pamphleteers, who worked overtime to record and trumpet every incident. Young boys and men took to rioting every Thursday on market day and it was only a matter of time before there were deaths.

- On 22 February 1770, a man loyal to the British and suspected of informing on others for customs avoidance was surrounded and trapped in his house by the Thursday mob. He fired on the crowd and killed an 11-year-old boy. Five thousand Bostonians attended the funeral.

1767 – Townshend Duties on tea, lead, glass, paint, china and wine introduced

1772 – November: First Committee of Correspondence is set up in Boston on the suggestion of Sam Adams, followed by almost all the other colonies by 1774

1774 – Coercive Acts introduced in direct response to the Boston Tea Party

September: Representatives of all the colonies meet in Philadelphia in the Continental Congress in response to the Coercive Acts

| 1767 | 1770 | 1771 | 1772 | 1773 | 1774 | 1775 |

1770 – 5 March: Boston Massacre takes place following weeks of unrest in Boston against the Townshend Duties

1773 – May: Tea Act allows the East India Company to trade directly with America rather than shipping through London

16 December: Boston Tea Party: patriots throw 342 chests of tea worth about £10,000 into the sea in protest against the Tea Act

1775 – 18 April: First shots of the war are fired between Lexington and Concord

17 June: Battle of Bunker Hill

- On 2 March, workers at a rope factory attacked some **redcoats** and a running street battle followed.

- On 5 March, a small detachment of troops guarding the Customs House fired into protesting Bostonians and five Bostonians were killed, including Crispus Attucks, the leader of the protest. The Boston Massacre had taken place.

KEY TERM

Redcoat
A British soldier.

SOURCE

The Bloody Massacre in King-Street, March 5, 1770, engraving by Paul Revere, a Boston silversmith and member of the Sons of Liberty. It is based on another engraving produced by Henry Pelham, who felt that Revere had unfairly taken credit for his work. The Boston 'Massacre' of 1770 occurred when much-tried British troops shot into the crowd of organised protestors against the Townshend Duties. This engraving appeared just three weeks after the event and was one of the most important pieces of anti-British propaganda of the period. British soldiers are shown being given the order to fire in an orderly line when in fact they were attacked by the crowd.

1776 – June: Process of drawing up a new constitution for the new nation begins

4 July: Declaration of Independence formally and unanimously adopted by Congress

1778 – June: France declares war on Britain

1781 –19 October: British surrender to the Americans at Yorktown, effectively ending the war

| 1776 | 1777 | 1778 | 1779 | 1780 | 1781 | 1782 | 1783 |

1777 – October: Burgoyne's retreat to Saratoga takes place following the failure of an ambitious campaign from Canada

November: New constitution approved by Congress

1779 – June: Spain enters the war as an ally of France

1783 – 3 September: Peace of Paris is signed by Britain, the USA, France, Spain and Holland

WHY DID TENSIONS BETWEEN THE COLONISTS AND THE BRITISH REACH A POINT OF NO RETURN BETWEEN 1770 AND 1775?

Issue of customs collection and tea duties

Nature of colonial society

Continuous English settlement in America was established by royal charter in the first colony in Virginia in 1607 and the second major settlement was in 1620 following the sailing of the *Mayflower* to Massachusetts. Between 1620 and the establishment of settlements in Georgia in 1732, the thirteen English colonies were founded (see Figure 3.1). The economy of the new colonies was agriculturally based, but with distinct differences between the colonies.

- The New England colonies were farmed by small subsistence farmers and had an extensive fishing industry.

- The Middle colonies and Pennsylvania were a major source of wheat and flour products.

- In the Southern colonies, tobacco was the predominant crop. Tobacco is very labour-intensive to farm so the majority of slaves were imported to provide labour for the Southern colonies (see Chapter 2, page 44).

Despite the differences between the colonies, it is possible to make some generalisations about all thirteen colonies and their settlers.

The majority of the settlers were **Protestant** and many of the British religious sects had chosen to make the journey to establish a new life in a new continent because of persecution at home. The availability of land meant that, unlike in England where most farm labourers rented from the wealthy landowning class, in America most white men worked and owned their own land. Most settlers were employed in agricultural production linked to very small communities spread over 1.1 million km². In the towns (in 1770 there were only five towns of any size; Boston for example had about 20,000 inhabitants), skilled workers and tradesmen were able to command better wages than in Europe because of the scarcity of labour. This meant that far more white men in the American colonies enjoyed a sense of independence and had status as landowners and voters than in Europe. Colonists' loyalties were to their local communities and churches. The colonies were 'British', but the colonists were not. However, before the 1770s, they were not in any real sense 'Americans' either.

American colonists had a much higher level of political experience than their European contemporaries. Each colony was governed by a governor appointed by the British Crown and a legislative assembly. The assemblies were responsible for money bills and controlling expenditure and the lower houses were elected by a very wide **franchise** of at least 50 percent and sometimes as much as 80 percent of the adult male population. This is in dramatic contrast to Britain, where just one in ten men were entitled to vote. The smallness of the colonies in terms of population and the extensiveness of the franchise meant that the majority of colonial men were used to participating fully in the political process. Of course, women and slaves could not vote and members of the colonial elite were commonly elected automatically because of their social standing. Nonetheless, it is fair to say that the colonists were highly involved in their own self-government and practised a form of democracy.

Colonial assemblies were legislative assemblies, whose role was meant to be raising revenue for the provision of local services, payment of local officials and the passing of local legislation. During the 1760s, the colonial assemblies had consistently overstepped their constitutional position. They provided a focus for discussion and reaction to the British taxes from the introduction of the Sugar Act in 1764 until the outbreak of hostilities between the two countries, at first sending representations and messages to London, then later petitioning against new taxation and finally beginning to consult and work together to formulate stronger and more unified responses. By doing so, they were clearly exceeding the scope of their responsibilities. The legislative assemblies were at the heart of opposition to new British taxes and provided a forum for debate and a coherent response to the new laws.

The fact that there were thirteen individual assemblies meant that opposition to the British came from each individual colony at the outset of the opposition to taxes, making it easier for the British to ignore than a national assembly might have been. When the colonies did form a national assembly, there was a high degree of agreement among the representatives because they had been involved in separate and unsuccessful protests for ten years.

Figure 3.1 The thirteen colonies before the American War of Independence.

Why were the British attempting to tax the colonies in 1770?

The latest round of the rolling century-long Anglo-French conflict was the Seven Years' War (1756–63), which ended with the Peace of Paris in 1763. The victorious British and colonial forces had driven the French out of Canada and had been ceded all French land east of the Mississippi and most of the French Caribbean islands. There had been a huge expansion in the British Empire with new borders to defend and new citizens to govern.

The French defeat was the key factor in the renegotiation of the political settlement between Britain and the American colonies. The new territories brought with them new defence and governmental responsibilities and the latest extension of empire had to be paid for somehow. To the British, it seemed simple.

- The American territories would require a defence force to protect them from possible revenge attacks by the French and to protect the westward boundaries of the colonies from the Native American attacks.

- Government needed to be provided for the 80,000 citizens of French Canada who now were part of the British Empire.

- There needed to be a period of consolidation. Therefore, there should be no further expansion west by the American colonies.

To defend and govern the new and existing colonies, the British believed they would require a permanent army of 10,000 men permanently based in North America. How the new army would be paid for was far more problematic. Britain had paid for the war with France by increasing the **national debt** and the annual debt interest repayments were £4.4 million annually out of a government income of only £8 million. Colonial administration and defence had risen from £70,000 in 1748 to £350,000 in 1763 and this was without the costs of the new army, which was deemed necessary to defend the new territories. The British now felt that the colonists must contribute to the cost of their own defence and, during the 1760s, attempted to raise revenue from the American colonies through more effective collection of duties outlined under the Navigation Acts.

KEY TERM

National debt
This is the term given to the money borrowed by the British government through the issue and sale of securities or bonds. The British national debt doubled during the Seven Years' War, from £75 million to £133 million.

To the colonies, it seemed that the British government was trying to illegally extend their power by the collection of these duties, and colonial protest increasingly became focused on the nature of the relationship between Britain and its colonies. The colonists, influenced by the politics of the Enlightenment, argued that British actions represented an exercise in tyranny and must be opposed. As colonial opposition to British policies increased during the 1760s, it became a point of principle for the British that the American colonies should contribute to their defence.

The colonial view was that the only proper way to raise money in the thirteen colonies was through colonial assemblies and this money was to be spent locally, not for the benefit of the Empire or Britain. However, had the British government asked the colonial assemblies in 1770 to finance the 10,000 troops they believed necessary to maintain the Empire, the assemblies would certainly have refused, arguing that such an army was unnecessary and that the British only wanted troops to suppress the colonials.

The colonists' intellectual opposition to British authority was steeped in the ideas of the Enlightenment philosophers and the Whig tradition of rebellion against a king who breaks his contract with his people. Their response to British attempts to change the status quo in the 1760s and 1770s was summed up by the phrase 'no taxation without representation'. At the outset of the crisis in the 1760s, colonial opposition was focused narrowly against British ministers advising the king but, as the decade progressed, colonial activists widened their net to denounce King George and the British parliament as well as individual ministers, and by 1770 this language was widely used by those opposed to British attempts at taxation.

KEY TERMS

Agents of the Crown
Agents of the colonial government, including customs officials.

Tarring and feathering
Public humiliation whereby the victim was stripped to waist, covered in liquid tar and then feathers, before being paraded through the streets.

Townshend Duties
The collective name for a series of Acts passed by the British from 1767 relating to the collection of customs duties from the American colonies. They were introduced by the Chancellor of the Exchequer, Charles Townshend. They included taxes on lead, glass, painter's colours and, most controversially, on tea.

Agents of the Crown tasked with collecting revenue duties during the 1760s found they were obstructed more and more as the debate became more heated and the colonists' position more entrenched. Thomas Hutchinson, who became the last non-military governor of Boston, had his house ransacked as early as 1765 for his loyalist sympathies during protests against the Stamp Act. Many others suffered **tarring and feathering** for their attempts to carry out their duties, and violence against agents reached such a pitch that official after official resigned.

As the events of 5 March in Boston suggest, the situation in 1770 was highly unstable in Massachusetts following the British attempt to introduce new duties on the colonies with the introduction of the **Townshend Duties**. Boston was the centre of opposition to the British under the leadership of Sam Adams, but by 1770 all the American colonies were at loggerheads with the British over the attempts that had taken place since 1764 to introduce new taxation. As there was no official method of consultation with the American colonies, the colonialists had no mechanism to influence the British parliament other than by protest and pressure.

EXTEND YOUR KNOWLEDGE

Sam Adams (1722–1803)
A prime agitator in Massachusetts, Adams organised some of the most important set piece events in the resistance to British tax collection, including the Boston Massacre and the Boston Tea Party. He helped form the Committees of Correspondence (see page 70), which proved vital in, first, spreading the revolutionary messages and, then, in assuming power as British power collapsed.

ACTIVITY
KNOWLEDGE CHECK

Relationship between American colonies and Britain
1 What were the reasons inherent in the nature of colonial society for tension in the relationship between Britain and its American colonies?

2 Explain the taxation deadlock that had been reached between the colonists and the British in 1770. What was the position of the colonists? Why did the British continue to insist on the necessity for the colonies to pay new taxes?

Townshend Duties

In the context of the unrest that had developed in response to earlier attempts to introduce new duties in the 1760s, the introduction of the Townshend Duties from 1767 by the British government was highly inflammatory. Duties were introduced on the imports of glass, wine, china, lead, paint, paper and tea. The duties were light and expected to raise £40,000 annually. As colonials, such as Benjamin Franklin, had argued against the Stamp Act by saying that the British had no right to tax internally but had conceded parliament's right to regulate trade, it could be argued that the British government had listened to and respected the arguments of the colonists. However, the successive attempts by the British to introduce new taxes or tighten up the collection of old duties during the 1760s meant that, by the time the Townshend Duties were introduced, most colonists were highly suspicious of Britain's intentions and did not interpret the duties in this way.

On a political level, the assemblies went further than they had ever done in presenting formal protests against the new duties. The Massachusetts Assembly published a denunciation of the Townshend Duties for violating the principle of 'no taxation without representation' and seven other colonial assemblies quickly endorsed this letter. Boycotts were organised once again, and again there was well organised and violent protest in Boston. This time, the British were determined to stand firm and there was no repeal. The New York Assembly, which had refused to pay for the quartering of British troops, was suspended until it agreed to support the troops based there, and British military presence, both naval and military, increased in Boston from 1768 to ensure the collection of duties and the protection of the American Board of Customs Commissioners (placed in Boston in 1767). The Bostonian resistance was led by the **Sons of Liberty**, a well-organised paramilitary organisation, associated with Sam Adams, which had been founded in 1765 in opposition to the British attempts at taxation. They were active in the resistance to the Townshend Duties and led the persecution of agents of the Crown who were attempting to collect the duties. Their campaign culminated in the Boston Massacre in 1770.

KEY TERM

Sons of Liberty
Paramilitary opposition, originally centred in Boston, set up to organise resistance to British taxation in the 1760s. They ensured Boston was at the centre of anti-British activity.

EXTEND YOUR KNOWLEDGE

Benjamin Franklin (1706–90)

It was only in the New World that Benjamin Franklin could have reached such an eminent position as the one he occupied upon his death. This self-made, self-educated man was able to reach the highest echelons of American society and his life story in many ways embodies the opportunities and freedoms the colonies offered. He is perhaps the most famous 18th-century American.

Franklin was born in Boston and his formal education ended aged ten. He was apprenticed as a printer, running away to Philadelphia aged 17 and then to London. He made his fortune in printing and publishing and, because of his position and energy, was elected to the Pennsylvania Assembly. He represented the colony in London during the 1760s, where he tried to argue the colonists' case against the introduction of taxes by the British. He argued that the British had the right to regulate trade, but not to tax unrepresented Americans and he endeavoured to show that America had already met its financial obligations to defence during the American Indian War. His hardening stance during the early 1770s is characteristic of that of the journey to revolution taken by many patriots from protest to outright rebellion.

During the struggle for independence, Franklin was one of the delegates involved in the drafting of the Declaration of Independence – the text of which reflects the influence that he, and many of the other delegates, owed to their study of John Locke and Enlightenment philosophy. Congress appointed him as the American ambassador to France and he was key in establishing a positive Franco-American relationship. He was wildly popular in Paris and lionised by French society. French intervention in the war proved decisive in American victory.

In addition to his contribution to the founding of the new nation, he was a prolific pamphleteer on politics, economics and religion. He is also famous for his science experiments, including those showing the conductivity of lightning.

SOURCE

From a speech by Edmund Burke, MP for Wendover in Buckinghamshire, who opposed the British attempts to tax the colonies. In this speech to Parliament on 19 April 1769, he outlined the deadlock which British and colonial relations had reached over the Townshend Duties during a debate on their possible repeal.

The Americans have made a discovery, or think they have made one, that we mean to oppress them. We have made a discovery, or think we have made one, that they intend to rise in rebellion against us. Our severity has increased their ill behaviour, we know not how to advance, they know not how to retreat. This is my opinion of our situation with regard to America. He is a bold man who can say what measures we can take. If the question stood to repeal, or enforce, I have no doubt to repeal. We can't repeal it this Session, it is a complicated, commercial system... Some party must give way, there is a disposition in that Country to meet us. If the disposition of that Country is alienated from us the law can't be executed.

Why was the Boston Massacre not the start of the American War of Independence?

Although in many ways the Boston Massacre does represent the crossing of a line with the shooting of civilians (if the mob whipped up by the Sons of Liberty can be termed as civilians) by British soldiers, the American War of Independence was by no means a foregone conclusion in 1770. The reasons for this pause on the road to open hostility are:

- the British repeal of the hated Townshend Duties

- the existence of a significant number of loyalists in the colonies

- the lack of unity between the colonists.

A last minute repeal of the Townshend Duties brought the colonies back from the brink of revolt in 1770, but the 'years of calm', 1770–73, were uneasy nonetheless. While the British were prepared to repeal the Townshend Duties, their fundamental position that the American colonies should pay taxes had not changed. Equally, the colonists were on the alert for any new infringements of their liberties. Without a new approach to the government and taxation of the thirteen colonies, confrontation was inevitable. The years of calm represent a dampening down of tensions but no resolution of the issues that divided the colonists from the British. On 5 March 1770 in London, all of the Townshend Duties, except for those on tea, were repealed. Once again, American agitation had forced a reversal of British policy. For the colonists, however, the continuation of duties on tea represented continuing British tyranny and very limited legal duties were ever paid, as tea merchants doubled as dealers in smuggled tea.

Patriot
An American colonist who was opposed to British taxation and prepared to fight to defend American liberties. American patriots where proud to call themselves Whigs.

Loyalist
One who remained loyal to the British Crown during the agitation before the American War of Independence and during the war itself. Also referred to as Tory in an echo of British political names. In Britain, the Tories had supported the rights of James II before the Glorious Revolution, as opposed to the Whigs.

Committee of Correspondence
First set up in Massachusetts and then in other colonies, they provided a means of communication and a network throughout the colonies, which the British could not control.

However, despite the best efforts of Sam Adams, by no means all Americans were revolutionaries and **patriots.** The estimate that one-third of the population were active rebels, one-third were **loyalists** (also known as Tories to the colonists) and one-third were neutral has been attributed to John Adams (the first vice president of the USA). Whether he actually said this about the American Revolution or the French Revolution remains disputed, but the statement identifies an important truism. In *any* revolutionary event, the population broadly divides into those who are in favour and prepared to act, those who are neutral (although they may have an emotional preference) and those who are prepared to fight to preserve the status quo. In 1770, the neutrals happily drank their smuggled tea and would certainly have been moved to protest against further efforts to tax them, but the repeal of the Townshend Duties broadly satisfied them. Loyalists accepted Britain's right to tax the colonies and deplored the violence of the paramilitary Sons of Liberty. Many had a personal interest in the system in the colony remaining as it was, as they were agents of the Crown.

The most recent historical surveys suggest that loyalists represented around 20 percent of the population. As estimates of patriot support at its highest are 40–45 percent of the population, with the remainder being neutral, it is clear that a significant minority of colonists were loyal to the British and that the rest were not prepared to join the conflict but merely wished to get on with their lives. By drilling down through the records and identifying area by area who were the loyalists, it is possible to say that, on the whole, they tended to be on the margins of colonial society and made up of small groups with varying interests and a wide geographical spread. On the whole, the wealthier members of colonial society did not support the British; the Virginian planter elite was patriot to a man. Loyalists included minority groups like the Southern back-country farmers, Anglicans in New England, the Germans and Dutch of New York, and some of the more recent Scots immigrants to the colonies. Once the conflict began, far more slaves fought for the British in exchange for promises of freedom than for the patriots. However, the British were unwilling to destabilise society by promising wholesale freedom for slaves and there was no large-scale recruitment of black Americans, who made up one in six of the population as a whole.

The patriots were more unified and drawn from the colonial elite than those who remained loyal to the British Crown. The loyalists suffered from this diversity. As for the neutrals, if the British wished to win them over during the years of calm, they needed to be more active than they were in promoting the benefits of British rule and the need for an army to defend America's borders.

The patriots may have appeared more unified than the loyalists and, indeed, they were lucky to have a cause and some very catchy slogans to align themselves behind, but nevertheless there were still important divisions in American society which hampered the patriot cause. As well as the ethnic and religious subdivisions in American society, there was a gulf between the rich and the poor and, in Virginina and the Carolinas, between those in the more extensively settled Tidewater areas (so called because their rivers were tidal) and those fighting to establish claims in the back country. The early 1770s was a period of virtual civil war in the Carolinas, when the Regulator movement, made up of small farmers, rose up against corrupt Tidewater officials, and this local conflict would have been far more pressing to its participants than events in Boston and Massachusetts. The patriots used the years of calm more effectively to promote unity than the British. In September 1771, Sam Adams proposed the setting up of a **Committee of Correspondence**, whose role was to communicate in writing colonial grievances to all the towns in Massachusetts and, by mid-1773, 50 other towns in Massachusetts had their own committees. By February 1774, every colony except North Carolina and Pennsylvania had its own committee. By setting up a system of news dissemination which the British could not control, the patriots had a powerful tool ready to use to convert neutrals into patriots should the need arise.

A Level Exam-Style Question Section A

Study Source 3 before you answer this question.

Assess the value of the source for revealing the extent and nature of opposition to the British in Boston in 1772.

Explain your answer, using the source, the information given about its origin and your own knowledge about the historical context. (20 marks)

Tip
Remember to focus carefully on the extent of opposition to the British.

SOURCE 3

From a pamphlet published in Boston in 1772 including the minutes of the first Committee of Correspondence. Following an earlier decision to establish such a committee, the new body met on 2 November 1772 to establish their aims. The document resonates with the language of the Enlightenment philosophy of the patriots.

The Honorable JOHN HANCOCK, Esq; Being unanimously chosen Moderator, The Chairman of said Committee acquainted him that he was ready to make Report, and read the same as follows.

THE Committee appointed by the Town the second Instant "to state the Rights of the Colonists and of this Province in particular, as Men, as Christians, and as Subjects; to communicate and publish the same to the several Towns in this Province and to the World, as the Sense of this Town, with the Infringements and Violations thereof that have been, or from Time to Time may be made. Also requesting of each Town a free Communication of their Sentiments on this Subject," – beg Leave to report.

First, A State of the Rights of the Colonists and of this Province in particular.

Secondly, A List of the Infringements and Violations of those Rights.

Thirdly, A Letter of Correspondence with the other Towns.

1. Natural Rights of the Colonists as Men. Among the natural Rights of the Colonists are these: First, a Right to Life; secondly, to Liberty; thirdly, to Property; together with the Right to support and defend them in the best Manner they can. These are evident Branches of, rather than Deductions from the Duty of Self-Preservation, commonly called the first Law of Nature.

All Men have a Right to remain in a State of Nature as long as they please: And in Case of intollerable Oppression, civil or religious, to leave the Society they belong to, and enter into another....

All Persons born in the British American Colonies, are, by the Laws of GOD and Nature, and by the common Law of England, exclusive of all Charters from the Crown, well entitled, and by Acts of the British Parliament are declared to be entitled, to all the natural, essential, inherent and inseparable Rights, Liberties and Privileges of Subjects born in Great-Britain, or within the Realm.

The Boston Tea Party

Without an imaginative response which gave the colonies actual self-government at the same time as tying them emotionally to the idea of being part of an empire, it is hard to see how the British could have saved the colonies for the Empire in the long term. However, they might have avoided the outbreak of hostilities in 1775 by considering how the Tea Act 1773 would play into the hands of Sam Adams and the patriots. Bungling and ill considered, the attempts by the British to enforce the Tea Act mark the tipping point in the making of the American Revolution.

Tea Act 1773

Simultaneous to the attempt to force new duties on the American colonies, the British had attempted to squeeze money out of the East India Company (see pages 136–37) with the payment of £400,000 in 1767 and 1768 as a means of paying off some of the national debt. This, combined with famine in Bengal in 1772 and rising administrative costs meant the company faced bankruptcy and collapse in 1773. The British introduced the Tea Act in 1773 in an attempt to shore up the East India Company, but the Act proved the final nail in the coffin for British colonial relations.

The Tea Act allowed the East India Company to trade directly with America, rather than obeying the mercantilist principle that everything must be traded through British ports. It was hoped that the outcome of the Act would be dramatically increased profits for the Company, thereby saving them from bankruptcy. This was because the East India tea would now be able to compete with the smuggled tea which colonists enjoyed – the tea would be cheaper because it was exempt from duties incurred by passing through British ports. The British also hoped for increased duties from the American colonies as the East India tea would remain subject to American duties.

The American reaction was predictable and followed familiar paths. The Act was greeted as another attempt to tax Americans illegally. The Committees of Correspondence sprang into action condemning the Act and encouraging boycotts and civil disobedience. Tea sent to Philadelphia and New York was rejected and sent back. Tea in Charleston was landed, but it was not offered for sale. Unsurprisingly, the most outrageous defiance took place in Boston.

EXTRACT 1

From Hugh Brogan in the *Penguin History of the USA* (1999) commenting on the dangerous decision by the British to introduce the Tea Act in 1773.

He (Lord North) had not consulted any of the American merchants or colonial agents in London before legislating. To judge by his later statements, he had assumed that the Americans would rush to buy cheap tea and given the matter no further thought. It certainly never occurred to him that the ordinary American tea-drinker would make common cause with the smugglers and legal importers to protest against a measure which substantially lowered the price of the stuff.... he took no warning from the fact that the colonies south of Connecticut had never accepted the duty. In 1770 the amount of dutied tea imported to New York was only 147 pounds; Philadelphia took only sixty five. Both cities drank enormous quantities of contraband tea instead. The plantation colonies showed a similar pattern. The duty was never accepted in principle anywhere, of course colonies had continuously petitioned against it. North's blindness to all this demonstrated, as had Grenville and Townshend how little fitted British ministers were to govern the Empire.... North should have known, or should have found out, that the colonies would be most unlikely to accept the Act: to barter their principles for cheap tea.

Sinking of the tea

On 28 November 1773, the *Dartmouth* sailed into Boston laden with East Indian tea, followed by the *Eleanor* on 2 December and the *Beaver* on 15 December. Governor Hutchinson, a prominent loyalist, appointed after the Boston Massacre, was determined that the tea should land (two of his sons were tea merchants). The patriots were equally determined that Boston should set an example to the rest of the colonies. After two weeks of discussions between the governor and the patriots, 60 Sons of Liberty boarded the three ships on 16 December and threw the cargoes, worth about £10,000, into the sea. The crowds watched in silence as 342 chests sank beneath the waves. It was obvious to all that a line had been crossed from which there would be no turning back. The British response was simple outrage. It was clear that Britain faced a fundamental challenge and, costly or not, the American colonies must be taught a lesson.

The British response was to try to isolate Boston and Massachusetts and lock down the city and the state under what was effectively military control. They certainly intended to punish the colony for their actions, but they totally underestimated the extent of intercolonial links and the level to which patriot support already existed in the other colonies. The impact of their hardline policies in Boston was to drive all thirteen colonies into outright rebellion.

SOURCE 4

Edmund Burke speaking in the House of Commons on 19 April 1774 during a debate which arose from a question proposing the reconsideration of the Tea Act 1773.

Again, and again, revert to your old principles,—seek peace and ensue it,—leave America, if she has taxable matter in her, to tax herself. I am not here going into the distinctions of rights, nor attempting to mark their boundaries. I do not enter into these metaphysical distinctions; I hate the very sound of them. Leave the Americans as they anciently stood, and these distinctions, born of our unhappy contest, will die along with it. They and we, and their and our ancestors, have been happy under that system. Let the memory of all actions in contradiction to that good old mode, on both sides, be extinguished forever. Be content to bind America by laws of trade: you have always done it. Let this be your reason for binding their trade. Do not burden them by taxes: you were not used to do so from the beginning. Let this be your reason for not taxing. These are the arguments of states and kingdoms. Leave the rest to the schools; for there only they may be discussed with safety. But if, intemperately, unwisely, fatally, you sophisticate and poison the very source of government, by urging subtle deductions, and consequences odious to those you govern, from the unlimited and illimitable nature of supreme sovereignty, you will teach them by these means to call that sovereignty itself in question. When you drive him hard, the boar will surely turn upon the hunters. If that sovereignty and their freedom cannot be reconciled, which will they take? They will cast your sovereignty in your face. Nobody will be argued into slavery. Sir, let the gentlemen on the other side call forth all their ability; let the best of them get up and tell me what one character of liberty the Americans have, and what one brand of slavery they are free from, if they are bound in their property and industry by all the restraints you can imagine on commerce, and at the same time are made pack-horses of every tax you choose to impose, without the least share in granting them. When they bear the burdens of unlimited monopoly, will you bring them to bear the burdens of unlimited revenue too? The Englishman in America will feel that this is slavery: that it is legal slavery will be no compensation either to his feelings or his understanding.

If this be the case, ask yourselves this question: Will they be content in such a state of slavery?

The Coercive Acts 1774 and their impact

The Coercive (or Intolerable) Acts were intended to isolate Boston and to force the patriots into submission and they were the final nail in the coffin for Anglo-American relations. The Acts' main aspects were:

- closure of the port of Boston from 1 June until all the tea was paid for

- revising the charter of the colony to allow the governor to appoint and remove most officials – the governorship passed from the unlucky Hutchinson to General Gage, commander-in-chief of the army

- arranging for the transfer of murder trials to England if deemed necessary (to prevent juries allowing patriots to literally get away with murder)

- giving more powers to military commanders to arrange the quartering of their troops.

These Acts were shortly followed by the Quebec Act dealing with the governance of Canada. American patriots pointed to the appointment of a governor without an assembly and the limits to trial by jury in Canada as further evidence of the intent of the British to erode the liberties of Americans and establish tyrannical rule in all of their colonies.

SOURCE

5 From a letter by the Boston Committee of Correspondence circulated on 8 June 1774 outlining parliament's actions following the introduction of the Coercive Acts and suggesting a common response.

There is but one way that we can conceive of, to prevent what is to be deprecated by all good men, and ought by all possible means to be prevented, viz, The horrors that must follow an open rupture between Great Britain and her colonies; or on our part, a subjection to absolute slavery: And that is by affecting the trade and interest of Great Britain, so deeply as shall induce her to withdraw her oppressive hand. There can be no doubt or our succeeding to the utmost or our wishes if we universally come into a solemn league, not to import goods from Great Britain, and not to buy any goods that shall hereafter be imported from thence, until our grievances shall be redressed. To these, or even to the least of these shameful impositions, we trust in God, our countrymen never will submit.

We have received such assurances from our brethren in every part of the province of their readiness to adopt such measures as may be likely to save our country, that we have not the least doubt of an almost universal agreement for this purpose; in confidence of this, we have drawn up a form of a covenant to be subscribed by all adult persons of both sexes; which we have sent to every town in the province, and that we might not give our enemies time to counteract us, we have endeavoured that every town should be furnished with such a copy on or before the fourteenth day of this month, and we earnestly desire that you would use your utmost endeavours that the subscription paper may be filled up as soon as possible, that so they who are in expectation of over throwing our liberties may be discouragd from prosecuting their wicked designs; as we look upon this the last and only method of preserving our land from slavery without drenching it in blood, may God prosper every undertaking which tends to the salvation of his people. We are, &c.

Signed by order and in behalf of the Committee of Correspondence for Boston.

William Cooper Clerk

BOSTON, JUNE 8, 1774.

ACTIVITY
KNOWLEDGE CHECK

The importance of tea

1 By comparing Sources 2 and 4, what differences can you find in Burke's analysis of the situation in America and his advice to the Commons regarding British action in 1769 and 1774?

2 Using the text and Source 5, explain why opposition to the Tea Act was centred in Boston and what action the British took to try to shut down what they believed to be a Bostonian problem.

A Level Exam-Style Question Section B

How far do you agree that the cause of the American Revolution was the introduction of the Tea Act in 1773? (20 marks)

Tip
Consider the long-term causes of tension between the colonies and Britain.

EXTRACT

2

From an online Q&A session by historian Christopher Hamner, who teaches at George Mason University, Fairfax, Virginia, and serves as editor-in-chief of *Papers on the War Department, 1784–1800*. He is also the author of *Enduring Battle: American Soldiers in Three Wars, 1776–1945*.

A near universal assumption of the founding generation was the danger posed by a standing military force. Far from being composed of honest citizens dutifully serving the interests of the nation, armies were held to be 'nurseries of vice', 'dangerous' and 'the grand engine of despotism'. Samuel Adams wrote in 1776, such a professional army was 'always dangerous to the liberties of the People'.

EXTRACT

3

From *Patriots, Settlers and the Origins of American Social Policy* (2003) by historian Laura Jensen.

As long as relations between the colonists and the British troops stationed in the colonies remained essentially peaceful, the anti-military philosophy infusing the pamphlets and sermons of the Revolutionary leaders could be dismissed, if uneasily. Public opinion about the British army's presence deteriorated from scepticism to open protest, however, when several thousand soldiers were dispatched to the colonies in 1763, and civil-military skirmishes became increasingly common. When five civilians were killed by British regulars in the streets of Boston in 1770, political theory and reality were finally and spectacularly merged.

THINKING HISTORICALLY Evidence (6b)

The strength of argument

1 Read Extract 2.

   a) Is this an argument? If yes, what makes it one?

   b) How might this argument be strengthened?

2 Read Extract 3.

   a) How have they expanded their explanation to make the claim stronger?

   b) Can you explain why this is the strongest claim of the three sources?

3 What elements make a historian's claims strong?

WHY DID CLASHES BETWEEN THE COLONISTS AND THE BRITISH DEVELOP INTO A STRUGGLE FOR INDEPENDENCE?

Following the introduction of the Coercive Acts, two parallel strands began the process of the struggle for independence by the thirteen colonies. In Massachusetts, open rebellion led to the first military engagements of the American War of Independence, while in Philadelphia delegates met at the Continental Congress and began the process of drafting and reaching agreement for a Declaration of Independence.

Rebellion to revolution, 1775–76

The Coercive Acts did not succeed in isolating Boston. Colonial assembly after assembly had to be dissolved by their governors but continued to meet in defiance of British law. They met together for the first time in September 1774 as the **Continental Congress**. This congress supported the views of the radicals (even in the autumn of 1774, there were moderates like Joseph Galloway who argued that the colonies should accept Britain's right to regulate trade within its empire) and called upon Massachusetts to arm for defence and proclaimed the right of each colony to determine its own need for troops. Committees of Correspondence became Committees of Safety and the day-to-day running of America largely passed into the hands of the committees by early 1775 (except ironically in Boston where Gage was able to maintain control with the troops he had to hand, while writing distractedly to London for more and more men).

Britain declared Massachusetts to be in a state of rebellion on 9 February 1775. At the very last moment, some of the brighter members of the English establishment had woken up to the danger they were in and the Earl of Chatham (Pitt the Elder) proposed the removal of all duties from the Americas, including the Sugar Act and recognising the power of the Continental Congress as an American parliament. This proposal was rejected by the House of Lords by 2 to 1 and Britain began to prepare for war.

KEY TERM

Continental Congress
A convention of delegates from the thirteen colonial assemblies which met for the first time in 1774 and became the *de facto* government of the United States, responsible for the drafting of the Declaration of Independence and the financing of the patriot army.

SOURCE

From the long, secret letter written by Lord Dartmouth, the American secretary in London, on 27 January 1775 to General Gage. The receipt of this letter was the prompt for Gage to attempt the seizing of rebel weapons from Concord, during which action the first shots of the war were fired.

The violences committed by those who have taken up arms in Massachusetts, have appeared to me as the acts of a rude rabble, without plan, without concert; and therefore I think that a small force now, if put to the test would be able to conquer them, with greater probability of success, than might be expected from a larger army...

With regard to the state of America in general, affairs there are now come to a crisis in which the government of this country must act with firmness and decision....

In reviewing the charter of Massachusetts I observe that there is a clause that empowers the governor to use and execute the martial law in time of actual war, invasion and *rebellion*. The enclosed copies of a reply made to me by the attorney and solicitor general contain and opinion, that the particulars in the papers you have transmitted to are the history of an actual and open rebellion in that province; and therefore I conceive, that according to that opinion the exercise of that power is strictly justifiable.

Military action in 1775

The early fighting occurred in and around Boston. The British under General Gage had only 4,000 troops available to them and what the first military actions of the American War of Independence demonstrated was that while the British might control Boston, they were unable to hold down Massachusetts, let alone the remaining 12 colonies. Messages from London could, and did, urge action, but the outcome of these actions proved disastrous for the British and the result of the early skirmishes was to support the political process towards revolution and the creation of a new nation and constitution.

- Lexington and Concord: General Gage knew where the rebel weapons were stockpiled and had unsuccessfully attempted to seize munitions from Salem in February 1775, despite being virtually besieged in Boston. Goaded by a letter (see Source 6) from the American secretary, Lord Dartmouth, Gage attempted a secret mission on 18 April 1775 to Concord (20 miles outside Boston) to seize or destroy a military store. Warned by the radicals, British troops were met by 75 volunteers at Lexington and the first shots of the war rang out. They pushed onto Concord and destroyed the stores, but were steadily fired on all on the way back to Boston and were saved from total disaster only by the arrival of relief soldiers. Total British casualties were 273, and 73 were killed. Shortly afterwards Boston was besieged and surrounded by 20,000 colonial militia.

- Bunker Hill: Reinforcements arrived in Boston in the shape of British generals Howe, Clinton and Burgoyne on 26 May 1775 with a few thousand more troops, and their arrival sparked the bloodiest engagement of the whole war. The British attempted a full frontal assault against the rebels at what is always known as the Battle of Bunker Hill on 17 June. (In fact, the battle took place on a neighbouring hill of an entirely different name.) More than 1,000 of the 2,500 British engaged in the battle became casualties. The Americans lost fewer than half that number. Although the British carried the position, the attrition rate they suffered (one-eighth of British officers killed in the entire conflict died in the engagement) means that it cannot be called a victory, especially as the British were shortly besieged in earnest by the new colonial army under Washington and in March 1776 were forced to evacuate Boston for Nova Scotia. As a result of the news of Bunker Hill, George III issued a Proclamation on 23 August 1775 declaring all colonies to be in a state of open rebellion.

Some historians have argued that this period represents a missed opportunity by the British and that, with sufficient soldiers (25,000 instead of the 4,000 increasing to 9,000 once reinforcements arrived) and decisive action, they might have taken hold of the situation. However, without a creative political solution for the thirteen colonies and a debt financing plan that did not involve taxing the American colonies or squeezing the East India Company until it collapsed, it is hard to see what kind of long-term solution might have been achieved.

The Declaration of Independence

While the first skirmishes of the war were taking place, the political journey to declaring independence began with the meeting of the second Continental Congress in Philadelphia on 10 May 1775. For many Americans, including Benjamin Franklin, the years 1775 and 1776 were the point when they crossed the line from being dissatisfied British colonists to becoming American patriots ready to be part of a new nation. The fighting in Lexington and at Bunker Hill contributed to this new mood. It became obvious to the colonists that George III would not see sense and furthermore that it was possible to beat the British army. Congress' deliberations added to the patriots' sense of purpose. The organisation of the American army and the Declaration of Independence were not Acts pushed through by extremists, but the result of careful democratic consultation and were the considered views of the democratic majority of those participating in the political process.

The immediate necessity was the finance and organisation of an army and Congress took two important decisions in June 1775.

- They issued paper money to try to meet some of the costs of a war.

- They made George Washington the commander of the new Continental Army.

The formal Declaration of Independence and establishment of a new formal government took longer for a number of reasons.

- The delegates were embarking on an intellectual and personal journey towards revolution and nationhood. The American Revolution involved the creation of a new nation and a new system of government and patriots undertook their personal journeys slowly towards the intellectual position of support for independence.

- Communication with local committees and assemblies took place at every step along the path to independence and, in an age of communication by print and transport by horse, this meant that it took time to reach an agreed resolution.

- Members of the Continental Congress worked hard to reach a consensus before moving forward and this meant demonstrating to moderates that every effort had been made to reach accommodation with the British. The Necessity of Taking up Arms Declaration adopted on 6 July 1775 disclaimed any intention of separation from Great Britain and the Olive Branch Petition of 8 July appealed directly to George III to cease hostilities so that a plan of reconciliation might be drawn up.

This approach by the Congress, cynical on the part of some, driven by democratic instincts on the part of others, paid off. George III refused to consider any such advances and on 23 August declared the colonies in open rebellion and called on all officials of the Crown, as well as soldiers and loyal subjects, to help suppress the rebellion. He thus justified the patriots' position of having no alternative but to consider the formation of a new government, as from the patriots' point of view he was manifestly behaving like a tyrant. By taking time to consult widely in 1775 and 1776, American patriots moved the revolution from being a Bostonian revolt led by street fighters to a something more formal and representing the democratic wishes of citizens. The most widely read and influential pamphlet of the period, *Common Sense*, by Thomas Paine was published in January 1776 and quickly sold 12,000 copies, helping to cement the opinions of many. It argued that reconciliation was no longer possible and that instead Americans should look to the future and the establishment of a new and fairer system of government.

EXTEND YOUR KNOWLEDGE

Thomas Paine (1737-1809)

Thomas Paine was an English radical who emigrated to the American colonies in 1774 with the help of Benjamin Franklin. His *Common Sense* pamphlet, published in 1776, was one of the most important documents of the revolution and its central demand was for independence from Britain. Paine moved to France in the 1790s and wrote the *Rights of Man* defending the French Revolution. He survived the French Revolution, despite spending some time in prison and returned to the USA in 1802.

Between April and July 1776, local assemblies authorised their congressional delegates to declare independence and after some last minute horse trading and changes of mind the Declaration of Independence was passed on 2 July 1776 with votes in favour by twelve out of the thirteen colonies and the abstention of one, New York. It was formally adopted by Congress on 4 July 1776.

SOURCE

Commissioned in 1817 from John Trumbull for the Rotunda at Washington, this image depicts the signing of the Declaration of the Independence. Trumbull decided to include as many likenesses of the signatories to the document as possible (42 of the 56) even though they were never in one room at the same time, as the Declaration was debated and signed over a period of time. Trumbull's motive was to commemorate the great events of his country's revolution and to show the likenesses of the people who had formed the Declaration.

Following moves within the Continental Congress in June 1776 towards independence, a committee was set up under Thomas Jefferson to draft a declaration. It was formally adopted on 4 July following a vote on 2 July. It was unanimously supported by the delegates of all the states as the two Pennsylvanians who opposed independence did not attend the session.

We hold these truths to be self-evident, that all men are created equal, that they are endowed by their Creator with certain unalienable Rights, that among these are Life, Liberty and the pursuit of Happiness.– That to secure these rights, Governments are instituted among Men, deriving their just powers from the consent of the governed, –That whenever any Form of Government becomes destructive of these ends, it is the Right of the People to alter or to abolish it, and to institute new Government, laying its foundation on such principles and organizing its powers in such form, as to them shall seem most likely to effect their Safety and Happiness. Prudence, indeed, will dictate that Governments long established should not be changed for light and transient causes; and accordingly all experience hath shewn, that mankind are more disposed to suffer, while evils are sufferable, than to right themselves by abolishing the forms to which they are accustomed. But when a long train of abuses and usurpations, pursuing invariably the same Object evinces a design to reduce them under absolute Despotism, it is their right, it is their duty, to throw off such Government, and to provide new Guards for their future security.–Such has been the patient sufferance of these Colonies; and such is now the necessity which constrains them to alter their former Systems of Government. The history of the present King of Great Britain is a history of repeated injuries and usurpations, all having in direct object the establishment of an absolute Tyranny over these States. To prove this, let Facts be submitted to a candid world.

He has refused his Assent to Laws, the most wholesome and necessary for the public good.
He has dissolved Representative Houses repeatedly, for opposing with manly firmness his invasions on the rights of the people.
He has made Judges dependent on his Will alone, for the tenure of their offices, and the amount and payment of their salaries.
He has erected a multitude of New Offices, and sent hither swarms of Officers to harrass our people, and eat out their substance.
He has kept among us, in times of peace, Standing Armies without the Consent of our legislatures.
He has affected to render the Military independent of and superior to the Civil power.
For Quartering large bodies of armed troops among us:
For cutting off our Trade with all parts of the world:
For imposing Taxes on us without our Consent:
For depriving us in many cases, of the benefits of Trial by Jury:
For transporting us beyond Seas to be tried for pretended offences
For taking away our Charters, abolishing our most valuable Laws, and altering fundamentally the Forms of our Governments:
He has abdicated Government here, by declaring us out of his Protection and waging War against us.
He has plundered our seas, ravaged our Coasts, burnt our towns, and destroyed the lives of our people.
He is at this time transporting large Armies of foreign Mercenaries to compleat the works of death, desolation and tyranny, already begun with circumstances of Cruelty & perfidy scarcely paralleled in the most barbarous ages, and totally unworthy the Head of a civilized nation.

KEY TERM

Constitution
The system of beliefs and precedents by which a country is governed. Britain has an 'unwritten' constitution, which does not mean there are no constitutional documents, but that there is a series of important laws and precedents by which Britain is governed. The American constitution is a written document agreed in 1789 to which there have been important amendments since, including the ending of slavery.

Articles of Confederation

If the Declaration of Independence was a long list of what the American colonists considered to be the crimes that the British king and parliament had committed against the innocent colonists, then the Articles of Confederation were a way of creating a national government which was as little like the British parliamentary system as the patriots could make it. In June 1776, Congress appointed a committee of thirteen (one man from each state) to draw up a constitution for government and to fight the war. It was not the **constitution** of the USA as we know it today, but a mechanism which allowed the states to work together without sacrificing too much power to a central executive body as that was what American thinkers believed was the root problem with the British system. Some of the most important articles were as follows.

- All powers not specifically granted to Congress were reserved by the states. Congress had no right to enforce taxes or regulate trade.

- All states had to agree to any amendment of the constitution.

- Congress could, however, declare war, borrow and issue money (paper money which was based on nothing as they could not raise any taxes), draw up treaties and alliances with foreign powers, deal with Native American affairs, requisition the states for money and men for fighting, set standards for weights and measures (important at a time when most taxes were collected on goods so the agreed weight of goods was an important issue) and regulate post offices. However, really important issues like treaties and alliances needed the agreement of at least nine states, not just a majority.

- There was no president, prime minister or cabinet. Instead, each state had one vote regardless of size. States sent delegations to Congress but only one congressman was elected for each state. They were elected annually (to prevent corruption) and could not be elected more than three times in every six years.

As they were in the middle of a war, the Articles of Confederation were not approved by Congress until November 1777 and were not ratified by every state until 1781 when Maryland ratified the document. Congress did function during this period, but the length of time it took to obtain formal agreement from each state emphasises the fear the patriots had of abdicating power to a central authority.

A Level Exam-Style Question Section B

How far do you agree that the primary cause of the American War of Independence was the ideological difference between the American and British points of view over taxation? (20 marks)

Tip
Consider the structural relationship between the two countries.

ACTIVITY
KNOWLEDGE CHECK

Declaration of Independence

1 Read the (edited) list of complaints made by the colonists about the king in the Declaration of Independence (Source 8). Use the text and your own research to find evidence to support the assertions made by the colonists.

2 Complete your own timeline of events from September 1774 to November 1777, highlighting actions by the British, military actions by the colonists and political actions by the colonists in different colours.

WHY DID BRITAIN LOSE THE AMERICAN COLONIES?

The British are generally held to have lost the war fought by the Americans for their independence with a combination of diabolical generalship and poor supply lines. However, it is also acknowledged that the Americans can hardly be judged to have 'won' the war. In George Washington, they had a truly great leader but their supply lines and resourcing were terrible too. The British did not give up on the fight and threw money into the war, but, by failing to win the hearts and minds of the majority of colonists, with hindsight their ultimate defeat appears inevitable.

The limitations of Britain's military resources

Britain was a long-established state with a population of around eight million, was developing into a major European power and had a powerful navy and financial system to depend on. Furthermore, Britain had only recently emerged victorious from the Seven Years' War against France in 1763. America, on the other hand, consisted of thirteen colonies that were only just beginning to work together politically, a population of 2.4 million, no regular army and no financial institutions with which to finance a war.

British strengths
Britain did not embark on the war in America expecting to lose and, as the gravity of the situation became apparent, it increased its spending and its military presence in the colonies in an attempt to defeat the patriots. Britain had significant strengths as a military power.

- Britain's armed forces had 48,647 soldiers (on paper) at their command in 1775 and were able to hire mercenaries from German principalities when necessary. However, these troops were not experienced and only about 8,000 were in America in 1775. During the war with America, Britain still had to meet its military obligations elsewhere in the Empire and at home.

- The Royal Navy had some 340 ships. They were able to reinforce British troops, and blockade and attack American ports. They were able to use Newfoundland, Canada and the West Indies as bases from which to launch their attacks. The first lord of the Admiralty, Lord Sandwich, was able and energetic but had first to re-equip and build up the navy, which had suffered from limited investment in the 1760s.

- Britain's economy was well established and diverse. It had the most sophisticated methods of public finance in the world and it was able to absorb increasing levels of debt to continue the fight. Britain's population was eight million at this point and growing rapidly. It could put large armies on the field thousands of miles away, while continuing to gather harvests and retain sufficient manpower for the developing industrial base. Although teaching the colonists was a lesson that most felt was worthwhile, when the war dragged on and debts piled further and further up then British political will to continue faded.

British weaknesses

The weaknesses of the British forces were a combination of logistical difficulties and those inherent in fighting an emerging nation.

- Logistically supplying and maintaining the troops in America was very challenging. Since loyalist support was in pockets, Britain's hold on the colonies was maintained by holding the seaboard and garrisoning the ports. Armies were then dispatched deeper into the landmass (although most Americans lived no further than 120 km from the sea) to pin down the Continental Army and score a decisive victory. This meant stretching supply lines further and relying on generals being able to pincer the colonials without being separated and defeated themselves. Britain's critical defeats at Saratoga and Yorktown were both the result of divided forces, elongated supply lines and delayed relief efforts.

- Although British generals were very mixed in terms of their abilities, they suffered from lack of direction from London in terms of strategy. They were not to fight a simple seaboard and defensive campaign, starving the colonists into submission, nor was there an obvious colonial centre for them to defeat. Instead, they were committed to chasing and destroying the Continental Army, which meant risking their supply lines. As long as the Continentals could melt away and reform, the British could not be the victors. Once the French entered the war, the focus of London again changed as the conflict was now global and America was reduced to a sideshow in the age-old Anglo-French struggle.

American strengths

The British thought of the colonists as rebels, not a nation, and the 1777 peace talks foundered during the opening phase of the war as the British commanders and peace commissioners were not empowered to sign a treaty with the newly formed independent nation. For Americans, however, this was not acceptable. Independence had been declared and the nation created, and until the British were prepared to treat them on equal terms then Americans were not prepared to negotiate a peace settlement.

- The formation of a nation on democratic principles was both an ideological dream and the developing reality, and the vibrancy of the new state drew neutrals to become patriots, leaving the loyalists isolated. Most Americans were convinced by the 'Glorious cause'. The arguments about the limits of British power had been raging for ten years by the time war broke out and the high level of participation in the process of declaring independence helped cement support for the new nation. The neutrals were not wooed by promises from the British and there was no decisive victory to draw them to the British side. Indeed, the use of Hessian mercenaries by the British had a detrimental impact on winning neutral support.

- The terrain and extremes of climate were familiar to the colonists and this knowledge helped the patriots whenever the British ventured inland from the seaboard or away from the navigable rivers. Armies always perform better on home ground and America was no exception. The new

Continental Army was not a professional army but made up of Americans of a new nation. The strength of a nation fighting for its survival was to be seen a decade later in the wars against the Revolutionary French Army, with the same result. When soldiers are committed ideologically to what they are fighting for and are fighting to defend their homes, they have the edge over paid professional soldiers.

- Washington was the true genius of the American War of Independence. Time and again, when it appeared that all was lost, he regrouped and retrained his forces. He was responsible for the formation of the Continental Army as he realised that the British would not be defeated by guerrilla fighting from militias but needed to be challenged conventionally. Over the long years of the war, he was responsible for the army's survival and increasing professionalism. Although he was disdainful of the militia, he was aided by the militia's ability to control parts of the country not actually occupied by the British. He also benefited from Congress' continuing support of his position, even in the darkest days of the war.

American weaknesses

America's weaknesses were those of a newly formed nation with limited economic development. They were reliant on the issuing of paper money for currency as Congress had no ability to levy taxes and this caused inflation in prices and a general unwillingness to accept the paper notes. Without a large manufacturing base, the Americans were very short of weapons throughout the war. However, the British could never completely blockade them into submission, as there was so much coastline to patrol and a strategy of completely starving the colonials into submission would have impacted on their loyalist support base. The intervention of the French lessened British effectiveness at sea still further as the navy now had more responsibilities globally.

EXTRACT

 From Hugh Brogan, *The Penguin History of the USA* (1999), writing about General Washington's capabilities as a commander.

> George Washington cannot honestly be called a great fighting general, though he was a capable and aggressive one. He made some bad mistakes in his campaigns, especially in the first year or two. Matched as he was against such limited opponents as Gage, William Howe, Clinton and Cornwallis, it scarcely mattered: they made more and worse mistakes than he. What did matter was that he possessed various other qualities that made him, if not unique amongst commanders, at any rate highly unusual... no detail was too small for his attention; yet he seldom lost his sense of proportion. Above all, his size and strength (he was a very big man) went with a tenacious, dignified, conscientious mind which never allowed difficulties, however great or disagreeable, to deflect him from the path of duty... General Washington was always at his post.

The war dragged on and on for seven bitter years. The British could only attack from the seaboard and up navigable rivers as they had no discrete territorial land base. The Americans suffered from lack of equipment, experience and organisation. British defeats occurred when they overstretched their supply lines or lost control of naval waters and these moments were the turning points in the war.

General Burgoyne's defeat at Saratoga, 1777

The retreat to Saratoga in October 1777 was the first key turning point of the war and the first rebel defeat of the British. General Burgoyne had penetrated 200 miles into America from Canada, but his forces were not joined by those of General Clinton from further south. Overstretched and surrounded, he began negotiations with Gates, the American general and surrendered on 17 October 1777. News of the surrender played a part in the French decision to enter the war against the British.

- Burgoyne had presented a plan to the king in February 1777, which was basically to lead a combined force of British regular soldiers, Hessian mercenaries, native Americans, Canadians and such loyalists as could be marshalled along the way, from the Canadian border south to meet the main British troops stationed around New York. The plan was not explicitly reliant on the forces of either Clinton or Howe meeting Burgoyne's forces and they were given no orders to that effect.

- Burgoyne was overconfident. He had placed a bet in his London club that he would be home by Christmas, victorious. Some of the difficulties he encountered were entirely of his own making (he was encumbered by an enormous baggage train including 30 vehicles for his wardrobe and champagne) and others easy to predict (American neutrals and loyalists did not flock to join an army which included native Americans). The major weakness in his plan was that it was not part of a co-ordinated plan with Generals Clinton and Howe, who were pursuing different objectives. At the point where retreat would have saved his army, Burgoyne chose to gamble that Clinton's army would progress north fast enough to prevent his troops bearing the full brunt of Gates' attack. As a result, he found himself in Saratoga effectively surrounded by double the number of American troops and was forced to surrender.

- The peace that was negotiated was fairly favourable to the British. Burgoyne's 5,895 troops were to lay down their arms and march to Boston to be embarked on British ships on the condition they did not fight again. However, Congress found reasons to reject the terms negotiated by Gates and the soldiers remained prisoners until the end of the war in 1783.

French and Spanish entry into the war

The diplomatic mission led by Benjamin Franklin was successful in persuading the French to ally themselves with the Americans, partly as a result of Franklin's success as ambassador, but largely because of the French reaction to the news of Burgoyne's defeat. The French were motivated by their long-term rivalry with the British and the possibility of regaining territory lost in the Seven Years' War, not by any revolutionary sympathies for the patriots, and proof that the patriots were a credible force resulted in their willingness to enter the war on the side of the Americans. Treaties were signed between the countries in February 1778 and the French declared war on the British in June 1778. Spain entered the war as an ally of France in June 1779. French and Spanish involvement in the war proved decisive in colonial victory, as the conflict was now opened on many fronts and, for the British, defeat of the French became more important than holding onto the colonies.

SOURCE

9 From a letter by John Sullivan, a member of Congress, writing to George Washington in May 1781. Sullivan was a member of the first Continental Congress, served as a general in the revolutionary army and again as a delegate at Congress from 1780.

Philadelphia May 28th 1781

My dear General

Though the Distresses of our Army, the Success of the Enemy in the Southern States; The certainty of the Second Division not coming to America; and the Disposition of the Sovereigns of Russia, and Germany, to dictate a Peace; when the **uti possidetes** if admitted would Operate to deprive us of very important parts of the united States: Yet I would forbear congratulating Your Excellency on the general Compleation of our Affaires which in my Opinion wear a more promising Aspect Than they have done for many Years.

The Reinforcement from France though far short of what was intended, will (I trust) Enable us to undertake Offensive Operations by Land & Sea. the Generous Donation of his most Christian Majesty with the measures adopted by Congress & by our Financier will Enable us to pay and Supply our Army. The Cloathing Arrived & now on its passage will Enable us to Cloathe our Army. The Measures adopted by the French Court will furnish us with the necessary Munitions of War. The Late important discoveries made by Congress have at Length convinced them that Honesty is the best policy; This will restore our Lost credit. The prospects of a peace being Dictated to us by an **Armed neutrality** will rouse Congress and the States to Exertions which may put us on a footing to negotiate on Terms of Equality.

The Scrupulous adherence of his Christian Majesty to the Terms of the Alliance; The favorable Disposition of the Spanish Court; and the interest which the powers of Europe have discovered in our becoming an Independant Nation promise us Every thing in a negociation which our Exertions & their political Interest may Dictate. but Amidst all those flattering prospects we are now called upon to make our Last desperate Struggle to pave the way to that peace and Independance for which we have so long contended. Congress do and I am convinced the States will feel the necessity to Exert Every nerve at this critical moment and I do not Entertain a Doubt of the Success.

A Level Exam-Style Question Section A

Study Source 9 before you answer this question.

Assess the value of the source for revealing American hopes and fears regarding the likely outcome of the war and future peace settlement.

Explain your answer, using the source, the information given about its origin and your own knowledge about the historical context. (20 marks)

Tip
Place the letter in the context of military developments and engagements 1779–81.

The entry of France and Spain into the war was enormously significant for the course of the war for the following reasons.

- Until 1778, 65 percent of the British army was in North America. By 1780, this had dropped to 20 percent as troops were required for the defence of Britain against a possible invasion. Similarly, in 1778, 41 percent of the British navy was in American waters; by 1780, this had dropped to 13 percent.

- The intervention of the French fleet at Chesapeake Bay under de Grasse was vital in the defeat of the British in Yorktown in 1781, in what proved to be the decisive battle of the war. Although there were fewer than 10,000 French troops in America and these were largely inactive until 1781, they did form part of the attacking force on Yorktown.

- By 1781, Spanish forces had cleared British troops from the Mississippi Valley.

The vital importance of the French–Spanish intervention into the conflict between the British and the colonists was the subsequent redrawing of British priorities. Britain was mobilised against invasion, it held its possessions in the West Indies (deemed vital to the economic life of Britain) and increased its presence in India. After Yorktown, the collateral loss of the American colonies came to be seen as acceptable to the British (see page 85).

General Cornwallis' defeat at Yorktown, 1781

Following Saratoga, the British had decided to move their focus south where they believed there to be more loyalists, in the hope that victory there would give them the base to move northwards and take the New England colonies one by one. Clinton's assault on Charleston in 1780 was successful and the British were able to move into the interior with relative success. However, British control in 1781 rested on their ability to control Chesapeake Bay and keep Yorktown linked to New York by sea. The British defeat at Yorktown was the result of Washington being able to lead an army of 16,000 American and French troops into the Yorktown peninsula and lay siege to the British for three weeks, while the French fleet held control of the Bay. Cornwallis surrendered on 19 October 1781. Reinforcements arrived five days too late. In London, Lord North responded to the news by saying 'Oh God, it is all over.' The campaign which culminated in the defeat at Yorktown bears all the hallmarks of the problems that the British were unable to overcome in America.

- The population in the South did not prove to be the loyalist stronghold that the British hoped for. When Cornwallis moved into the interior, he had the same problem that the British faced in the North. Victories did not mean that territory was held and loyal.

- After the siege of Charleston and the butchering of American troops attempting to surrender at Waxhow Creek, Virginia, by Colonel Tarleton, General Clinton returned to New York leaving Cornwallis to fight the southern campaign with just 4,000 men. Once again, the British were obliged to split forces and weaken their attacking army to ensure that the seaboard

was held and the ports garrisoned. This put them at the mercy of inadequate communication and open sea lanes.

- The southern campaign, like the northern one that ended in disaster at Saratoga, relied on Britain's ability to hold the ports. Clinton had blithely assured Cornwallis that the French would not be able to hold superiority of the seas for any length of time. However, they proved strong enough to repulse the first British fleet on 5 September and Clinton's relief force and reinforced fleet failed to arrive in time to prevent the surrender of Yorktown on 19 October 1781.

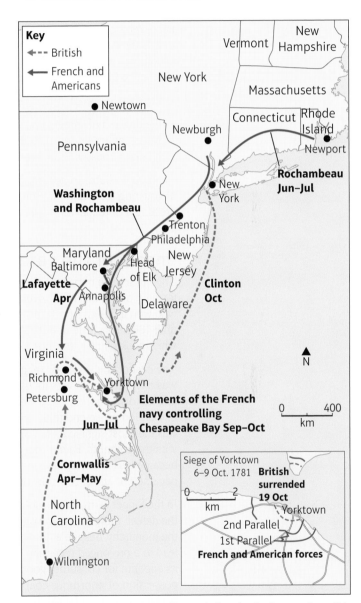

Figure 3.2 British and American forces during the final campaign of the war in 1781.

ACTIVITY
KNOWLEDGE CHECK

The turning points of the war
Which of the three events, the defeats at Saratoga and Yorktown, and the entry of the Spanish and French into the war, do you consider to be the most significant turning point of the war? Support your answer with evidence from the text and sources.

The decision to seek peace and accept the Peace of Paris

Yorktown resulted in the end of the war, not because the British position in America collapsed overnight, but because the political will in London was no longer there. The City of London and parliament put pressure on the king and his ministry to end the war, which was perceived as being bad for trade, and speaker after speaker in the debates highlighted the impracticability of continuing to fight after Yorktown. Defence priorities had changed following the entry of the French into the war and, by 1782, the British were prepared to accept the loss of the colonies. Despite holding New York, Charleston and Savannah, and with over 30,000 troops left in America, the British Commons resolved to end military measures against the Americans in February and Lord North resigned on 20 March.

Peace of Paris

Peace talks commenced in April under the new ministry led by Shelburne, whose principal concern was to split the Americans from their French allies and was therefore prepared to be generous to the new nation. The evacuations of the British strongholds were ordered and the Peace of Paris was signed by Britain, the USA, France, Spain and Holland on 3 September 1783. Its most significant clauses were:

- the recognition of American independence and its new boundaries

- the division of imperial possessions between Britain, France and Spain: Spain gained Florida and Minorca; Britain regained the Bahamas; France regained St Lucia, Goree and Pondicherry, and retained Tobago; Britain returned Trincomalee to Holland, but regained Negapatam in India.

America was able to achieve far more favourable terms than they expected because of their strong negotiating team and the British concern to cement reasonable relations with America with a view to creating a potential ally against the French in the future.

Impact of the defeat on Britain

The immediate impact of the defeat on Britain was the resignation of Lord North in 1782 and the formation of a coalition government. This was shortly replaced by a new ministry under William Pitt, who won a decisive (in 18th-century terms) election victory in 1784 and remained prime minister until 1801. As prime minister, he was the mastermind of the next phase of the Anglo-French conflict which took place in the 1790s.

The cost of the war was staggering and, by 1783, the national debt was £232 million. Britain's trade was disrupted, both with its European neighbours and with the colonies. The financial cost of war and the disruption of trade were important causes of pressure placed on parliament by the City of London for an end to the war. However, the intervention of the French and Spanish in the war was the most significant factor in the redrawing of British priorities and the decision to seek peace with the colonists. Faced with possible invasion from France, teaching the thirteen colonies a lesson became less important in the minds of the British political elite. Making terms with the Americans became not just acceptable, but desirable.

In the longer term, Britain showed remarkable economic resilience and social cohesion. Following the defeat, there was no revolution. Political power remained in the hands of the landed gentry and the monarchy, despite a flurry of agitation calling for reform of the political system. Defeat did not lead to a prolonged recession. Britain's population continued to grow (always a sign of optimism) and its appetite for consumer goods combined with the happy circumstance of Britain being an island in possession of enormous coal deposits meant that entrepreneurs were able to benefit from the stable banking system and build the mills and factories on which Britain's Industrial Revolution was based. By 1785, Britain's trade with its former colonies had reached its pre-war levels and the value of British exports to Europe doubled between 1783 and 1792.

SOURCE
10

From *Memoirs of the Life of the Right Hon William Pitt* by George Tomline, published in 1821. The memoirs describe in exhaustive detail the debates in parliament surrounding war in America following Yorktown and the King's eventual reply to the House of Commons accepting the points made there during the debates.

His majesty returned the following answer. 'There are no subjects nearer to my heart than the ease, happiness and prosperity of my people. You may be assured, that, in pursuance of your advice, I shall take such measures as shall appear to me most conducive to the restoration of harmony between Great Britain and the revolted colonies, so essential to the prosperity of both; and that my efforts shall be directed in the most effectual manner against our European enemies, until such a peace can be obtained, as shall consist with the interests and permanent welfare of my kingdoms.'

British policy in Ireland, Britain's first colony, does suggest that some lessons were learned along the way by the political establishment as a result of Britain's defeat at the hands of the colonists.

- In 1780, the British altered the mercantilist system in Ireland, which was causing protest, to allow Ireland to trade directly with British colonies.

- In 1782, the Irish were granted effective legislative independence as the British repealed the Declaratory Act 1719.

The reaction to the loss of the American colonies is interesting because it is so different to the anguish and self-searching which resulted from the end of empire and decolonisation in the 20th century. This is because the concept of empire was an essentially 19th-century creation and the loss of Britain's empire in the 20th century was accompanied by Britain's decline as a great power. In 1783, British identity was far more defined by the concept of 'Britishness' created by their victory over France than by an imperial identity. They accepted that there had been a revolution by British citizens in the American colonies and moved on; within five years, they were sending convict ships to Australia in a new venture. The loss of the American colonies did not curtail new imperial ventures or dent the self-confidence of what was about to become the richest, most powerful country in the world.

ACTIVITY
KNOWLEDGE CHECK

The war and the peace

1 To what extent does Source 10 support the view that the entry of the French into the American War of Independence was key in Britain's decision to enter peace talks?

2 What were the results of the end of the war in Britain?

ACTIVITY
SUMMARY

The loss of the American colonies, 1770-83

1 What was the American view of British attempts to impose new taxation on them? Support your summary notes with quotations from the sources and evidence from the text of the chapter.

2 Summarise the British and American strengths and weaknesses and use your summary to write an explanation of American victory.

WIDER READING

Brogan, H. *The Penguin History of the USA*, Penguin (1999)

Farmer, A. *Britain and the American Colonies*, Hodder Education (2008)

Farmer, A. *The American Revolution and the Birth of the USA*, Hodder Education (2015)

Weintraub, S. *Iron Tears: America's Battle for Freedom, Britain's Quagmire: 1776-1783*, Free Press (2005)

The website www.masshist.org has a huge collection of sources relating to the period available online.

3.4 The birth of British Australia, 1788–1829

KEY QUESTIONS

- How did the first British penal colony in Australia develop as a settlement?
- What was the impact of British settlement on the Aboriginal people in Tasmania and New South Wales, 1788–1829?
- What was the extent and nature of colonial control in Australia in the years 1803–29?

First Fleet
The First Fleet consisted of 11 ships that set sail from Portsmouth on 13 May 1787, bound to found 'Australia'. The fleet was made up of six convict transport ships, three storage ships and two navy ships. Their route was approximately 15,000 miles and took 252 days, with the fleet arriving in Botany Bay, Australia, on 18 January 1788.

INTRODUCTION

On 18 January 1788, the **First Fleet** sailed into Botany Bay. Those on board were not free settlers looking to establish a home, but British convicts under the command of Arthur Phillip, a retired naval officer. They had been transported 5,000 miles in a journey that took at least six months to serve their sentences in a new continent, establishing a new British colony in the process. The eleven ships sailed into Botany Bay in good order having survived the passage of 252 days with no ships lost and only 69 deaths, discharges or desertions within the entire fleet which carried over 1,400 people, including convicts, seamen, marines and a small number of civil officials (there is no exact available number of seamen on the journey). Having landed and following their instructions from London, they discovered that Botany Bay lacked both water and fertile soil so they sailed out again on 26 January to Port Jackson, landing at Sydney Cove, a far more suitable venue for settlement, and the new colony was founded. The little that was known about the new continent that this strangely assorted group found themselves on had been recorded by Cook's expedition which had returned to London in 1771, 17 years before. Governor Phillip read aloud to the entire colony the Act of Parliament founding the colony and his commission as governor on 7 February 1788. For the convicts, it must have been obvious that they would live and die in this new unfamiliar place 5,000 miles away from their former homes. For Phillip, the immensity of his task in establishing a settlement, dependent only on his supplies and the promise of relief ships in two years, all being well, must have been nearly overwhelming.

1770 – 22 August: Cook claims New South Wales for the British as *Terra Nullis* (Nobody's Land)

1788 – 18 January: First Fleet arrives in Botany Bay after a passage of 252 days at sea

1790 – Governor Phillip dispatches 300 convicts to Norfolk Island

1796 – John Macarthur introduces merino sheep to Australia

| 1770 | 1775 | 1780 | 1785 | 1790 | 1795 |

1776 – American War of Independence disrupts transportation of criminals to America

1789 – Smallpox breaks out among Aboriginal population with catastrophic results

1791 – Whaling begins in the colony on the *William and Ann* and the *Britannia* of the Third Fleet

James Ruse is granted land at Rose Hill (Parramatta) as a reward for growing the first crop of wheat in the colony

HOW DID THE FIRST BRITISH PENAL COLONY IN AUSTRALIA DEVELOP AS A SETTLEMENT?

Why had the British chosen to establish a penal colony at Botany Bay?

The establishment of a penal colony in New South Wales came about with very little serious consideration by the British government. Once Cook's expedition returned, it was well known that a vast land was lying ready for the taking in the southern hemisphere. Furthermore, the Cook expedition reported favourably as to the fertility and emptiness of the land. (Cook did not consider the Aboriginal people to have any claim to the land as they did not appear to him to be using it.)

The American War of Independence meant that **felons** could no longer be transported to the American colonies and so the Pitt government judged that this new continent would be a suitable destination for felons currently crowded into rotting frigates moored on the Thames. Botany Bay was picked on the suggestion of Banks, the botanist on the Cook expedition, and James Matra, also a member of the expedition, spoke favourably of the possibility of growing flax for sail making in the area chosen. The suggestion that American loyalists be settled there was dismissed out of hand and the First Fleet came into being, under the command of Phillip, with very little further thought by the British. The cost of **fitting out the fleet** was £84,000, which, although not exactly cheap, appeared to be money worth spending to the government of the day.

Some weight was given by the British government to the fact that, by settling a colony in Australia, they would be preventing any French territorial claim to the territory. Weight was also given to reports of Norfolk Island, a small island 877 miles east of Sydney in the Pacific Ocean, which were positive regarding its pine trees and flax, both of which were crucial to the building of ships. However, the fundamental reason for the decision to transport convicts to Australia was the crisis in the prison system in Britain. By the late 1780s, the prisons in Britain were filled to bursting point with convicts.

By the 1780s, the penal system was in crisis. **Urbanisation** and slum poverty resulted in more and more crime, undeterred by severe punishments. Moreover, the system of trial by jury meant that increasingly juries were finding defendants not guilty rather than hanging them for crimes of desperation. The introduction of transportation of felons to the American colonies in the early 18th century had provided a temporary stop gap to ease the crisis and George III in particular was assiduous in his exercise of his prerogative in dispensing mercy to those who appealed to him. Transportation provided a third and more merciful option to death and allowed the system to continue unreformed in its fundamentals. The American War of Independence put an end to transportation to America and the Pitt government opted for transportation to the new continent of Australia rather than attempting the overhaul and reform of the prison and justice system that was glaringly necessary.

KEY TERMS

Felon
One who has committed a serious crime.

Fitting out the fleet
The preparation of ships to ensure their seaworthiness and the purchase of all stores necessary for a journey.

Urbanisation
The social process in which cities grow and societies become more urban. The growth of cities is rarely matched by provision of sanitation or controlled by planning regulations and tends to be accompanied by slums, disease and crime.

1808 – 26 January: Rum Rebellion – Governor Bligh is removed from office by a mutiny of the New South Wales Corps and free settlers

1813 – Blaxland, Lawson and Wentworth are the first Europeans to cross the Blue Mountains

1828 – November: Martial law is declared against the Aboriginal people in Tasmania by Governor Arthur

| 1800 | 1805 | 1810 | 1815 | 1825 | 1830 |

1803 – A small military outpost is established in Van Diemen's Land to prevent any settlement by the French

1810 – 1 January: Lachlan Macquarie becomes governor of New South Wales

1823 – New South Wales Act establishes a legislative council in the colony

1829 – August: First British settlers arrive in Western Australia

A Level Exam-Style Question Section A

Study Source 1 before you answer this question.

Assess the value of the source for revealing the reasons for the choice of Botany Bay as Britain's first settlement in Australia and the hopes the government had for the colony.

Explain your answer, using the source, the information given about its origin and your own knowledge about the historical context. (20 marks)

Tip

Consider the influence that Banks was likely to have on the debate surrounding the establishment of such a colony in Australia.

SOURCE

From the report of the Bunbury Committee on Transportation (1779). Joseph Banks was appearing as an expert witness (only a handful of people had actually seen Australia and he had been a member of the Cook expedition) for the parliamentary committee investigating the option of transporting convicts to Australia.

J Banks Esq, being requested, in case it should be thought expedient to establish a colony of convicted felons in any part of the Globe, from whence their escape might be difficult, and where from the Fertility of the Soil, they might be able to maintain themselves, after the fifth year, with little or no Aid from the Mother County, to give his opinion what place would be most eligible for such settlement? informed your Committee, that the Place which appeared to him best adapted for such a Purpose, was Botany Bay, on the Coast of New Holland, the Indian Ocean, which was about seven Months Voyage from England; that he apprehended that there would be little Probability of any Opposition from the Natives, as during his stay there, in the year 1770, he saw very few, and did not think there would be above Fifty in all the Neighbourhood, and had Reason to believe the Country was very thinly populated; those he saw were naked, treacherous, and armed with Lances, but extremely cowardly, and constantly retired from our People when they made the Appearance of Resistance: He was in this bay in the End of April and beginning or May 1770, when the Weather was mild and moderate; that the Climate he apprehended was similar to that of Toulouse in the South of France, having found the southern Hemisphere colder than the Northern;... the Proportion of rich soil was small in proportion to the barren, but sufficient to support a very large Number of People;... And being asked, whether he concurred the Mother Country was liable to reap any Benefit from a Colony established in Botany Bay? he replied – If the people formed among themselves a Civil Government, they would necessarily increase, and find Occasion for many European Commodities; and it was not to be doubted that a Tract of Land such as New Holland, which is larger than the whole of Europe, would furnish Matter of advantageous Return.

Who were the first British settlers?

Approximately 1,420 people boarded the First Fleet in Portsmouth, 775 of whom were convicts and 14 were children born to convict mothers. They were escorted by nearly 300 non-convicts responsible for guarding them and ensuring the safe transportation of the fleet.

Convicts

Existing records suggest that 732 convicts landed (543 men, 189 women and 22 convicts' children – 11 boys and 11 girls), but no precise record of the number of seamen and their families who made the voyage exists. The youngest convict was John Hudson, aged nine, who had been given seven years' transportation for stealing, and the oldest a women of 82, Dorothy Handland, was transported for housebreaking (she hanged herself from a gum tree a year later).

- Two-thirds of the convicts had been sentenced for minor theft and the average age was under 30.

- The majority of women were listed as domestic servants and sentenced for theft, but it was likely that many were also prostitutes. (Prostitution was not a transportable offence.)

- As well as the English and Scots, there were Americans (black and white), Germans and Norwegians, and Jews made up a significant religious group.

A stereotype grew up in late 19th- and early 20th-century Australia of convict ancestors transported for petty theft, poaching or stealing to feed a family, but fundamentally honest and decent nonetheless. This has largely been demolished by statistical analysis. The convicts transported in the First Fleet and in later ships were overwhelmingly city dwellers and a half to two-thirds of the convicts had at least one previous conviction. They were not murderers (a capital offence), but in the most part they were criminals rather than innocents caught up by unfortunate events. Only a tiny minority, even of the Irish felons, were transported for political activity.

Others

The remaining personnel (more than 600 in number) were marines, their wives and families, seamen and their families, and civil officers. The marines, under the command of Major Robert Ross, were to prove a thorn in Governor Phillip's side as they were disinclined to do anything other than military duties, which were effectively non-existent. Instead, Phillip relied on seamen and convicts to act as overseers and even police as he got on with the tasks in hand of building shelter and maintaining food supplies for all in the new settlement.

The role of governors

Governors exercised absolute power and military discipline over the penal colony. The length of time it took for communications to reach and return from London (and even between Sydney and Hobart) meant that effectively they were completely reliant on their own judgements. There were several notable governors in addition to Macquarie (see page 93) during the early years of the settlement.

- Arthur Phillip (in office 1788–92): He was responsible for the highly successful journey of the First Fleet and the establishment and survival of the colony in the first years. Thorough and pragmatic, he was a tough disciplinarian but fair. He gave the first land grants to ex-convicts, thereby ensuring the future subsistence of the colony. His fairness was extended to the Aboriginal people, who interested him deeply and with whom he was non-confrontational and offered some protection.

- William Bligh (in office 1806–08): To suffer one mutiny can be considered a misfortune, to suffer two suggests a personality flaw. Seventeen years after being marooned by the crew of the *Bounty*, Bligh was removed as governor of New South Wales by the New South Wales Corps and other free born settlers angry at his attempts to curb their privileges. There was little punishment of the perpetrators, suggesting London recognised his fatal flaw.

- Thomas Brisbane (in office 1821–25): He reversed the paternalistic and high-spending approach of Macquarie, limiting early pardons and land grants to convicts. During his governorship, power and wealth in the colony was consolidated in the hands of the freeborn settlers, who formed a wealthy farming class.

- George Arthur (Tasmania) (in office 1824–36): He devised a system of punishments and rewards for convicts. He also extended his control over the free settlers of the colony to run a police state, refusing convict labour to any settlers whose actions he disapproved of. Under his governorship, Van Diemen's Land was as close to a totalitarian state as was ever reached in the British Empire.

Initial settlement

Botany Bay had been chosen on the advice of Joseph Banks, the botanist who accompanied the Cook expedition, who had strongly advocated the founding of a penal colony in Australia and appeared before the Parliamentary Committee as an expert witness (see Source 1). To those charged with establishing a colony, the choice of Botany Bay must have seemed bizarre as the area lacked a fresh water supply and the soil was obviously unsuitable for cultivation. The rapid move through Port Jackson and into Sydney Cove, after a brief reconnaissance, was a matter of immediate survival, although in the first few months of the settlement Governor Phillip revisited Botany Bay several times, as if he was afraid to accept that his orders, based on Banks' recommendation, could have been so wrong.

However, Sydney itself was to prove such a challenging environment that the first settlement was lucky it did not repeat the fate of the settlement at Roanoke in Virginia, where all 107 settlers perished between 1587 when they arrived and 1590 when the relief ship arrived. Although the settlement established in Sydney was much larger than that at Roanoke, it is not beyond the realms of possibility that the entire colony could have collapsed. Within six months, the livestock that had been bought with the Fleet had either been eaten or disappeared. There was no plough available to till the soil or animal suitable to pull a plough and the thin soil around Sydney Cove did not yield much of a crop to the miserable hand-hoed efforts of the non-farming convicts. Even Governor Phillip was initially lodged under a canvas structure, which let in the wind and rain, and building efforts were hampered by the difficulty of making bricks and lack of mortar available. The settlement existed on supplies they had bought with them and whatever fresh fish or birdlife they could kill. The settlers traded with the Aboriginal people, whose superior hunting skills enabled them to kill kangaroo, but their meat intake was largely limited to dried supplies.

The task of forming a working society was a hard one. Phillip had, in order of priority, to ensure subsistence for all in the colony, control the convicts, build adequate shelter and housing, command the marines, manage smooth relations with the Aboriginal peoples, encourage respectable and godly behaviour thereby reforming the convicts, encourage settlement once convictions were spent, build a township and develop economic life – and this was all without recourse to advice from London and in an unfamiliar environment. Furthermore, the material he had to work with, the convicts themselves, were not the knowledgeable farmers, skilled carpenters or hunters he desperately needed. On the whole, they were town dwellers and petty, or more hardened, criminals. Their skills, if they had any, were generally of an undesirable nature and they were unused to working as part of a team.

Phillip often had to resort to harsh physical punishment to maintain control and lashings were commonplace and hangings frequent.

Phillip's instructions left a great deal to his own initiative. London initially envisaged that the colony would be self-sufficient within four years and the government costed the venture at just over £70,000. All supplies of food and clothing within the settlement were the property of the government and distributed at the governor's discretion. Likewise, all produce grown or income derived from the planned flax industry in Norfolk Island (which never materialised as the flax proved to be the wrong type) was to be the property of the government. The governor's instructions called for the appointment of a surveyor and the allocation of plots of land to those convicts who had served their terms, and Phillip duly complied with this instruction. He was also instructed to offer encouragement to any serving officers who decided to stay on in the colony and, although most of the First Fleet marines opted to return to Britain, some stayed and were granted land. The development of private land holding did not ease the demands on government supplies, however, as former convicts did not necessarily prove adept at farming and there was no real internal market due to the universal reliance on the Government Store for supplies.

Phillip allocated work on the basis of the skills he found among the convicts and, by the time he sailed for Britain, everyone was housed in rudimentary wattle and daub dwellings and there was a brick-built governor's mansion. There was also a Government Farm at Paramatta and 66 grants of land had been made, of which 53 were to those whose convictions were now spent, and by 1792 there were 1,000 acres under public cultivation and 516 under private cultivation. Phillip's powers over discipline in the colony were absolute and included the power to sentence to death if he saw fit. His even-handed exercise of his powers prevented any mutiny. In addition, he had used the powers granted to him to buy extra supplies for the colony at the government's expense opportunely in 1788, which helped to tide the colony over until the arrival of relief ships.

In many ways, credit for the survival of the colony in its first few years must be given to Governor Phillip. This semi-retired naval officer, with a relatively undistinguished career up to this point, not only pulled off one of the greatest sea journeys ever undertaken by transporting the First Fleet with such tiny loss of life, but his calm practicality ensured the survival of the colony in its most vulnerable years. The survival of the British in the first two years after the departure of the ships for home was the result of four main reasons.

- *Preparations for the journey*: Phillip's preparations for equipping the First Fleet had been thorough and painstaking, evidenced both by the high level of survival of those sailing in the First Fleet (the ships' logs recorded a death rate of only three percent of all those on board for the outward journey) and the survival of the colony until 1790 and the arrival of the Second Fleet. Had the expedition set sail in December 1786, as Lord Sydney, the home secretary, wished, rather than spending the next six months preparing for departure as Phillip insisted, the story of the first British colony might indeed have been one of starvation and total failure.

- *Establishing a second colony at Norfolk Island*: Phillip decided, in 1790, to send 183 convicts, 28 children and 81 marines to Norfolk Island (the potential site of the flax-making, ship-building trading post in the minds of the British government) where there appeared to be a better chance of survival. Although the island was to become synonymous with extreme hardship and was largely evacuated in 1807, in 1790 it was a softer option than Sydney largely because it was the habitat of the 'mutton bird' (*Pterodroma melanopus*) until most were eaten by the colony. (By 1796, they were much reduced in numbers; by 1804 they were almost gone; and by 1830 they had disappeared from the island altogether.) The removal of the 183 convicts from Sydney Cove meant that the miserable rations were just about enough to ensure the survival of the remaining people. One convict, Joseph Owen, did die of starvation in May 1790 having lost or sold his cook pot and no other convict being willing to help him.

- *Phillip's control of food stores*: Phillip's insistence that rations be shared equally from 1 April 1790 was hugely resented by the marines but a critical part of the community's survival. It meant that while food was very meagre, there was enough to tide everyone over (with the exception of Joseph Owen) until the arrival of the Second Fleet. As rationing was completely fair, there were no riots over rations as would have been the case had the marines continued to receive the extra rations. Hours of convict labour had to be cut at the same time as the ration was really too small to sustain manual labour.

- *Relocation to better farmland*: Phillip decided to settle the colony 16 miles from Sydney Cove in Parramatta (he renamed the area Rose Hill), which appeared more fertile, and to grant lands to former convicts in that area. In 1791, James Ruse, who had been a farmer in Cornwall before his conviction and transportation for breaking and entering, received the first land grant of 30 acres in New South Wales in Rose Hill and was able to grow wheat and other crops successfully. Phillip was a rational man and it appeared obvious to him that in the absence of free settlers, to whom convicts could be indentured, as had been the system in America, the best thing to do was to get men off Government Store supplies and enable them to be able to subsist from their own land as quickly as possible. If this meant making former convicts landowners, then so be it.

- Nevertheless, the survival of the colony hung in the balance, especially after the flagship *Sirius* was wrecked at Norfolk Island on its way to Canton for more supplies. A relief ship, the *Guardian*, from England, never reached the colony and she sunk near the Cape. As all the other ships of the Fleet had left apart from the *Supply*, which no one wanted to risk, the future of the colony was not assured until the arrival of the Second Fleet with more vital supplies from Britain.

SOURCE 2

First interview with the native women at Port Jackson, New South Wales, 1788, by William Bradley. Bradley's watercolours form an important record of the early days of the penal colony. Officers were taught to draw coastal profiles, charts and views accurately for naval purposes. Bradley was interested in the Aboriginal people and recorded some of the early meetings between the British and the Aboriginal peoples.

The Second Fleet

The arrival of *Lady Juliana*, the ship devoted to transporting the female convicts of the Second Fleet, on 3 June 1790 with letters from home, 222 female convicts and provisions for those they carried on board was solid evidence that the colony had not been forgotten and that further help was on its way. The store ship the *Justinian* arrived two weeks later, followed by the rest of the horrific transport ships of the Second Fleet with their cargoes of suffering and dying convicts. At least a quarter of those transported had died during the voyage, and a further 150 died soon after landing, from a combination of starvation, scurvy, poor sanitation and louse-borne diseases. Rather than entrust the Second Fleet to an officer, as they had done with the First Fleet and Phillip, the government had chosen to contract the journey out to a private firm, Camden, Calvert and King, with tragic results.

In today's world of instant news delivered to your mobile phone, it is worth remembering that apart from the bizarre coincidence of the contact with two French ships shortly after the First Fleet arrived, there had been no communication with the Old World for over two years. News from home included reports of the French Revolution and the madness of George III, big stories by any measure.

Despite the human tragedy, the arrival of the Second Fleet dramatically increased the chances of the colony's survival because they brought vital supplies of livestock and crops on the store ship *Justinian*. Phillip augmented the colony's supplies further by dispatching the *Atlantic* of the Third Fleet to Calcutta to buy rice for the colony, and this eked out supplies until London sent further supplies in reply to messages sent home on the return leg of the Third Fleet voyage. At the end of his governorship, Phillip was able to sail home in 1792, and to retirement in Bath, secure in the knowledge of a job well done. He had carried out his orders and more, using his initiative to secure the survival of the settlement through its first five years. Even the government's orders regarding the establishment of a settlement on Norfolk Island had been executed and over a thousand people were now living there. In Sydney and Paramatta, there were just over 3,000 split between the two settlements.

Further fleets remained in private hands and the government dealt with the public response to the reports of losses on the Second Fleet by appointing a Royal Commission into the affair which resulted in no prosecutions. As the years went on, the regulations for transportation became more and more proscriptive, particularly under the governorship of Macquarie, and although the conditions remained grim they were never as inhumane again. Transportation meant exactly that, it was not lottery for survival as the transportation of slaves from Africa to America was, where conditions were so bad that up to 50 percent of slaves might die during the journey across the Atlantic.

ACTIVITY
KNOWLEDGE CHECK

Initial settlement and survival

1 Read Source 1. Banks predicted easy settlement and quick financial reward for the government from the colony. Why was this not the case in 1777–92?

2 Assess Phillip's role in the survival of the settlement in its first years. How close did the colony come to starvation and failure in its early years?

Irish prisoners

The first ship of Irish prisoners reached the colony in 1791 and they formed the largest single group within the colony. They were regarded as particularly dangerous by the authorities in the colonies, partly because some of them were political dissidents in the struggle for freedom from Britain and partly because of the distrust all Englishmen felt for Catholics in this period. The Irish convicts stuck together and in 1804 there was an attempted rebellion by the Irish against Governor King that was foiled by the New South Wales Corps. Although the Irish did number political prisoners among their number, the vast majority were convicted for theft. Whatever the reason for their sentences, the Irish convicts shared a common sense of grievance against the English and this, combined with their Catholicism, made them an important grouping within the settlement.

Inadvertently, the penal colonies did help to reform convicts. Most, once free of the slums and poverty of Georgian England flourished in the warmth of the Australian sunshine. However, some convicts, unable to comprehend the vastness of the Australian continent, bolted from the colony intending to walk to China. (This practice tailed off once the colony extended towards the Blue Mountains and the bleached bones of 'bolters' were found lying on the ground.) Others escaped by sea and were either lost at sea or eked out an existence in miserable conditions as beachcombers on whichever coastline they landed on.

The importance of Lachlan Macquarie (governor 1809–21) to the development of New South Wales

While it seems unlikely that the British would ever have abandoned the colony, it is certainly true that Macquarie's mark on Sydney was enduring and his explorations into the Blue Mountains hastened the economic growth of the colony. His tenure was fruitful and productive, and a distinct turn for the better when compared to the **Rum years** that had preceded his arrival. Macquarie's impact on the colony partly derives from the length of his tenure and partly from his paternalistic vision for the place. He liked the widespread powers he held and was determined to use them to improve the colony, both in terms of its morality and its appearance. His tenure coincided with two important developments which aided the growth of the colony economically.

- The British government sent the first shipment of sterling silver coins to the colony in 1812. This replaced the mishmash of currencies, **promissory notes**, barter, IOUs and rum on which the colony's economic life had previously existed.

- The end of the Napoleonic Wars in 1815 saw an increase in prisoners sent to the colony as economic conditions in Britain worsened and crime increased as a result. Three-quarters of convicts shipped to Australia were transported after 1815, providing labour for the growing colonial economy. The arrival of increased numbers of convicts enabled the growth of the nascent economic life of the colony and Governor Macquarie's ambitious public works' programme absorbed a significant proportion of the new arrivals.

How did Macquarie change the colony?

The first significant change to the colony during Macquarie's governorship was the removal of the **New South Wales Corps**. In 1792, the marines who had been the initial military force and prison guard of the convicts were replaced by the New South Wales Corps. They, in turn, were replaced in 1809 once they had mutinied against Governor Bligh in the **Rum Rebellion** and it was obvious to London that the affairs of the colony were badly awry. Governors had almost limitless powers within the colony, but could only exercise them with the support of their officers and, in the hiatus between Governor Phillip's departure and Governor Hunter's arrival in 1795, the Corps had assumed significant powers within the colony which they maintained until 1809. They were assigned up to ten male convicts and three female as farm labourers (far more than freed convicts were granted) for their farms and had taken control of the import of alcohol into the colony using their wages in London as credit with the merchant captains. Officers were able to write IOUs to merchant captains, which could be drawn in London against their regimental pay, in exchange for alcohol. As there was no actual money in the colony and not much else by way of desirable goods to trade, they effectively controlled the economic life of the colony. It is impossible to over-emphasise the importance of alcohol in the colony at this period. Everyone drank, to excess if possible, and, until silver money was dispatched to the colony in 1812, rum was the default currency on which the colony operated.

In addition, as communications between London and Sydney became more frequent, London received information not just from their governor in the colony but from influential free settlers, almost all of whom were retired members of the New South Wales Corps and they were thus able to undermine governors if they chose.

Nevertheless, the action by free settlers and the Corps removing Bligh from office in 1808 and taking over the colony in his absence (he was dispatched to Hobart) indicated to London that the Corps were out of control and needed reining in and they took action accordingly. Influenced by reports from free settlers and Bligh's previous history, London did, however, deem Bligh to be partly responsible for his own fate and the perpetrators of the mutiny were not punished. Macquarie was dispatched from London with a new regiment and under his governorship the colony ceased to operate as a cartel run by the freeborn officers whose actual role was meant to be the overseeing of the prisoners.

KEY TERMS

Rum years
A period of time during which the New South Wales Corps dominated the colony, 1792–1809.

Promissory note
A signed note promising to pay the bearer the stated sum at a specific date.

New South Wales Corps
An army regiment formed in 1789 to replace the marines who accompanied the First Fleet. They were the military force in the colony until they were disbanded in 1809 following their mutiny against Governor Bligh in 1808.

Rum Rebellion
Term given to the mutiny removing Bligh from his position of governor in 1808.

3.4 Britain: losing and gaining an empire, 1763-1914

The New South Wales Corps, who generally stayed on as settlers once their commissions were finished, were naturally keen to retain their hold on the wealth of the colony and were the founders of the growing wool industry. For them, Australia's development of a **gentry** of landowners was of first importance and they felt that governors should actively promote their interest group. The **Emancipists** and the **Currency**, who made up the small farmers along the new settlement of the Hawkesbury River, resented the stranglehold that the Corps had on the colony and wanted the Corps reined in and Macquarie tended to side with the Emancipists and the Currency over the **Exclusives**, which was a source of tension throughout his tenure in office.

KEY TERMS

Gentry
The group whose wealth derives from agricultural landownership.

Emancipist
A convict who had served his or her term or been given full or conditional pardons and was now a settler. Also known as 'government men'.

Currency
A free child born to a convict. They were notably healthier looking and taller than their parents, reared on the abundant food the colony provided. They were also notably law abiding. The freeborn children of settlers rather than convicts were known as 'Sterling'.

Exclusive
A free settler and their descendants. This included members of the New South Wales Corps who elected to remain in the colony.

A score of privates were transferred to the new regiment, the 73rd Regiment, under Macquarie's command, but the bulk of the Corps were sent to garrison duty to the Isle of Guernsey. The leaders of the rebellion, mostly ex-officers of the Corps, who formed the backbone of free settlement in the colony, were not punished by the British government, suggesting they realised that in many ways Bligh was the author of his own downfall. However, the dismantling of the Corps as a whole was deemed necessary for the smooth development of the colony. Macquarie's term of governorship was able to proceed peacefully, safe in the knowledge that the soldiers stationed in Sydney were under his full control.

By ending the rule of the Corps, Macquarie limited the power of the Exclusives and he was viewed as being sympathetic to the Emancipists. He argued for Emancipists, for example that the lawyer George Crossley should be able to plead in court. Although this measure was blocked, surgeon and ex-convict William Redfern delivered Macquarie's wife's baby, and Macquarie shocked society by inviting four Emancipists to dinner at Government House. In his view, convicts could be transformed into citizens and Macquarie personally greeted every new ship transporting convicts in the colony to exhort convicts on the opportunities open to them if they worked hard and what they could expect for good behaviour. His speech extolled the virtues of the new colony, explained the system of pardons and land grants for convicts whose behaviour merited such reward,

and outlined convict rights in the colony. Discipline was harsh and convicts would have expected that. This was mitigated by the fact that the punishments were not doled out by masters indiscriminately, but only after a hearing by a local magistrate. Macquarie's tone was paternalistic and encouraging for he truly believed in the colony's abilities to reform criminals and give them a second chance.

Convicts generally knuckled down under the carrot-and-stick approach of the New South Wales system. The promise of landownership and independence to those generally drawn from the very poorest sections of Georgian society was alluring. Most convicts, once their terms were spent or they obtained pardons, took up their land grants and remained in the colony. The distance travelled, the time elapsed away from Britain and the circumstances which had led to their transportation provided no incentive to try to return to Britain. Those who reoffended and proved intractable in New South Wales were sent to Van Diemen's Land once that colony was established. Notorious penal colonies were established at Port Macquarie in 1822 and on Norfolk Island in 1824. (The previous settlement had been largely evacuated in 1807 and totally abandoned by 1814.)

SOURCE

3 *Van Diemen's Land*, a convict ballad from the 1820s. Although it is impossible to know the identity of the original author, the number of variants of the song suggests that it was an important part of the collective folklore of convicts and resonated with individual experience.

... my fellow sufferers

I'm sure I can't tell how,

Some chained to a harrow

And some unto a plough

No shoes or stockings had they on,

No hats had they to wear,

Leather breeches and linen drawers,

Their feet and hands were bare.

They drove about in two and two

Like horses in a team

The driver he stood over them

With his malacca cane.

As we marched into Hobart Town

Without no more delay

A gentleman farmer took me,

His game keeper for to be:

I keep my occupation,

My master loves me well,

My joys are out of measure

I'm sure no tongue could tell.

Under Macquarie, the colony also became less drunken and more respectable. He passed a proclamation against cohabitation without **benefit of clergy** (he was a high-minded Anglican), which while it did not instantly transform the sexual politics of the colony did contribute to a gradual change over the following decades. Marriage improved women's economic status slightly as, if their husbands predeceased them, they were able to inherit property and businesses and to run them independent of male control. There were some notable widows in the colony, including Mary Haydock, who inherited a shipping and trading business from her husband and expanded it aggressively after his death in 1811, and Elizabeth Macarthur, the wife of John Macarthur, regarded as the father of the Australian woollen industry, who managed his farms while he made journeys back to England and once his health declined. These women were the exception and in many ways early convict women were the prisoners of prisoners, However, the less it became acceptable to pick women off the boat and then return them to the Government Store when they became pregnant, the better the lot of convict women became. Likewise, Macquarie's efforts to limit the consumption of alcohol did not solve the addiction the colony had to rum, but began the process of limiting the sale of alcohol which was very necessary. Public houses were to be closed during religious services and their number reduced. The traffic in spirits was reduced and he attempted to cut down the consumption of alcohol among the labourers within the colony.

KEY TERM

Benefit of clergy
The conducting of a ceremony such as a marriage by a priest or vicar.

Convict experience

The four governors and one deputy governor between 1788 and 1810 had the first choice of convicts for government service and, until 1810, the needs of the government were paramount within the colony. Convicts were needed to work on Government Farms, build roads and erect government buildings. Female convicts worked weaving cloth for the coarse clothing worn in the colony and as domestic servants. As the colony became more secure, the balance shifted and convicts were increasingly assigned to private masters involved in the growing wool trade. Whaling, which had begun following the arrival of the Third Fleet, was the most important source of income for the colony until the 1830s and tended not to rely on convict labour but was the preserve of freed convicts.

Whether in government service or assigned to an individual, convicts worked nine hours a day for five days a week and five hours on Saturday. Beyond this, they sold extra labour to their employer for wages (as there was no effective monetary system in the early years, this meant goods or rum). The convict workforce acted as workforces normally do when they are not free by working slowly and badly and stealing was a serious problem. Punishments were extremely harsh to try to maintain discipline. Minor transgressions meant 100 lashes by an experienced flogger and the gallows were frequently used.

Nevertheless, the rights of convicts were protected to some extent as punishments were only carried out once they had been brought before a magistrate and convicts had rights to food, shelter and the vital rum ration. The system developed by governors in the colony was intended to prevent abuses and the lot of a convict was certainly preferable to the lot of an American slave.

The place of women within the system was the most miserable. New South Wales was an overwhelmingly male colony. Male convicts outnumbered females by six to one; the 1805 census records 4,000 men and 1,300 women in the colony. The history of women begins with the 'festivities' that took place when the first female convicts landed on 6 February 1788. Male convicts were joined by seamen in 'welcoming' the women ashore with what historians have used a variety of terms to describe, but it is certain that the first experience that many female convicts had in Australia was rape. Those who escaped rape on that first night did so because they were already under the protection of a seaman or marine, established during the journey out. These relationships were in some cases enduring but in many cases were transitory, ending with the sailing of the ships for home.

Women who had not found protectors on the voyage were grimly aware that their best chance in the colony rested on doing so once their ships landed and the docking of a ship of women was marked by a market of the available women, who were assigned to officers, soldiers and ex-convicts as domestics. Domestic service was generally a form of cohabitation. If women were lucky, the relationship prospered; if they were unlucky, they were thrown back on the Government Store pregnant. In 1806, the Reverend Samuel Marsden, the senior Anglican minister in the colony at that time, drew up his notorious Female Register categorising women as either 'married', of which he counted 395, and 'concubine', of which he counted 1,035. Discounting the fact that Marsden ignored Catholic and Jewish marriages, and took no account of long-term cohabiting relationships where people would have seen themselves as married, it is clear that the fate of most convict women was to live under the protection of a man they had not chosen in exchange for a home and food and to secure a future for their children.

SOURCE

4

Michael Hayes, an Irish convict, wrote to his sister in 1798 telling her not to join him in Australia because of the fate that awaited convict women in the new colony. He was a political prisoner and therefore more literate than the average convict.

[He warned her of the...] distress that generally accompany unprotected Females coming to this distinct part of the world... Even were you with me your life would be a solitary one, (unless) you were to associate with Prostitutes. In this country there is Eleven Hundred women I cannot count Twenty out of that to be virtuous. The remainder support themselves through the means of Ludeness... This way of life was sanctioned by the Governors, from the first day of landing.

Skilled labour, known as Specials, was much in demand in the colony and the governors, from Phillip to Macquarie, made use of all the skills they could discover within their convict body, including Macquarie's commissioning of public buildings designed by the colony's first architect, Francis Greenway, convicted for forging a financial document. Forgers with useful skills as painters were set to record the developing colony and literate convicts were heavily in demand as servants and skilled workers. Having no free lawyers in the colony meant that George Crossley, convicted for forging a client's will, was able to practise law (although not plead in court) and even advised Governor Bligh during the Rum Rebellion. William Redfern, convicted for participating in a mutiny while serving as a surgeon's mate, delivered the Exclusives' babies and those of the convicts in the Rum Hospital alike.

Land grants to ex-convicts and the development up the Hawkesbury River

The system for convict work set up under Phillip was broadly used by subsequent governors in New South Wales and Van Diemen's Land and interpreted by Macquarie in a particularly generous and open-minded spirit. Original thinking (as far as this had happened back in London) had imagined that the Aboriginal people might serve as a workforce for the colony and that convicts would serve their terms and then be freed. Phillip's original instructions had included the provision of land grants to freed convicts and, because of the vast distances involved, London's intention had always been that freed criminals would stay in Australia, although a tiny number did return to Britain. Emancipists were able to apply for convict labour to be assigned to them. Likewise, the Exclusives, the free settlers who trickled in and the serving marines and later the New South Wales Corps, were all entitled to convict labour. Macquarie was well known for issuing early pardons and **tickets of leave**, and for treating the emancipated convicts as full members of society.

The First Select Committee Report into Transportation of Convicts in 1812 was broadly supportive of Macquarie's liberal interpretation of the penal system devised by Phillip, although it thought fewer tickets of leave should be granted and opposed the granting of pardons by the governor. This recommendation was flatly turned down by Earl Bathurst, the colonial secretary, who thought that the governor's authority should be absolute, but Exclusive complaints against Macquarie's liberal attitude to pardons rumbled on and were upheld by the Bigge Report later in Macquarie's governorship.

The original land grants made to convicts were made at Paramatta and Rose Hill under Phillip and his decision to do so was one of the reasons for the survival in the first years. The numbers in the colony were split from 1791 and during the first decade of the 19th century, with roughly half based around the harbour and the other half based at Paramatta. The first land grants in Hawkesbury, 65 km north-west of Sydney, were made as early as 1794 and, between 1800 and 1809, there was slowly expanding settlement in the area as it was easier to transport goods, people and crops by water than by any other method. The land near the Hawkesbury River was fertile and the mouth of the estuary was a good source of oysters. This new settlement was essential to feed the ever-growing population of Sydney and received strong support from Macquarie who founded five towns in the Hawkesbury region between 1810 and 1811. Steady expansion of European settlement was

KEY TERM

Ticket of leave

A document allowing convicts to hire themselves out or be self-employed before their sentence expired, on condition that they remain in a specified area, report regularly to local authorities and, if possible, attend church every Sunday. Governor King granted tickets of leave on arrival to convicts able to support themselves financially (gentlemen convicts). This was altered under Macquarie to ensure that such convicts served some of their sentences, but the system remained at the governor's discretion and a formal system was only developed under Governor Brisbane.

at the expense of the local Darug band of Aboriginal people, who frequently came into conflict with the settlers and were 'pacified' by various formal expeditions organised by governors from Hunter to Macquarie and by a bloody guerrilla conflict fought by the settlers in the Hawkesbury region against the Aboriginal people of the area. In 1816, Macquarie authorised a punitive party against the Aboriginal people in response to attacks on Hawkesbury farmers and 14 Aboriginal people were killed. The Hawkesbury farmers, who benefited significantly from Macquarie's support, were naturally supportive of the governor and his land policies. However, their support was not sufficient counterweight against the Exclusives. The Exclusives resented the land grants to convicts and wished to see instead much larger land grants being made to themselves to develop sheep stations, with the use of convict and ex-convict labour. Many of them had connections in London and, after the Bigge Report and the end of Macquarie's governorship, they were able to ensure a swift change from the pattern of land grants and settlement established under Macquarie.

The growth of Macquarie towns

Macquarie's paternalistic vision meant he oversaw the development of significant public buildings and infrastructure in the colony, spending far more money than London might have wished but leaving the colony vastly improved. London paid the wages for the regiment and the governor's salary. The colony was self-sufficient but, although it made a profit under Macquarie, no money was sent back to London (as originally planned in 1788) as he reinvested it in the colony's infrastructure. He built roads, schools, barracks and churches, utilising the skills of convict architect, Frances Greenway, whose designs showed genuine talent and helped to develop Sydney from a motley collection of dwellings into a city. 'Macquarie' townships were developed in Castlereagh, Richmond, Windsor, Pitt Town and Wilberforce in 1810 and 1811, along the fertile Hawkesbury River. Each Macquarie town followed a set plan and was built with a school (badly needed by the fast-growing population), a church and an inn.

In the centre of Sydney, he built a hospital at no cost to the colony by awarding the licence for trade in spirituous liquor to the builders (inevitably, the hospital was nicknamed the Rum Hospital). The building programme had the fortunate upside that it helped cushion the colony through economic depression, droughts, floods and caterpillar plagues by providing employment and income for convicts and Emancipists alike. The road that was built over the Blue Mountains opened up the grazing plains beyond, which were to boost development of the wool industry in the 1820s and lead to it becoming the pre-eminent industry of the continent.

SOURCE

5 From Macquarie writing to Lord Bathurst in 1822, having come under sustained criticism for his style of governorship.

I found the colony barely emerging from infantile imbecility, and suffering from various privations and disabilities; the country impenetrable beyond forty miles from Sydney; agriculture in a yet languishing state; commerce in its early dawn; revenue unknown; threatened with famine; distracted by faction; the public buildings in a state of dilapidation and mouldering to decay; the few roads and bridges formerly constructed rendered almost impassable; the population in general depressed by poverty; no public credit, nor private confidence; the morals of the great mass of the population in the lowest state of debasement, and religious worship almost totally neglected. Such was the state of New South Whales when I took charge of its administration on 1st January, 1810. I left it in February last, reaping incalculable advantages from my extensive and important discoveries in all directions, including the supposed insurmountable barrier called the Blue Mountains, to the westward of which are situated the fertile plains of Bathurst; and, in all respects, enjoying a state of private comfort and public prosperity, which I trust will at least equal the expectation of His Majesty's Government. The change may indeed be ascribed in part to the natural operation of time and events on individual enterprise: how far it may be attributed to measures originating with myself, as hereinafter detailed, and my zeal and judgment in giving effect to my instructions, I humbly submit to His Majesty and his ministers.

SOURCE

6

St Matthew's Anglican Church, Windsor. This is the oldest Anglican church in Australia, built in the Macquarie town of Windsor and designed by the convict architect Frances Greenway.

ACTIVITY
KNOWLEDGE CHECK

New South Wales, 1788–1821

1 How useful would Extract 1 be to a student explaining the importance of Macquarie in the development of New South Wales? What other evidence can you find in the text to help you analyse the importance of Macquarie's governorship to the colony?

2 Make notes from the text in two columns:

- Features of the penal system and its administration which aided the growth and development of the colony, 1788–1821.

- Features of the penal system and its administration which may have hampered the growth and development of the colony, 1788–1821.

3 Using your work for the questions above, complete your own analysis of Macquarie's importance to the colony.

WHAT WAS THE IMPACT OF BRITISH SETTLEMENT ON THE ABORIGINAL PEOPLE IN TASMANIA AND NEW SOUTH WALES, 1788–1829?

The population of Aboriginal people

As far as carbon dating can establish, *Homo sapiens*, in the form of the Australian Aboriginal people, has existed on mainland Australia for at least 50,000 years. A probable ice barrier prevented human occupation of the south-eastern part of the continent and Tasmania until the end of the last ice age, as settlement in these areas appears to have taken place at a much later date.

The Aboriginal nations lived in harmony with their harsh environment and their civilisation was based on hunting not cultivation. Their ancestor worship, or Dreaming, combined their knowledge of the land, its past and its creatures into a tool for living in harmony with their environment. Their national systems and language were complex. Their survival skills and ability to survive in the harsh environment of the continent were unmatched, but their technological advancement was weak by any measure. Mainland Aboriginal people had fire, those in Tasmania did not, and they were able to fashion fishing materials and build canoes, but as they did not cultivate the soil they had no farming implements and they had not developed the wheel.

At the point in history when British settlers arrived in the continent, there where at least 300,000, and possibly as many as 750,000 to one million, Aboriginal inhabitants in Australia. Their fate is one of the worst chapters in all the history of the British Empire. Phillip, always an accurate observer, reckoned that there were about 1,500 Aboriginal people in the area he explored in the first months, which would suggest a population density of about three people per square mile on the New South Wales coast.

British arrival

When Captain Cook ignored the part of his orders that told him to claim land for the king having first obtained the 'consent of the natives' by claiming Australia as *Terra Nullis* (Nobody's Land), he was making a value judgement about the Aboriginal people, which was shared by the first settlers. It was the basis for the devastation wrought on the Aboriginal peoples in Australia and in particular events in Tasmania, which are commonly termed as a **genocide** by some recent historians. He deemed it unnecessary to engage with the Aboriginal people because, as far as he could see, they did not lay any claim to the land by cultivation. To Georgian Englishmen, the Aboriginal people were savages; their way of life was primitive and not quite human, and they acted accordingly.

SOURCE

Surgeon George Bouchier Worgan made these observations in his journal in 1788 about the Aboriginal people he encountered.

It does not appear that these poor creatures have any fixed Habitation; sometimes sleeping in a Cavern of Rock, which they make as warm as a Oven by lighting a Fire in the middle of it, they will take up their abode here, for one Night perhaps, then in another the next Night. At other times (and we believe mostly in Summer) they take up their lodgings for a Day or two in a Miserable Wigwam, which they made from Bark of a Tree. There are dispersed about the woods near the water, 2, 3, 4 together; some Oyster, Cockle and Muscle [sic] Shells lie about the Entrance of them, but not in any Quantity to indicate they make these huts their constant Habitation. We met with some that seemed entirely deserted indeed it seems pretty evident that their Habitation, whether Caverns or Wigwams, are common to all, and Alternatively inhabited by different Tribes.

The Eora of New South Wales

There were perhaps 2,500 Aboriginal people of the Eora nation in the area where the first settlement in New South Wales was established and some friendly meetings took place between the two groups, although demonstrating complete mutual incomprehension. Tensions quickly developed. Although Phillip issued instructions that the convicts should not steal from the Aboriginal population, this was largely ignored and the Aboriginal people retaliated by stealing the convicts' shovels, spades and pick-axes. Stealing developed into violence. On 30 May 1788, two convicts were murdered by the local Aboriginal people and their bodies mangled and butchered.

SOURCE
8 From Governor Phillip's instructions from the government of King George III, 1787. The official instructions given to Phillip before his departure for New South Wales included the following passages.

You are to endeavour by every possible means to open an Intercourse with the Savages Natives and to conciliate their affections, enjoining all Our Subjects to live in amity and kindness with them. And if any of Our Subjects shall wantonly destroy them, or give them any unnecessary Interruption in the exercise of their several occupations It is our Will and Pleasure that you do cause such offenders to be brought to punishment according to the degree of the Offence. You will endeavour to procure an account of the Numbers inhabiting the Neighbourhood of the intended settlement and report your opinion to one of our Secretaries of State in what manner Our Intercourse with these people may be turned to the advantage of this country.

And it is further Our Royal Will and Pleasure that you do by all proper methods enforce a due observance of Religion and good order among all the inhabitants of the new Settlement and that you so take such steps for the one celebration of publick Worship as circumstances will permit...

... It is our Will and Pleasure that in every such case you do issue your Warrant to the Surveyor of Lands to make surveys of, and mark out in Lots such Lands upon the said Territory as may be necessary for their use; and when that shall be done, that you do pass Grants thereof with all convenient speed to any of the said Convicts so emancipated, in such proportions, and under such conditions and acknowledgements, as shall hereafter be specified. Viz To every Male shall be granted, 30 Acres of land, and in case he shall be married, 20 Acres more, and for every child who may be with them at the Settlement, at the time of making the said Grant, a further quantity of 10 Acres, free of all Fees, Taxes, Quit Rents, or, for the space of Ten years, provided that the person to whom the said Land shall be been granted, shall reside within the same, and proceed to the cultivation and improvement thereof.

A Level Exam-Style Question Section A

Study Source 8 before you answer this question.

Assess the value of the source for revealing British attitudes towards the Aboriginal population of Australia and the impact of settlement.

Explain your answer, using the source, the information given about its origin and your own knowledge about the historical context. (20 marks)

Tip
Consider the impact of settlement and cultivation on Aboriginal hunting grounds, as well as treatment of Aboriginal people.

When Phillip tried to demonstrate the fairness of British justice by ordering that convicts be flogged in the presence of the Aboriginal people for stealing fishing gear, the mutual incomprehension between the settlers and the indigenous population was clear. The Aboriginal people watching the spectacle showed their disdain by turning their backs and their tears showed clear sympathy for those being punished, rather than gratitude to Phillip. It is possible that these tensions might have developed into a more substantial challenge to the First Fleeters by the Aboriginal population,

despite Phillip's best efforts, had they not been struck down by an epidemic of smallpox in 1789 for which the most probable explanation is transportation of the virus by the First Fleet. As no cases were recorded on the ship's log, how this actually happened remains as much of a mystery today as it did to Phillip in 1789.

It has been estimated that the smallpox epidemic among the Aboriginal people wiped out 50 percent or more of the coastal population, as they had no resistance to the disease and the strain proved the most virulent one. The impact of the epidemic was to depopulate the area very significantly (of the Cadigal nation of Aboriginal people closest to the settlement in Sydney as few as three remained of an original 50 to 80). The source of the epidemic has been the subject of lively debate among historians and a range of theories exist, including:

- deliberate biological warfare by the British (vials of the disease were transported by Surgeon White, the doctor who travelled on the First Fleet, to enable inoculation of the young if necessary)

- transmission from the **Makassan** sailors further north, who came to trade with the Aboriginal population

- accidental transmission from clothing and goods aboard the First Fleet (although nobody aboard suffered from smallpox during the journey and the disease cannot lie dormant in individuals)

- the possibility that it was a virulent form of chickenpox rather than smallpox.

KEY TERM

Makassan
An inhabitant of Makassar, the principal trading port of Indonesia. They traded with the Aboriginal people for *trepang* (sea cucumbers), which were valuable to the Chinese for culinary and medical purposes.

EXTEND YOUR KNOWLEDGE

Smallpox
Smallpox is a contagious virus that was endemic in 18th-century Britain. It is recognisable by its distinctive rash and, in its most severe variant, had about a 30–35 percent mortality rate. Its incubation period is similar to that of chickenpox and the virus cannot lie dormant in carriers. Inoculation against the disease by injecting patients with small amounts of the virus had taken place in Britain for 70 years before the First Fleet sailed for Australia and the surgeon carried vials of the disease with him for this purpose.

Vaccinations against smallpox began after the observation by Edward Jenner in 1796 that milkmaids who had contracted cowpox were immune to smallpox and inoculation with the smallpox virus was replaced with injecting patients with cowpox, a much safer option. By 1800, his observations had been translated into all the major European languages, an indication of the deep interest in the new vaccine and its quick spread.

Phillip was mystified as to how smallpox had appeared in the colony as no cases were recorded on the journey. After quarantine of the original cases and investigation (White was adamant that the vials were untouched), Phillip concluded that the source of the outbreak must be from a different transmission point than the First Fleet. One seaman from the *Supply* caught the disease from the Aboriginal people and died, but the rest of the convicts remained immune.

Despite the terrible ravages of smallpox, there were clashes between the Aboriginal people and the convicts in the 1790s. Phillip was interested in the Aboriginal population (he took Bennelong, who had been captured and then lived with the settlement, back to England when he left the colony – see Source 2) and favoured a non-aggressive policy where possible. He refused to order reprisals when he was injured by a spear thrown by an Aboriginal individual. Nevertheless, he did organise punitive expeditions in the 1790s in response to attacks on settlers and subsequent New South Wales governors did the same, including Macquarie, who was also fairly well disposed towards the Aboriginal population. As a result of settler action and denied access to their traditional fishing grounds, the Aboriginal population of New South Wales was effectively destroyed.

Aboriginal genocide in Van Diemen's Land

If the fate of the Aboriginal people in New South Wales was to be nearly wiped out by smallpox and then to suffer an ongoing frontier conflict as the settlement expanded, the **Black War,** the fate of the Aboriginal people in Van Diemen's Land, was very similar. Disease there took its toll in the form of venereal disease and the usual viruses, to which the Aboriginal people had no resistance, brought first by the whalers and, from 1803, by the settlers when a formal colony was established. As the interior of what is now Tasmania was later cleared to make way for farms to produce wool, the original inhabitants were hunted, starved and poisoned until the population was wiped out. Settler violence was not checked by the authorities and when the Aboriginal population resisted settler encroachment, Governor Arthur declared martial law against the Aboriginal people in 1828, the ostensible purpose of which was to find the Aboriginal population and 'settle' them in **Settled Districts**, thus calming settler fears.

KEY TERMS

Black War
A period of violent conflict fought between the Aboriginal people and settlers of Tasmania in the 1820s.

Settled Districts
Governor Arthur wanted the Aboriginal population to remain in land set aside for them and even proposed their removal to Bruny Island, near Tasmania, for their protection.

There were about 3,000–4,000 Aboriginal people in Van Diemen's Land when formal settlement began in 1803. Part of the reason for their complete extinction rests on the particular circumstances of the colony established. Tasmania, like New South Wales, faced starvation in its first years of colonisation. Survival of the colony rested on hunting the kangaroo. As a result, guns were placed in the hands of convicts and a class of armed and uncontrollable bushmen was created, who regarded the Aboriginal people as vermin and had no compunction about killing them. This is unlike New South Wales, where control rested far more clearly with the governor and as a result limits were placed on violence against the Aboriginal population.

Free settlers who trickled into Tasmania from 1804 provided no protection for the Aboriginal population, for with the settlers came farming and the introduction of the merino sheep in 1821 hastened their fate. By 1827, there were 436,256 sheep in Van Diemen's Land and some stock breeders were getting three lambings every two years. Earlier governors, Collins, Davey and Sorrell, had issued proclamations instructing settlers not to persecute the Aboriginal population. However, by the late 1820s, with the increase in the white population, retaliatory raids began against the settlers by the Aboriginal people as their food supplies were destroyed and the ensuing settler hysteria meant Governor Arthur was forced to change policy towards the Aboriginal population. A proclamation was passed restricting Aboriginal people to settled districts in the north-eastern corner of the island and, when this failed (the Aboriginal population could not read, after all), Arthur issued a proclamation of martial law on 1 November 1828 to force their relocation.

SOURCE 9

From a letter to Governor Arthur from George Frankland, the surveyor general, in 1829 regarding his Proclamation to the Aboriginal People.

I have lately had an opportunity of ascertaining that the aboriginal natives of Van Dieman's Land are in the habit of representing events by drawings on the bark of trees… In the absence of all successful communication with these unfortunate people, with whose language we are totally unacquainted, it has occurred to me that it might be possible through the medium of this newly discovered facility, to impart to them to a certain extent, the real wishes of government towards them, and I have accordingly sketched a series of groups of figures in which I have endeavoured to represent in a manner as simple and as well adapted to their supposed ideas as possible, the actual state of things (or rather the origin or the present state) and the desired termination of hostility.

The policy of relocating the Aboriginal people away from farmlands failed; the last Tasmanian Aboriginal person died in 1876.

The history of Australian Aboriginal people has provoked fierce debate among historians and political commentators over the last 40 years. It is linked to debates on the rights of the Aboriginal population in Australian society today, the kind of Australian history that should be taught in schools and the extent of racism in Australia today.

SOURCE 10

Following the advice from Frankland (see Source 9), Governor Arthur's Proclamation to the Aboriginal people was produced in the form of a pictogram. In 1830, copies were pinned to trees in Tasmania for the Aboriginal people to view.

EXTEND YOUR KNOWLEDGE

The historical debate

From the 1960s, historians rewrote Australian history to reflect the experiences of the Aboriginal people since 1788, which had been absent from earlier, older histories. A narrative of a **frontier war** between settlers and Aboriginal people emerged and the events in Tasmania were labelled as genocide, a position that has been widely accepted.

Revisionists to this approach, notably Keith Windschuttle, take the position that claims of both a frontier war and a genocide are wildly exaggerated and inaccurate. There are a number of articles focused on the statistics and the methodology of the two historical camps. As any estimates of deaths of Aboriginal people are very difficult to substantiate, it is likely that the debate will continue, revealing as much about current Australian politics and attitudes to race as they reveal about the past.

A Level Exam-Style Question Section B

How accurate is it to say that policy towards the Aboriginal people in Australia was determined by the settlers of New South Wales and Van Diemen's Land? (20 marks)

Tip
Consider who else influenced policy regarding the Aboriginal people.

KEY TERM

Frontier war
Clashes between Aboriginal people and Australian settlers as the Aboriginal population resisted the settlement of Australia.

EXTRACT

From Henry Reynolds, *Why Weren't We Told?* (2000). Reynolds is one of the historians responsible for the now widely accepted interpretation of the treatment of Aboriginal people in Tasmania as genocide. This book has appeared on the Australian school curriculum.

The more I read about frontier conflict, the more certain I became that the central problem had been there from the beginning. It was always at the heart of things. The settlers came to acquire the land which was already owned and occupied and had been so for many thousands of years. The British decided they would take the land without a treaty, without negotiation, and without any attempt to purchase it. Whenever and wherever the indigenous landowners resisted the European incursion that attempted to impose their law on newcomers, the only answer was force. It is hard to see how it could have been otherwise. The result was predetermined. The Europeans would get all the land they wanted, but to effect the expropriation they would have to kill some of the Aborigines and terrorise the others into acquiescence. This recipe for successful colonisation was well understood by early governors. As we have already seen Governor Phillip decided in 1790 to 'infuse an universal terror... to prevent further mischief'. In 1816 his successor, Governor Macquarie, planned to attack the tribes on the outskirts of the settlement 'so as to Strike them with Terror against Committing Similar acts of violence in the future.' Twelve years later, in Tasmania, Governor Arthur's Executive Council declared martial law, the purpose of which was 'To inspire them with terror...' which would be 'the only effectual means of security for the future.'

EXTRACT

From a speech by Keith Windschuttle, *The Fabrication of Aboriginal History* (2003).

The truth is that there was nothing on the Aborigines' side that resembled frontier warfare, patriotic struggle or systematic resistance of any kind. The so-called "Black War" was a minor crime wave by two Europeanised black bushrangers, followed by an outbreak of robbery, assault and murder by tribal Aborigines. All the evidence at the time, on both the white and the black sides of the frontier, was that their principal objective was to acquire flour, tea, sugar and bedding, objects that to them were European luxury goods. The full-blood Tasmanian Aborigines did die out in the nineteenth century, it is true, but this was almost entirely a consequence of two factors: the 10,000 years of isolation that had left them vulnerable to introduced diseases, especially influenza, pneumonia and tuberculosis; and the fact that they traded and prostituted their women to convict stockmen and sealers to such an extent that they lost the ability to reproduce themselves. Despite its infamous reputation, Van Diemen's Land was host to nothing that resembled genocide, which requires murderous intention against a whole race of people.

THINKING HISTORICALLY   Evidence (6c)

Comparing and evaluating historians' arguments
Read Extracts 1 and 2.

1 Compare the two accounts and identify factual statements or claims that they both agree upon. Make a list of these points.

2 Look carefully at how the historians use language. Do they both use equally cautious language in making their claims or is one more confident and assertive than the other? Is one (or both) of the historians over-claiming?

3 Look back at Sources 8, 9 and 10. Do both historians appear to have made equally effective use of the sources available?

4 Are both of the historical accounts equally credible or are there reasons to prefer one account more than another?

ACTIVITY
KNOWLEDGE CHECK

The impact of British settlement on the Aboriginal people of New South Wales and Tasmania

1 How useful would Sources 9 and 10 be to a historian explaining the Black War in Tasmania?

2 The use of the term 'genocide' is often debated on the basis of the intent of those who carry out the killing of another group. While it is used by many historians to describe events in Tasmania, there are others who question the use of the term. How justified do you think the use of the term is to describe the fate of Aboriginal people in Van Diemen's Land?

WHAT WAS THE EXTENT AND NATURE OF COLONIAL CONTROL IN AUSTRALIA IN THE YEARS 1803–29?

In all, around 168,000 convicts were transported to Australia between 1788 and 1868. A graph of transportation to Australia from 1788 to 1830 would show a slow upward trend until 1815 and then a steeper rise. By 1800, only 42 ships had gone to Australia and transportation numbers did not reach 1,000 in a single year until 1814.

After 1815 and the end of the Napoleonic Wars, Britain had more shipping available for transportation and the end of the wars was marked by short-term economic problems in Britain with increased crime as a result. Furthermore, Britain's population was growing extremely rapidly during this period, effectively doubling between 1801 and 1841; the decade with the fastest rate of growth was 1811–20. Transportation increased steadily from 1815 to 1830 and then rose again sharply.

Phases of transportation	Male convicts	Female convicts
1788–1810	9,300	2,500
1811–20	15,400	2,000
1821–30	28,700	4,100
1831–40	43,500	7,700

Figure 4.1 Numbers of convicts transported to Australia between 1788 and 1840. Based on data from Robert Hughes, *The Fatal Shore* (1986).

The number of men transported always far exceeded that of women transported (see Figure 4.1), reflective of crime statistics in general.

Transportation was the major source of new inhabitants to the colony as free settlers were few, because of the enormous distance involved. The officers of the New South Wales Corps and their successor regiment tended to remain in the colony and formed the basis of the free settlers to the country.

The native-born population, however, grew rapidly due to a very high birth rate. The rough census of 1807 showed a total white population of 7,563 in New South Wales, but the proportion of children was one in four. By 1828, the free population (20,870) outnumbered the prison population (15,728) and, as the colonies grew in maturity, the desire for political representation of the free population grew, especially among those who fancied themselves a group apart, the free settlers or Exclusives and their descendants.

Free settlement was largely the result of soldiers sent to guard the convicts remaining once they had served their terms. As the economic life of the colony developed, some settlers were attracted by the opportunities offered, although they were a tiny handful. In 1829, the first organised attempt to develop a free settlement in Australia took place in Western Australia.

Penal settlement in Van Diemen's Land, 1803

By the time Van Diemen's Land was settled by the British in 1803, the colony in New South Wales was secure enough to contemplate the establishment of a second branch of settlement. Port Risdon, renamed Hobart, was chosen because of its strategic value (sailing through the Bass Strait took weeks off the passage from England to Sydney) and because Tasmania was a key area for whaling, which the economy of New South Wales depended on. Van Diemen's Land operated as an adjutant part of the main settlement until 1824; although governors there could operate semi-independently from Sydney because of the time it took for orders to be communicated. The island, like Norfolk Island, operated as a useful dumping ground for the most hardened prisoners and acquired a fearsome reputation.

In Van Diemen's Land, under the governorship of Sir George Arthur (in office 1823–37), a more totalitarian version of the system developed in New South Wale was operated. The island was divided into police districts under the control of a police magistrate and control over free settlers, as well as convicts, was exercised by the withholding of assigned labour (unlike New South Wales, emancipated convicts were not assigned labour). Convicts themselves were made to work through each of the seven levels of punishment devised by Arthur before gaining their freedom. There were no early pardons in Van Diemen's Land. Arthur's stern religious views meant that settlers discovered having friendly relationships with convict labour, such as asking them to share a Christmas dinner, resulted in their assigned labour being removed at once (black listing) and those who committed acts such as standing convicts a drink were warned and red listed.

The development of whaling and sealing

The wool industry was to become so dominant in terms of Australia's economy in the 19th century and the story of early settlement so inextricably linked to land grants for freed convicts, that it is important to note that until the 1830s wool was the second most important source of income for the colony. The success and survival of the early years of the colony rested far more on the whale and seal trade than it did on agriculture. Every part of the seas off south-eastern Australia teemed with whales and seals and, in the early 1800s, it was dangerous to sail into Hobart's estuary in a small boat, so full was the water with pregnant and calving black whales. Exports of whalebone, whale oil and sealskins enabled the colonies to buy the goods they needed for the new colony and, of course, the rum that was consumed so universally.

Whaling began following the arrival of the Third Fleet in 1791 under Captain Thomas Melvill of the *Britannia* and was a significant industry for the colony for the next 70 years, until the demand for whale oil was superseded by demand for petroleum. The whaling and sealing industries were dominated by Emancipists and the Currency lads. The contractors for the transportation of the Third Fleet, Enderby and Champion, had an agreement with the British government that, once they had delivered the convicts, they would be able to go whaling and then return to London.

From 1805, local whaling was able to make serious money for the colony. Robert Campbell, a Scottish merchant, broke the East India Company's monopoly (see page 24) on the trade by sailing direct to England in 1805 on *Lady Barlow* with 260 tons of oil from the rendered skins of 13,700 seals (in large cast-iron whaling pots). He was followed shortly afterwards by the *Hondurous Packet* carrying 34,000 skins bound for England. Despite the East India Company attempting to seize the ships and cargo, Campbell was successful in establishing the free trade of skins and oil between the colony and England from this date and returned to the colony to a warm welcome.

SOURCE
11
The Flurry, painted by William Charles Duke (1848). The painting demonstrates the dangers of whaling in small boats. The level of danger meant that whaling crews were not made up of convict labour, but instead by free men willing to risk their lives for an income. Duke was Irish-born and worked as a mechanist of dioramas and as a scene painter, travelling in both Australia and New Zealand.

The fact that the large harbour in Sydney and the estuary in Van Diemen's Land were teeming with whales meant that the trade could be plied from small **open-bottom dories** rather than ocean-going ships, which enabled the trade to be established cheaply and easily in both Sydney and Hobart.

> **KEY TERM**
>
> **Open-bottom dories**
> The dory is a small boat, about 5–7 metres (16–23 feet) long. It is usually a lightweight boat with high sides, a flat bottom and sharp bows. They are easy to build because of their simple lines and designed to be used in estuaries or harbours rather than for sea voyages.

The sealers simply clubbed the seals to death on the beaches and, by 1826, officials were warning Governor Arthur in Tasmania that the trade was threatened with annihilation because there was no limit to seal killing during the breeding season.

Gradually, however, the wool industry became more and more significant within the colony as the great sheep stations were established and the wool trade boomed. By 1805, the colony grew enough grain to feed itself and agriculture shifted from mere subsistence. Sheep numbers had risen to about 20,000, of which John Macarthur, who came out with the Second Fleet as an ensign with the New South Wales Corp, owned about a quarter. He, supported by his redoubtable wife Elizabeth, was the driving force in the development of the woollen industry in the colony. Macarthur imported merino sheep into the colony and took Australia's first export bale back to Britain when he was sent for trial for his part in the Rum Rebellion.

The industry exploded between 1820 and 1840. In 1821, the first bale was sold in Garraways Coffee House in London and exports of wool were valued at £2 million by 1830.

The first crossing of the Blue Mountains

The crossing of the Blue Mountains in 1813 took place after a period of drought and in search of more grasslands and pasture for the burgeoning wool industry. The successful expedition by Blaxland, Lawson and Wentworth, led by an Aboriginal guide, managed to survey a route over the Blue Mountains and, upon arrival at what was renamed Blaxland, they saw a vast expanse of bush and grasslands. Blaxland reported back to the governor that there was enough grazing land west of the mountains to support the colony for 30 years. Macquarie instructed the surveyor general to follow the path mapped out by the explorers and commissioned a road across the mountains in 1814. The road was built with convict labour in less than six months and settlers began to populate the area shortly afterwards.

In 1818, the surveyor general pushed further west and north-east, discovering the Liverpool Plains, and Charles Throsby's expedition in 1819 opened up even more of the land beyond the Blue Mountains to settlement. He wrote to Macquarie with some justification that the rich fertile land would be equal to any population increase for many years.

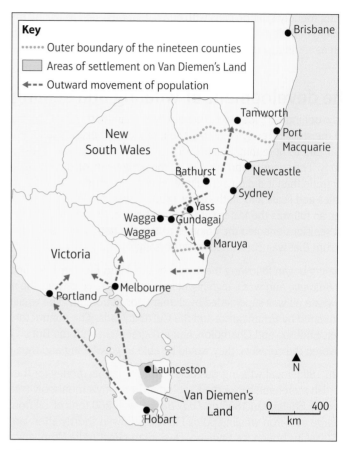

Figure 4.2 The settlement of New South Wales, Van Diemen's Land and Victoria by 1835.

In 1824, the Australian Agricultural Company was established by Royal Charter in Britain, and given one million acres (4,047 km²) in New South Wales for agricultural development. The area selected ran from Port Stephens to the Manning River. Sheep farming operations began in 1825. Cheap labour was sourced through convicts, Aboriginal workers and indentured labourers on seven-year contracts.

First British settlements in Western Australia, 1826

Western Australia was settled for the usual mix of reasons: to forestall any such move by the French; to provide a useful trading link with India, China and the islands to the North; and on the enthusiastic recommendation of someone (in this case, Captain James Stirling) who knew very little about agriculture. The coast was surveyed and claimed for the British in 1791 by George Vancouver and, in 1826, the British established a small military outpost in King George Sound in what was later to become known as Albany. In the meantime, Captain Stirling had persuaded the government to back a different kind of settlement to the penal colonies of Eastern Australia and established the Swan River Company in 1828. The Swan River Company undertook to send out 10,000 free settlers in exchange for a large land grant. The syndicate gave 40 acres for every £3 settlers had in assets.

Western Australia's first settlers arrived in 1829 at Swan River and, on 29 May 1829, Captain Freemantle officially laid claim to all of Australia that did not make up New South Wales from the mouth of the Swan River.

The first free colony struggled and was threatened with famine in its early years. By 1832, it had only 1,500 colonists. However, the nature of the settlement of Western Australia demonstrates an important change in the official British thinking about Australia. Britain no longer viewed Australia as an open prison but as a source of potential wealth and opportunity. As a result, future settlements in the continent followed the more familiar pattern of British imperialism through the mechanism of private finance, facilitated by government protection and, in the case of Australia, the provision of convict labour.

Political development

Australia's initial settlement by the British was essentially a vast open prison and the distance from London meant that early governors had almost unlimited power to run the colony as they saw best. Unless events in the colony got totally out of hand, as in the Rum Rebellion against Governor Bligh, the British government had little actual involvement in the running of the new colony, although they could of course discipline governors or members of the New South Wales Corps under the system of army or naval discipline.

Macquarie's governorship is credited with transforming the settlement from a prison camp to a colony. The political powers of the governor remained the same, but the size of the free population in the colony and the increased frequency of communications with London meant there was far more scrutiny of the colony and the governor. Macquarie's paternalistic style and investment in the infrastructure of Sydney proved to be his downfall. The Exclusives were not prepared to take his promotion of Emancipists lying down. Actions such as appointing an ex-convict as a magistrate acted as a red rag to the Exclusives and wild rumours began to circulate in England about the colony once more. Civil servants confronted with the accounts of costs for Macquarie's public building programme, and the mounting number of convictions in Britain, began to wonder if the colony was acting as the deterrent it was meant to as there were reports from judges of defendants requesting transportation at sentencing.

In 1819, Lord Bathurst, the secretary of state for the colonies, appointed John Thomas Bigge as a commissioner of inquiry to report on whether transportation was any longer efficient as punishment. Bigge travelled across New South Wales and Van Diemen's Land between 1819 and 1821 and came to the conclusion that Macquarie had taken the colony in the wrong direction. He recommended that:

- convict labour should primarily be assigned to the sheep farms, rather than used in public works programmes

- the early pardons and tickets of leave granted under Macquarie and the land grants for Emancipists should cease

- positions of responsibility should not be given to Emancipists.

EXTRACT 4

From *Turning Points in Australian History*, by Martin Crotty and David Andrew Roberts (2008). The Bigge Report has received criticism for ending the egalitarian direction the colony took under Macquarie, but it is also true that the 1820s saw considerable private investment in the colony.

Bigge's Commission reflected a renewed interest in the Australian settlement, after 30 years of near neglect by Great Britain and languid local progress. The importance of his recommendations in the decade after 1822 saw New South Wales transformed from a minor and inadequate penal settlement into a thriving economic and social concern. New policies adopted in the wake of these reports allowed for the beginnings of mass convict transportations and the influx of private capital on a grand scale... Ultimately the Bigge Reports were also crucial in setting a new tone for penal administration, intended to make transportation an 'object of real terror'. These innovations underpinned the expansion of colonial industry and wealth and also consolidated the Australian colonies reputation as places of dire punishment, depravity and immorality.

The extent of colonial control by 1829

Following Bigge's research and report, the New South Wales Act was passed in Britain in 1823 which altered the power and position of governors in the existing colonies and paved the way for self-government (in the hands of an established and wealthy landed class) later in the century.

- A legislative council was created. Members were not elected but worthy citizens (Exclusives) were asked to serve in the assembly to advise the governors.

- The justice system became independent of the governor and a supreme court was established with a chief justice.

- Van Diemen's Land was to operate as a separate colony (in practice it already did so) and a legislative council and supreme court were to operate there too.

The legislative councils were enlarged in 1828 from seven members to 15, of which seven were nominated by the governor and the remainder were government officials. (This was also the year in which the number of free men and women in New South Wales first outnumbered the number of convicts.) This was a similar structure for governance to that which existed in Britain's colonies in Canada and the Caribbean at that point in time.

A Level Exam-Style Question Section B

'By 1829, British settlement in Australia had effectively been transformed from an outdoor prison into an imperial colony.'

How far do you agree with this comment on the Australian colonies in the late 1820s? (20 marks)

Tip
Include changes in the economy of the colony as well as political developments.

By 1829, the almost unlimited powers of early governors had been restricted by more frequent communication and interventions from London, and by the requirement to formally consult the free citizens of the colony. These were not of course elected assemblies, but nevertheless the Exclusives exercised considerable power when they needed to by lobbying their connections in London and by their participation in the legislative council.

A further indication of the way the British intended the future settlement and economic life of Australia to develop were the land grants made to the Australian Agricultural Company in 1824, the Van Diemen's Land Company in 1825 and the Swan River Company in 1829. These companies were granted land in Newcastle, Van Diemen's Land and Western Australia respectively and, although they were supported by the British government continuing to transport convict labour, the pattern of imperial settlement had changed from direct government-sponsored operations run by the navy and army to a far more typical form of British imperialism in which private companies and settlers bore the risks of imperialism.

The settlement of Australia is unique in the story of the British Empire. There had been transportation to the American colonies but only as part of a wider flow of immigrants. The establishment and settlement of a penal colony on a new continent as the only form of British settlement and then its slow transformation into a settler colony has no other parallels. Its initial survival was by no means a foregone conclusion and when the Select Committee recommended the establishment of the colony at Botany Bay they could not, and did not, predict its transformation into the colony it became, although they were of course hopeful that it would make a profit while solving their immediate concern, which was the overcrowding of prisons.

ACTIVITY
KNOWLEDGE CHECK

Penal settlements to Crown colonies

1 What were the three most important changes that took place in the development of the colony's economic life between 1800 and 1829?

2 How important are the Bigge Report, the Royal Charter of the Australian Agricultural Company and the Swan River Company in helping to explain the way in which imperial settlement in Australia was changing?

ACTIVITY
SUMMARY

The birth of British Australia, 1788–1829

1 Write a description explaining the reasons why the nature and function of British settlement changed between 1788 and 1829. Include the following:

- the original purpose of the colony

- the economic basis of the colony

- the political developments following the Bigge Report

- the indications for the future implicit in the way in which the settlement of Western Australia took place.

2 What were the key turning points in terms of the fate of the Aboriginal peoples of New South Wales and Van Diemen's Land?

WIDER READING

Books

Clarke, M. *A Short History of Australia*, Penguin, 4th edition (1995)

Hughes, R. *The Fatal Shore*, Vintage (2003)

Grenville, K. *The Secret River*, Canongate (2006)

Keneally, T. *Australians: Origins to Eureka*, Allen & Unwin (2010)

Reynolds, H. *Why Weren't We Told?*, Penguin (2000)

Online

Lachlan Macquarie: Visionary and builder – a digital gallery of documents: http://www2.sl.nsw.gov.au/archive/discover_collections/history_nation/macquarie/governor/

Oakum's Razor presentation: *Smallpox in Sydney, 1789* – audio and transcript available to download: http://www.abc.net.au/radionational/programs/ockhamsrazor/smallpox-in-sydney-1789/3145560

An online index of articles relating to the debate on the fate of Aboriginal people in Australia: http://www.kooriweb.org/foley/indexb.html

3.5

Learning from past mistakes: Canada and the Durham Report, 1837–40

KEY QUESTIONS

- To what extent did the political nature and government systems of Upper and Lower Canada minimise the perceived threat from the USA?

- What was the significance of the revolts against British rule in the Canadas in the years 1837–38?

- How significant to the development of Britain's relationship with its colonies was the Earl of Durham's report on Canada published in 1839?

INTRODUCTION

John George Lambton, 1st Earl of Durham, a flamboyant and high-handed aristocrat, might at first appear to be an unlikely candidate for the title 'the man who saved the Empire'. His *Report on the Affairs of British North America*, published in January 1839, the writing of which was triggered by revolts in Britain's remaining North American provinces in what is now Canada, was in many ways the key document in the political development of the white settler colonies of the Empire in the second half of the 19th century. Despite the seismic upheaval of the American Revolution, Britain continued to control executive authority in its colonies. The concept of responsible self-government, as proposed by Durham in his report, appears so obvious with hindsight that it is hard to appreciate its real importance and significance for the mid-19th-century contemporary debate. His suggestion that colonies should elect governments and govern themselves in all domestic matters broke the intellectual deadlock on the future of the remaining North American colonies and had immense wider significance on the white settler colonies of the Empire. Until Durham proposed his solution, politicians in London fatalistically accepted that it was inevitable that at some point Canada would follow the same path as America, while in Canada the term 'responsible government' was used by various individuals to mean better government, and nothing more.

Durham's, and his advisers', proposal was a genuinely innovative solution to the age-old problems of taxation, representation and Empire, and one that was eventually adopted in the colonies with large white populations. These colonies contributed hugely to the economic and military strength of the

1791 – British parliament passes Constitutional Act establishing the provinces of Upper and Lower Canada and their system of government

1835 – Sir Francis Bond Head arrives in Upper Canada as lieutenant governor

Earl of Gosford leads a parliamentary commission to enquire into the grievances of Lower Canada

1831 – Howick Act passes in Britain

| 1790 | 1828 | 1829 | 1830 | 1831 | 1834 | 1835 | 1836 |

1828 – The parliamentary select committee, the Canada Committee, reports recommending no change in the system of government in the Canadas

1834 – February: Papineau's 92 Resolutions are presented to the legislative assembly in Lower Canada

1836 – November: Gosford Commission publishes their sixth and final report

British Empire through two world wars and the Great Depression of the 1930s, and without them Britain would not have been able to maintain its position as an imperial and world power for as long as it did.

TO WHAT EXTENT DID THE POLITICAL NATURE AND GOVERNMENT SYSTEMS OF UPPER AND LOWER CANADA MINIMISE THE PERCEIVED THREAT FROM THE USA?

While the British were establishing the thirteen North American colonies, which eventually became the USA, the French were colonising further north, fanning out from the eastern seaboard into what is present-day Canada.

The Seven Years' War and the Peace of Paris in 1763 resulted in Britain gaining all of **New France** and its efforts to absorb and defend its new imperial possessions resulted in the revolt by its thirteen original colonies against the new taxation Britain deemed necessary to protect its new territories (see Chapter 3). The evacuation of the loyalists from the American colonies led to the restructuring of the provinces closest to the American border into Upper and Lower Canada by the **1791 Constitution**. Upper Canada had a largely British population, whereas Lower Canada was a combination of the descendants of French settlers to New France and the new loyalist influx. Because of their differing histories of settlement, Upper and Lower Canada had different land tenure systems, languages and religion, but their political systems, as ordained by the British, were broadly similar. The remaining British colonies, such as Newfoundland and Nova Scotia, were ruled directly from London as self-contained colonies with their own governors and assemblies. Canada as a country or a nation did not exist.

KEY TERMS

New France
The French colonies and possessions in North America until 1763.

1791 Constitution
The political system of government in the newly created Upper and Lower Canadas was established by the British by the passing of the Constitutional Act in 1791 in the British parliament. The Act created a system for political representation in the provinces and assured French Catholics of continuing religious freedom.

EXTRACT

1 From *Lord Durham: A Biography of John George Lambton, First Earl of Durham*, by Chester W. New (1929). Here, the author analyses the relationship between Canada and Britain.

The British Government learned singularly little, so far as colonial policy was concerned, from the American Revolution. Misunderstanding the cause of that movement to be a dispute over taxation, it was scrupulously careful in that field; but the political history of both Lower and Upper Canada in the period preceding Lord Durham's Report is to a remarkable extent a repetition of that of the American colonies. An English Executive, in conflict with colonial Assemblies, well-meaning Governors tied up by instructions from London which were the result of ignorance rather than tyranny, colonial legislatures increasingly resentful of oversees restrictions on their legislation, the Assembly seeking to get its way through the control of appropriations, conflicts over a suggested Civil List, the refusal to vote supplies, the exaggerated importance and undisciplined ambitions of the demagogues who constituted themselves tribunes of the people – they had been the staples of political warfare in the colonial days on the Atlantic sea-board, and there they recurred in the history of the Canadas. Some better constitutional way had to be discovered.

1838 – January: Both rebellions are effectively over and rebels are either in prison or have fled over the border to the USA

28 May: Lord Durham arrives in the Canadas with executive powers and to compile a report on the future of the provinces for the British parliament

9 October: Lord Durham resigns and returns to Britain

1840 – July: British parliament passes the British North America Act for the provinces, commonly known as the Act of Union

1837	1838	1839	1840	1848

1837 – March: British parliament passes the ten Russell Resolutions

10 November: British cavalry exchange shots with the patriote militia in the revolt in Lower Canada

5 December: Revolt in Upper Canada begins

1839 – January: Lord Durham's Report on the Affairs of British North America is published

1848 – February: The British grant responsible self-government to Nova Scotia

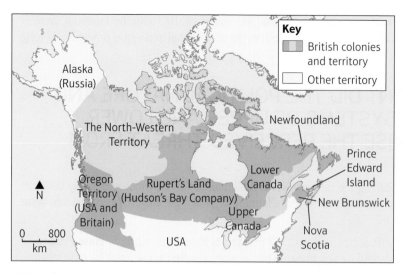

Figure 5.1 British North American territories in 1825.

Upper Canada

Upper Canada had far more British settlers than Lower Canada and the number of those who considered themselves British increased considerably during the evacuation of loyalists during the American War of Independence. 'Loyalist' settlers from America continued to arrive from the 1790s, principally seeking free land available in the province and their actual loyalty to Britain was in some cases questionable. Immigration in the province continued to grow in the 1820s and 1830s in what was a conscious effort to populate and develop the province. In 1825, the cash-strapped administration of the province moved from the system of free land grants to settlers to one of sale by auction and in 1825 the private land company, the Canada Company, was given a royal charter to aid the colonisation and development of the province.

The province of Upper Canada was governed by a lieutenant governor, appointed by London, but reliant on the tax-raising powers of a locally elected legislative assembly. There was a further complicating factor in the form of an appointed council, who exercised executive power in addition to the lieutenant governor. The British lieutenant governor, whose role was like that of the governor in Britain's Australian colonies (see Chapter 4), ran the province with the aid of the executive council, whose members took on the role of ministers. Power was exercised by the lieutenant governor and executive council in tandem, but they were responsible to London, not to the locally elected legislative assembly. Members of the executive council were chosen and could be removed by the lieutenant governor and could remain on the council for life. A number of notable families, known as the **Family Compact**, maintained control of the council, exercising power largely for their own benefit.

There was a legislative assembly, of no fewer than 16 representatives, elected by a fairly wide franchise of landowning males, and an appointed legislative council (an 'upper house' modelled on the British House of Lords) of seven, whose members were appointed for life. Members of the legislative assembly were not usually members of the executive council, but members of the legislative council often were. Laws passed by the legislative assembly had to be approved by the members of the legislative council, meaning that the appointed members could block laws passed by the elected representatives.

The unifying factors which bound the individuals of the Family Compact were their loyalist tradition, their adherence to the **Anglican Church** and their reluctance to countenance any changes to the constitution which might loosen their grip on power. Lord Durham called them 'a petty, corrupt, insolent Tory clique' with all of a great Whig Lord's contempt for colonial upstarts aping the traditional aristocracy in Britain. (The term 'Tory' was adopted in Canada for those who supported direct rule from Britain.)

Landownership in Upper Canada

Land tenure in Upper Canada was based on the British freehold tenure. Most of the land was held by the Crown and therefore judged to be free to grant to settlers. However, the British did recognise that the indigenous peoples of Canada had claim to the land (unlike in Australia) and treaties were signed at various points with native groups to increase Crown lands, providing the indigenous people with some remuneration in exchange. One-seventh of all lands in Upper Canada were designated as clergy reserves, with the profits from their sale or rental going to support the Anglican Church in the province. The British were convinced that one of the best ways to maintain Canadian loyalty was through the support and establishment of the Anglican Church and the Family Compact were devout Anglicans. However, Anglicans were not in a majority in the province and, although the Upper Canadians were mostly Protestant, they were Baptists, Congregationalists and, increasingly, Methodists. The clergy reserves grated with the non-Anglicans, but the control of the Family Compact and their absolute loyalty to the Anglican Church meant that no reform of the system of the clergy reserves was possible. Even if the legislative assembly had voted for change, its laws would immediately have been stifled by the Family Compact.

Tensions in Upper Canada

In some ways, the province had the potential to make better economic progress than the more populous Lower Canada because of its land tenure system. However, Upper Canada lacked infrastructure and capital investment and had a very small population from which to raise revenues. Investment in infrastructure like canals and roads meant that the government itself was cash-strapped but, instead of working with the legislative assembly to raise taxes, it attempted to raise revenue by other means, thus sidestepping the assembly and denying them the opportunity to influence spending within the province. Revenue was raised by the sale of land to the Canada Company and was used to pay the salary of officials, which added to the frustrations of the **Reformers** in the assembly as they were unable to influence the actions of the lieutenant governor through the traditional means of refusing to vote money to pay for salaries. The population of Upper Canada was only 350,000 in 1835. The province was on the extreme frontier of the British Empire with fragmented settlements and limited resources.

KEY TERM

Reformer
A member of the legislative assembly in Upper Canada who wished for greater economic and political control of the province. More widely in the province, the Reformers in the assembly were supported by the Upper Canada Central Political Union founded in 1832, which copied the organisational structures of the reform movement in Britain.

Opposition to the Family Compact grew in the 1820s and 1830s around the issue of the clergy reserves allotted to the Anglican Church and there were calls for 'responsible and cheap government'. The Reformers meant a number of things by the term 'responsible government': first and foremost, the removal of the Family Compact and their stranglehold on places in the legislative and executive councils, but as time went on they made more sophisticated calls for constitutional change. Robert Baldwin, a lawyer in Upper Canada, can certainly claim to be 'the father of responsible government', as the term came to be understood. He wrote to Lord Glenelg, the colonial secretary, in 1836 suggesting constitutional reform to establish responsible government in the colony, whereby the executive was responsible to voters in Canada rather than London (see Source 1).

SOURCE

1 Robert Baldwin, a Reformer from Upper Canada, visited London in 1836 and wrote the following letter as part of a series to Lord Glenelg, the colonial secretary, to try to explain the Reformers' position.

If it is the desire of the mother country, which I, of course, assume it to be, to retain the colony, it can only be done either by force or with the consent of the people of Upper Canada themselves. I take it for granted that Great Britain cannot desire to exercise Government of the Sword, and that she will therefore only govern Canada so long as she can do so with the concurrence of the people. For the purpose therefore of placing the connexion upon this footing, it is absolutely necessary, first that the political machinery of the Provincial Government should be such as shall work harmoniously within itself, without collision between any of its great wheels; and secondly, that it should be such as that the people may feel that they have an influence on it sufficiently powerful to secure attention not only to their abstract rights, but to their feelings and prejudices

[To that end, Baldwin recommended that the British]

put the Executive Council permanently on the footing of a local Provincial Cabinet, holding the same relative position with reference to the Representative of the King (i.e the Governor) and Provincial Parliament, as that which the King's Imperial Cabinet stands with respect to the King and the Parliament of the Empire; and apply to such Provincial Cabinet, both with respect to their appointment to and continuation in office, the same principles as those which are acted upon by His Majesty with respect to the Imperial Cabinet in this country... as the only remedy by the application of which these objects can be attained, and Upper Canada preserved to the mother country...

I assure your Lordship that I am, in my own mind, most firmly persuaded, that, unless the course of above is promptly adopted and pursued, it will be wholly out of the power of the mother country to preserve the affections of the Upper Canadian people, although it may, of course, for a time continue to retain them in subjection to their authority.

A Level Exam-Style Question Section A

Study Source 1 before you answer this question.

Assess the value of the source for revealing the attitude of the Reformers in Upper Canada to the connection with Britain in the late 1830s and the proposals for reforms in the system of government.

Explain your answer, using the source, the information given about its origin and your own knowledge about the historical context. (20 marks)

Tip
Consider the typicality of the source carefully. How widespread do you believe Baldwin's views to be?

ACTIVITY
KNOWLEDGE CHECK

British settlement in Canadian North America

1 Use Source 1 and the text to compile a list of the principal grievances of the Reformers of Upper Canada to the system of British rule in the province.

2 What strengths and weaknesses can you identify in the system established by the Constitution of 1791?

KEY TERMS

Seigneur
A landlord of a large estate.

Civil law
Laws governing private relations in a community. Under French civil law, property rights in Lower Canada divided at death among all the sons in a family rather than passing to the eldest son, as would happen in British law.

Chateau Clique
A group of wealthy families in Lower Canada who controlled economic and political power in the province through appointment to the executive council. They were mostly British, rather than French-Canadian.

Lower Canada

Landownership in Lower Canada

As the area that became Lower Canada had been colonised by pre-Revolutionary France, the system of land tenure in Lower Canada differed from that of Upper Canada. Land was granted to a *seigneur*, who would then grant the land to tenants to subsistence farm in exchange for rents. This was an essentially feudal system of land tenure and can be contrasted unfavourably with the freehold tenancy system of Upper Canada, whereby landownership encouraged investment and improvement in the land by its owners. However, Canadian *habitants* (tenants) under the seigneurial system were protected by contracts and the relationship between tenant and *seigneur* was overseen by the state. In Lower Canada, 75–80 percent of the rural population lived in seigneurial land until the mid-19th century as the British continued with the system when they gained New France from the French in 1763.

Tensions in Lower Canada

In addition to maintaining the system of land tenure, the British had guaranteed the free practice of Catholicism in the Quebec Act 1774 as well as accepting the use of French **civil law** for matters of private law. Lower Canada was principally French-speaking, although the official language of the legislative assembly was English. The French–Canadians remained fiercely attached to their identity, language and institutions and formed an important political block in the assembly. The influx of British loyalists from the American colonies caused ongoing racial tension in the province and the French speakers remained wary of any attacks on their cultural identity or way of life.

Lower Canada was brought into being by the 1791 Constitution with the same political structure as Upper Canada. Governors tended to select members of their executive councils from the loyalists and British members of the colony, who were generally successful businessmen, creating an English-speaking oligarchy known as the **Chateau Clique**. The French-speaking population was larger than the English, which meant that their views dominated the legislative assembly. They were very quick to oppose any moves by the Chateau Clique which they deemed to be an attack on their French identity.

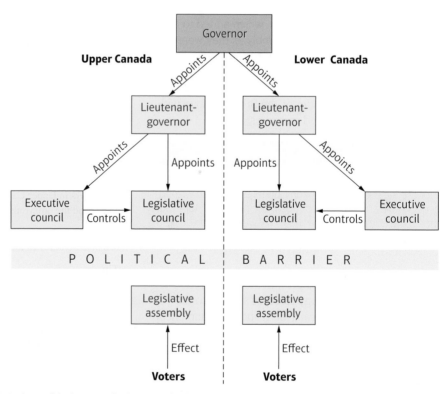

Figure 5.2 The political system in the Canadas in the 1830s.

The 1820s saw rural stagnation and genuine hardship for the *habitants* of the seigneurial estates. The ruling elite, made up as it was of English-speaking businessmen, had no hesitation in attributing the economic problems of the province to the backwardness of the French colonists. Their solution was to propose the passing of an Act in the British parliament in 1822 to unite Lower and Upper Canada as this would have resulted in a large English-speaking majority. French-Canadians mobilised opposition to the plan, and it was swiftly dropped in London on the basis of being not worth the trouble it had generated. Nevertheless, general mistrust of the English-speaking Chateau Clique among the French-speaking majority resulted. In the cities, a new group of French-speaking professionals began to seek reform of the political system to protect their French identities and to represent the interests of the small merchant and farmer. They were the **patriotes** and they represented a wide diversity of views, from those seeking inspiration from the French and American revolutions to those who wanted to uphold the seigneurial land system purely because it was French, not English, in origin.

The governor of Lower Canada from 1820 to 1828 was Lord Dalhousie, whose actions in his next posting in India were to prove a significant cause of the Indian Rebellion. In Lower Canada, he was soon at loggerheads with the French-speaking majority of the legislative assembly and by the time he was recalled to London events had reached the point whereby the assembly were refusing to vote money for the payment of officials and Dalhousie had **prorogued** the elected assembly in 1827 because he refused to accept the *patriote* leader as speaker of the house. Lobbying by the Lower Canadians in London and the presentation of a petition signed by 87,000 resulted in the end of his governorship as London was highly sensitive to unrest in colonial assemblies, without having the time and knowledge to actually sort out the fundamental issues.

SOURCE
2

Following the proroguing of the assembly in Lower Canada in 1827, Governor Dalhousie wrote to Bathurst, the colonial secretary, expressing his hopes that the 1791 Constitution would be suspended and summing up his views on the racial situation in Lower Canada. When he refers to Canadians, he means French-speaking Canadians. His letter is quoted in his biography in the *Dictionary of Canadian Biography*.

Instead of uniting the Canadian and British subjects in mutual friendship, and social habits; instead of uniting them in admiration of the principles of the Constitution which had been given them – [it] has had exactly a contrary effect;... a Canadian hates his British neighbour, as a Briton hates a Frenchman, by an inborn impulse." "The Canadians have succeeded," he added, "in obtaining a majority of votes in the House of Commons of this Province – a jealousy & hatred of the superior education, & superior industry of his British neighbour have led him to believe, that if he loses that majority, he loses also, liberty, laws, religion, property, and language, every thing that is valuable on earth.

The threat from the USA

The 1791 Constitution, which allowed French-Canadians religious freedom and preserved their system of land tenure, followed the precedent set by the **Quebec Act 1774**. The British intended by this to prevent possible revolts in their new territory by French-Canadians over religious and cultural matters. The continuation of this policy from 1791 until after the 1837 rebellion in Lower Canada can partly be attributed to the perceived threat to Canadian loyalty from the influence of the USA. By allowing French-Canadians religious freedom and preserving their legal system, the British hoped that any attempts by the USA to stir rebellion in the Canadas would be unsuccessful.

The political structure established in the Canadas by the 1791 Constitution was informed by the lessons the British had drawn from the American War of Independence. They believed, not unreasonably, that the thirteen colonies had revolted because of taxation. By establishing legislative assemblies with financial autonomy, they hoped to prevent a similar situation developing in their Canadian colonies in the future. In terms of constitutional development, the 1791 Constitution for the Canadas represented a considerable advance in terms of the colonial relationship from that which had previously existed in Britain's colonies. However, the fact that executive power rested in the hands of a British-appointed lieutenant governor meant that at some point tensions between the colonies and Britain were inevitable. This was a result of the actions of individuals and the impact of lengthy time delays and misunderstandings due to the slow communication between London and the provinces.

KEY TERMS

Patriote
A supporter of reform to the system of political power in Lower Canada.

Prorogue
To discontinue a session of parliament without officially dissolving it.

Quebec Act 1774
This was passed by the British parliament to incorporate New France into their Empire following their victory in the Seven Years' War. Religious freedoms to French-Canadians were guaranteed and the Catholic Church was granted the right to collect tithes. French laws were maintained in civil matters which maintained the land tenure system and the system of dividing land for inheritance rather than passing onto the eldest son.

A Level Exam Style Question Section B

How far do you agree that Britain's decision to allow the continuation of French land tenure was the most important cause of the revolt in Lower Canada in 1837?

Tip
Consider the role of the patriote leader and other grievances of the French-speaking population in Lower Canada.

ACTIVITY
KNOWLEDGE CHECK

The political systems of the Canadas
1 Look carefully at Figure 5.2. Create two mind maps and, using the text, identify which groups would have wished the system of government in the Canadas to remain as it was and which groups would have argued for change. Annotate your mind map, by adding for each group the arguments they would have used to support their points of view. Use Source 3 to help you complete the British argument. Use your work to debate the question of the nature of continuing British rule in Canada.

2 Explain why discontent was greater in Lower Canada than in Upper Canada in the late 1820s and early 1830s.

WHAT WAS THE SIGNIFICANCE OF THE REVOLTS AGAINST BRITISH RULE IN THE CANADAS IN THE YEARS 1837–38?

The British were not unaware of tensions building in the Canadas. In 1828, they received a delegation from Lower Canada and reports of petitions and agitation for political reform in Upper Canada. As the Lower Canadian petition was signed by 87,000 people and the delegation was actually in London, the British felt tensions to be higher in Lower Canada and took the problems there more seriously, but they were keen to see a resolution of the problems in both the Canadas. London's solution was to appoint the Canada Committee, a parliamentary select committee, to report to the British government on the underlying grievances in the Canadas and suggest remedies. The Committee's report, published in 1829, demonstrates the fundamental problem which was to lead to the revolts in both the Canadas in 1837. The British simply had no solution to offer for the constitutional problems inherent in the 1791 Constitution. When the Committee reported, it advised against amendment of the 1791 Constitution, arguing that proper management of the constitution by the lieutenant governor and governor would solve the problems in the Canadas. The rest of the report was devoted to the issues raised by Lower Canada and on every point, other than constitutional reform, the Committee upheld the complaints of the assembly, but suggested no mechanism for change.

SOURCE

From the *Report of the Select Committee on the Civil Government of Canada* (1829). The British parliament had ordered a select committee to complete a report on the Canadas following the standoff that had developed in 1827 between Governor Dalhousie and the legislative assembly in Lower Canada and upon the receipt of a petition from the province signed by 87,000 people.

> At an early part of their investigation, Your Committee perceived that their attentions must be directed to two distinct branches of inquiry: – 1st To what degree the embarrassments and discontents which have long prevailed in the Canadas, had arisen from defects in the system of laws and constitution established in these Colonies – 2nd How far those evils were to be attributed to the manner upon which the existing system has been administered.
>
> Your Committee has clearly expressed their opinion that serious defects were to be found in that system, and have ventured to suggest several alterations that have appeared to them necessary or convenient. They also fully admit from these, as well as from other circumstances, the task of the Government of these colonies (and especially with regard to the Lower province) has not been an easy one; but they feel it their duty to express their opinion that it is the second of the causes alluded to that these embarrassments and discontents are in great measure to be traced. They are most anxious to record their complete conviction that neither the suggestions they have presumed to make, nor any other improvements in the laws and constitutions of the Canadas, will be attended with the desired effect, unless an impartial, conciliatory and constitutional system of Government be observed in these loyal and important Colonies.

The report was published in July 1829 at the tail end of the Duke of Wellington's Tory ministry, which was replaced by the Whigs in November 1830. The Whig ministry of 1830 had its sights set on greater tasks than the reform of the constitutional system in Canada. They were about to embark on long overdue reform of the British parliamentary system, which was completely unrepresentative. The hopes of the *patriotes* and the Reformers were not fulfilled in the early 1830s because of difficulty the Whigs faced in introducing British parliamentary reform in Britain. As a result, the British did not capitalise on any goodwill generated by the Canadian Committee report by failing to act on its recommendations fast enough.

EXTEND YOUR KNOWLEDGE

The Great Reform Act 1832

The question of electoral reform dominated British parliamentary activity between 1830 and the actual passing of the Great Reform Act 1832. This Act, introduced and fought for by the Whigs, ended some of the worst abuses in the political system whereby derelict hamlets sent two MPs to parliament and some of the new industrial centres had no representation at all. The Act increased the electorate from 366,000 to 650,000, which was about 18 percent of the total adult male population in England and Wales. Some of the newer industrial cities gained representation for the first time and derelict boroughs like Old Sarum were abolished.

They were, however, prepared to move a considerable distance on the matter of finance and in 1831 the **Howick Act** was passed, which transferred to the assemblies the revenues from duties. In return, the British expected that the assemblies would agree to their **Civil List** for the payment of officials. The assemblies in both provinces were now highly frustrated with the failure to institute constitutional reform and the Civil List was not agreed at any point by the Lower Canadians in the 1830s. In both Upper and Lower Canada, Reformers and *patriotes* began to look more and more towards America as a model for government and were in no way satisfied with the increased financial powers offered to them by the British and the conciliatory efforts of British representatives in both provinces who tried to include Reformers and *patriotes* in the councils.

Causes of the revolt in Upper Canada

The political system and tight control of the Family Compact and the Anglican Church in Upper Canada were the underlying causes of the rebellion organised in Upper Canada by William Lyon Mackenzie in 1837. The situation deteriorated quickly in the 1830s as a result of a number of short-term causes:

- the emergence of a more **radical** voice within the Reform Party
- the concerns of the established settlers about the impoverished new emigrants from Britain arriving in the province in the 1830s
- the actions of two successive lieutenant governors, Colborne and Head
- the results of the 1836 election.

Radical Reformers

The constitutional and moderate Reformers were led by Robert Baldwin and his father, who from 1828 had been developing their definition of responsible government and trying to present their ideas to the colonial secretary with no success. During the rebellion of 1837, Robert Baldwin was actually in London protesting about his removal from the executive council by the lieutenant governor and events were led by the far less moderate voice of the Reformers, William Lyon Mackenzie. Mackenzie ran a newspaper, which had been attacked by the some of the sons of the Family Compact in 1826, making him a genuine victim of persecution and aiding his reputation as a reformer enormously. Mackenzie began his career, like Baldwin, arguing that reforms to the current system would be sufficient but, as the 1830s progressed, he looked more and more to America for his inspiration and argued that Upper Canada should follow the example of the American colonies and seek independence.

KEY TERMS

Howick Act 1831
An Act of Parliament in Britain that transferred the revenue from duties on Canadian goods to the control of local assemblies in the provinces. It reflects the commonly held belief that the American Revolution had stemmed solely from issues to do with taxation and an assumption that what needed to be fixed in the Canadas was financial control.

Civil List
Amount of money provided for the payment of government officials.

Radical
From the Latin word *radix*, meaning root. The term refers to those campaigning for fundamental changes from the roots.

Ops Township scheme
A scheme that administered official help by the Upper Canadian government for poor immigrants. The scheme was administered by Peter Robinson, businessman and fur trader, on behalf of the Upper Canadian government and with the strong support of the British Colonial Office.

EXTEND YOUR KNOWLEDGE

William Lyon Mackenzie (1795–1861)
Born in Scotland, Mackenzie arrived in Upper Canada in 1820. He quickly established a name for himself with his political journal, *Colonial Advocate*, and was elected to the legislative assembly in 1828. He was elected the first mayor of Toronto in 1834. He lost his seat in the legislative assembly in the controversial 1836 election and led the abortive rebellion in 1837. He spent ten years in America, having served a short prison term in America for his actions during the revolt. He was pardoned by the Canadians in 1849 and returned to Canada, where he resumed his journalism and his political career. His publications lack coherence, but his radical democratic rhetoric added considerable vigour to the debate about the nature of politics in Canada.

Emigration into the province

Irish emigration into Upper Canada in the 1830s meant that virtually the whole of Upper Canada east of Toronto and north of the older loyalist settlements became noticeably Irish in character. American aliens emigrating into the province from the 1790s to the 1820s had traditionally been regarded with suspicion and in the 1830s the longer-standing residents of Upper Canada shared all the prejudices against poor Irish emigrants common in Britain: that the Irish were feckless, criminally inclined and carried disease. Poor immigrants were assisted by the **Ops Township scheme** with temporary shelters and cheap supplies funded by the government. Reformers objected to the costs of the programme designed to assist immigration and the lack of consultation with the legislative assembly, and the Family Compact objected to the increase of poor immigrants who were unlikely to support their control of the power and influence within the colony and whose swelling numbers threatened the status quo. Concern regarding emigration was intensified by the cholera epidemics of 1832 and 1834 and the impact of a financial crisis in America in 1837, which affected the economic stability of Upper Canada.

Action of the lieutenant governors

Sir John Colborne (in office 1828–35) and Sir Francis Bond Head (in office 1835–38), lieutenant governors of Upper Canada, both shared a similar interpretation of the constitution, which was that they were there to govern and that the executive council was there to be consulted. When they encountered opposition, they simply carried on regardless.

Colborne was more successful than Head. He, at least, had some previous experience as a colonial administrator and his interest in improving the infrastructure of the province was clearly positive. However, he bypassed the legislative assembly by using tax revenues to pay officials' salaries and by setting up a classic English preparatory school, rather than the university some voices in the colony were calling for, using public funds. His most controversial action prompted his removal from his political position and appointment in the subordinate role of military commander-in-chief for Canada. It was the allocation of the income from clergy reserves for the ongoing support for 44 Anglican parishes across the province in an attempt to establish yet more firmly the Anglican Church as settlement across the province increased. This was highly provocative and one of the principal grievances leading to the rebellion.

EXTEND YOUR KNOWLEDGE

The disestablishment of the Church

The debate over clergy lands in Canada reflected the debate going on in Britain during the 1830s regarding the source of wealth of the Anglican Church. In England, Wales and Ireland, the Church held substantial lands and the clergy were supported partly from incomes drawn from these lands and partly from a tithe or tax collected from all those living in a parish. Members of other churches objected strongly to payments made to support churches in which they did not worship.

In 1836, the Whig government passed an Act which replaced the collection of the tithe with a cash payment from each parish, which was far less onerous, but the obligation to support Church of England clergy continued in Ireland (mostly Catholic) until 1869 and Wales (mostly Methodist) until 1914 and remained an ongoing source of dissatisfaction to non-Anglicans.

The appointment of Sir Francis Head remains something of a mystery. He had no previous colonial experience and the evidence suggests that he was plucked from obscurity by the British government on the basis of his local administration in Kent of the newly amended Poor Law. He arrived in Canada with the totally unjustified reputation as a reformer. His initial action in inviting some moderates onto the executive committee seemed positive, but he then forced them from office when they complained that they had not been consulted on issues they deemed to be within their remit. This prompted the 1836 election in which he campaigned vigorously against the Reformers in a departure from tradition, whereby the lieutenant governors did not campaign in elections. He was successful in removing the Reformers from the legislative assembly, but this made the situation even more volatile as the Reformers were now convinced they had no legal means to influence the government of the province and that rebellion was now the only option.

The 1836 election

The 1836 election was a victory for Head in that it delivered a pro-government majority after his personal intervention in the campaign. The new legislative assembly passed a number of laws intended to shore up their position and prevent the Reformers challenging their position. The laws included:

- a law extending the session of the legislative (King William IV was very ill and traditionally elections had to be called within six months of a monarch's death; the new law meant the expected election would not be carried out)

- a law preventing members of the legislature from serving as executive councillors; this rarely happened in practice, but to codify with legislation was an obvious attempt by the Family Compact to perpetuate their hold on government as future governors would be prevented from appointing Reformers from within the legislative assembly to the more powerful executive body.

In response, and under Mackenzie's leadership, many Reformers came to believe rebellion was now necessary and established Committees of Correspondence (see page 70) and secret councils, and began drilling men in what was a conscious imitation of the American model. Both sides engaged in flurries of propaganda and Mackenzie prepared a declaration of independence and made wild promises of confiscation and redistribution of land and property to his supporters.

SOURCE

4

William Mackenzie was the voice of the radical Reformers in Upper Canada and his writing shows the influence of the ideas of the American Revolution. His newspaper published a declaration of independence on 1 December 1837, written by him shortly before violence broke out in Upper Canada.

The time has arrived, after nearly half a century's forbearance under increasing and aggravated misrule, when the duty we owe our country and posterity requires from us the assertion of our rights and the redress of our wrongs.

Government is founded on the authority, and is instituted for the benefit, of a people; when, therefore, any Government long and systematically ceases to answer the great ends of its foundation, the people have a natural right given them by their Creator to seek after and establish such institutions as will yield the greatest quantity of happiness to the greatest number.

Our forbearance heretofore has only been rewarded with an aggravation of our grievances; and our past inattention to our rights has been ungenerously and unjustly urged as evidence of the surrender of them. We have now to choose on the one hand between submission to the same blighting policy as has desolated Ireland, and, on the other hand, the patriotic achievement of cheap, honest, and responsible government.

The right was conceded to the present United States, at the close of a successful revolution, to form a constitution for themselves; and the loyalists with their descendants and others, now peopling this portion of America, are entitled to the same liberty without the shedding of blood more they do not ask; less they ought not to have.

The events of the revolt in Upper Canada

The events in Upper Canada were far less serious than those in Lower Canada and the outcome of the revolt was never really in question, although Head's decision to send the province's small garrison of troops off to Lower Canada to help deal with the rebellion there weakened the government forces in Upper Canada somewhat. Fortunately for the British, Mackenzie's vacillating leadership and confused aims meant the British were able to deal with the revolt speedily and efficiently.

- In December 1837, following the news of the revolt in Lower Canada and the arrest of *patriote* leaders, Mackenzie decided to launch a revolt in Upper Canada. About 1,000 men, mostly farmers of American origin, gathered for four days in December at Montgomery's tavern on Yonge Street in Toronto. They were unclear about their objectives, but the general plan was to attack property and businesses of those identified as members of the Family Compact.

- On 5 December, several hundred poorly armed and organised rebels marched south on Yonge Street and exchanged gunfire with a smaller group of loyalists. The bulk of the rebel force fled in a state of confusion once the firing started.

- Three days later, the remaining rebels were dispersed following the arrival of loyalist reinforcements in Toronto by steamboat. There was a small, second confrontation soon afterwards in Brantford, but again the insurgents were dispersed.

- Although the revolt was effectively over, Mackenzie and other rebel leaders fled to Navy Island in the Niagara River, where he declared a provisional state. Numbers swelled to around 600, some of them responding to Mackenzie's promises of 300 acres of land for supporters. Their supply ship, the American steamer *Caroline*, was burned and on 13 January 1838 Mackenzie fled the island under heavy bombardment from the militia. He was captured by the US military and sentenced to 18 months for violating neutrality laws.

Results of the revolt in Upper Canada

Following the government's victory, hundreds, possibly thousands, of rebels and rebel sympathisers left the province for America. Those who stayed were often arrested and two were hanged. For those that remained, the political complexion of the province had changed considerably. After 1837, those who advocated an American-style revolution either fled to America or kept their opinions to themselves. The talk in Upper Canada was solely of loyalty to Britain and how to keep the province British. The British were convinced that the events were largely down to the actions of the Family Compact over many years and that something must be done to sort out the governance of the province. In such an atmosphere, the moderate reforming voices, like those of Baldwin, were bound to come to the fore and command the attention of Lord Durham, who was dispatched to the province tasked with finding a solution.

ACTIVITY
KNOWLEDGE CHECK

The Upper Canadian revolt

1 Which of the short-term causes of the 1837 revolt in Upper Canada do you consider to be the most significant? Explain your answer.

2 Explain the British position regarding constitutional reform for the Canadas in the 1830s.

Causes of the revolt in Lower Canada

The long-term tensions in Lower Canada were the result of the exclusion of the French-speaking majority of the population from the executive arm of government, as governors of the province tended to appoint British and loyalists to the executive council. In the short term, the revolt was sparked by the raising of expectations for change following the appointment of the Canada Committee in 1828 and then the failure of the British government to exercise any real changes to the system of government. The short-term causes of the revolt were:

- the leadership of the *patriotes* by Papineau

- economic and social issues in the province

- the Gosford Commission of Inquiry and the British decision about the colony which resulted from its findings.

Papineau

Louis-Joseph Papineau was the descendent of an old seigneurial family and had been prominent in Lower Canadian politics for many years. From 1830 onwards, his position became more and more anti-British and under his leadership the assembly refused to accept any of the compromises offered by the British regarding control of finances in the province and he steadfastly refused to agree to vote in favour of the Civil List to pay the salaries of officials. Although he borrowed the language employed by the patriots of the American Revolution, Papineau was not influenced by ideas of equality or revolution. His opposition to the British stemmed from his French-Canadian nationalism and he was opposed to any change in the seigneurial land system, unlike the more liberal members of the Patriot Party (*Parti patriote*).

EXTEND YOUR KNOWLEDGE

Louis-Joseph Papineau (1786–1871)
Papineau was the leader of the Patriot Party in the 1820s and 1830s and was responsible for the refusal of the assembly to accept any of the compromises offered by the British in the 1830s over financial affairs. In the 1820s and 1830s, his opposition to the British stemmed more from his French nationality than coherent radical politics. He was responsible for drafting the 92 Resolutions and his son was a founding member of one of the paramilitary organisations that fought against the British in the revolt in Lower Canada. Despite having spoken at large demonstrations at the beginning of the revolt, when armed insurrection began Papineau departed for America. It is not completely clear if this was from cowardice or because of the warrant for arrest issued by the British. Papineau remained in exile until pardoned and returned to Canada in 1845. He re-entered politics and advocated American-style democracy in later years.

The reasons for his change of heart post-1830 are obscure as previously he had viewed the British constitution as perfect and that Canadian local institutions should be based on the British parliamentary system. It seems likely, however, that he was influenced by the more radical mood of the times (there was a revolution in France in 1830) and by the general discontent regarding the economic situation in Lower Canada. Certainly, adopting a more hard-line stance ensured the continuation of his position as the acknowledged leader of the opposition to the British. In February 1834, **92 Resolutions** were published by the *patriotes* demanding constitutional change, including elective councils and seeking to protect the French-Canadian identity.

Economy

Lower Canada's economy did not perform well during the 1830s and the hardship suffered by the *habitants*, combined with general social unease resulting from increased immigration, meant that the population became increasingly radical. The immigrants brought with them the dreaded cholera and there was an outbreak in 1832, which increased tensions to the point that the military fired on a crowd during the 1832 election and two men were shot. The *patriotes* benefited from the hard times as so much of their rhetoric was that of the American Revolution that their supporters could be forgiven for confusing them with genuine radicals. Certainly, by 1834, the more radical wing of the Patriot Party was emerging as a stronger voice in the assembly and in the province as a whole.

For the British, the most pressing economic problem of the period was how to pay the salaries of officials, as the assembly, led by Papineau, was intransigent in its opposition to British proposals for shared economic control of the province.

The Gosford mission

The arrival in Canada in 1835 of a commission of inquiry led by Lord Gosford (the Royal Commission for the Investigation of all Grievances Affecting His Majesty's Subjects in Lower Canada) did little to ease the situation in Lower Canada. Gosford himself was experienced in the complicated politics of Ireland and might have been able to make some progress with the very recalcitrant *patriotes* had Sir Frances Head not disclosed the full terms of the inquiry to the assembly in Upper Canada in January 1836. This caused outrage in Lower Canada as the full terms of the inquiry's brief showed that the British had no intention of engaging in the kind of constitutional reform that the *patriotes* were calling for. The multiple reports of the commission led by Gosford worsened the situation by their failure to address the issues that the *patriotes* deemed important, and the issue of Canadian reform was referred to the British parliament. The debate on Canada in Britain demonstrated a hardening of British attitudes on all sides and the ten **Russell Resolutions** were passed by the House of Commons on 6 March 1837, rejecting the constitutional reform called for in the 92 Resolutions and allowing the governor the use of public funds without the consent of the assemblies. It was also calculated that the government of Lower Canada owed the British government £142,160 14s 6d for the payment of British officials, which had gone unpaid over the crisis years.

When the news of the Russell Resolutions reached the province in April, it resulted in widespread unrest and agitation. The *patriotes* held large public meetings throughout May and called for the boycott of British goods and free trade between Lower Canada and the USA. Lord Gosford responded by increasing the British military presence in the province and issuing a proclamation banning protest meetings, which was followed by a second proclamation the following month banning all public meetings. The banks closed their doors on 18 May, adding further to the general unrest. The assembly met in August and refused to accede to the demands of the British government, and on 26 August it adjourned and the *patriotes* began to prepare in earnest for revolt.

KEY TERMS

92 Resolutions
A long list of political demands of the *patriotes*. They were drafted by the *patriote* leader, Papineau.

Russell Resolutions
Resolutions passed by the British House of Commons, named after their proposer Lord John Russell, relating to the political demands of Lower Canadians.

KEY TERM

Société des Fils de la Liberté
A paramilitary organisation of the *patriotes*, similar to the Sons of Liberty in the American Revolution.

TIMELINE: EVENTS OF THE 1837–38 REVOLT IN LOWER CANADA

September–October 1837
500 or more form themselves into the paramilitary *Société des Fils de la Liberté*, holding public meetings in Montreal

26 October 1837
The Confederation of the Six Counties meets at St-Charles. Papineau speaks against rebellion, but Wolfred Nelson declares 'the time has come to melt our spoons into bullets', becoming the new voice of the *patriotes*

6 November 1837
Street fighting breaks out between the Doric Club (British and Anglican settlers) and *Société des Fils de la Liberté* and the offices of the pro-British newspaper, *The Vindicator,* are destroyed

10 November 1837
British cavalry and *patriote* militia exchange shots in Montreal

16 November 1837
A rebel force ambushes a small military detachment sent to arrest *patriote* leaders and several wounded on both sides. Lord Gosford issues warrants for the arrest of *patriote* leaders on the charge of treason

23 November 1837
A surprise victory for *patriote* forces at the village of St Denis under the leadership of Nelson

25 November 1837
British General Wetherall defeats the *patriote* forces at St Charles

29 November 1837
General Wetherall enters Montreal with 30 prisoners captured at St Charles

5 December 1837
Martial law is declared

14 December 1837
100 *patriotes* fleeing from a burning church in St Eustache are shot

The British burn houses of known *patriotes* and those who are believed to have sheltered them

December 1837–January 1838
Gosford has the situation in Canada under control and the *patriotes* are either prisoners or have fled to America

November 1838
Lord Durham's departure is followed by raids along the border by exiled *patriotes*, aided by American citizens acting independently of their government, in what is known as the 'Second Rebellion'. The raids are unsuccessful and quashed by action by Canada and the USA

SOURCE

5 From a letter from General John Colborne, the commander-in-chief, to Sir Francis Bond Head, the lieutenant governor of Upper Canada, following the victory by the *patriotes* at St Denis, requesting help with the situation emerging in Lower Canada in November 1837.

The Civil War has now commenced in this Province, I entreat you, therefore, to call out the Militia of Upper Canada and endeavour to send to Montreal as many corps as may be inclined to volunteer their services at this critical period.

SOURCE
6
Defeat of the insurgents by Sir John Colborne at St Eustache, 25 November 1837, an engraving by John Henry Walker (1831–99) and published in Canada in 1877 in *A Popular History of the Dominion of Canada.*

Results of the revolt in Lower Canada

The extent of the rebellion in Lower Canada was far greater than that in Upper Canada. Once order was restored, there were over 500 *patriotes* in the jails of Montreal and wild estimates as high as 13,000 were made of the number of rebels involved. The British passed an Act on 10 February 1838 suspending the 1791 Constitution of Lower Canada and Governor Gosford was empowered to run the province with a special council of appointed members. He revoked martial law in Montreal on 27 April 1838, judging that the ring leaders had now been apprehended and the situation had calmed.

The lessons the British drew from the events in Lower Canada were slightly different from those that they drew from events in Upper Canada. The rebels in Lower Canada were ethnically French-Canadian and this racial division coloured the views of the British. It was imperative that Lower Canada was reorganised in such a way that the French-Canadians could no longer command a majority in any assembly, at the same time as reining in the Chateau Clique of British loyalists who had undeniably contributed to the situation. London now accepted that a new constitutional settlement must be found for the province but were very alive to the needs of the British settlers in the province. Any solution for Lower Canada must be one that protected the rights of British settlers while tackling the system of land tenure which the British viewed as a principal cause of *habitant* poverty and discontent.

Was there a real threat of revolution in the Canadas?
Although the numbers involved in the revolts were small, the largest gatherings in Toronto and Montreal numbered about 1,000 rebels in each case, and the revolts were put down by the military with relative ease; the British took the revolts in Canada seriously. They judged, probably rightly, that the situation in Lower Canada was more serious than in Upper Canada because of the distinctive French-Canadian identity of the *patriotes*. However, both revolts raised the unpleasant spectre of the American Revolution 50 years before. In many ways, the British assessment of the revolts as very serious was correct. The number of rebels may have been relatively small, but these were after all sparsely populated provinces and events took place during the cold Canadian winter. Greater trouble might well have occurred during the summer of 1838 had the British not taken immediate steps to placate Canadian opinion.

The fleeing of rebels over the border to the USA was also a matter of some concern to British politicians. Since the American War of Independence, they had fought another brief campaign against the USA in 1812 and, while relations were relatively cordial during the 1830s, the bogey of possible American involvement in the Canadas was never far from British politicians' minds.

ACTIVITY
KNOWLEDGE CHECK

The revolt in Lower Canada

1 What were the similarities and what were the differences in the causes of the two revolts in the Canadas?

2 What evidence can you find in the text and sources that the Lower Canadian revolt had more widespread support than the revolt in Upper Canada?

EXTRACT

From Professor Steven Ellis, writing for the BBC in 2011, discussing the perception of the Irish by the English.

Ireland in 1558 was divided politically and culturally into English and Gaelic parts. The predominantly Gaelic west and north had a scanty, shifting population, with scattered, largely impermanent settlements, and a predominantly pastoral economy. A common legal system, social and cultural institutions also stretched across the North Channel into the Scottish highlands and islands, imparting some measure of unity. Yet Gaelic politics were intensely local, with the numerous rival clans and chieftaincies. This was, according to English officials, 'a land of war', inhabited by a rude and savage people ('the wild Irish') living in bogs and mountains.

SOURCE

From King James I discussing the English, Scottish and Irish temperaments (in remarks widely attributed to him). The monarch was James IV of Scotland from 1567, becoming King of England (after the union of the Scottish and English Crowns) and Ireland from 1603 as James I.

The Scots are a middle temper, between the English tender breeding and the Irish rude breeding and are a great deal more likely to adventure to plant Ulster than the English.

EXTRACT

From a synopsis of 'The Plantation of Ireland in the Counties of Armagh and Tyrone', an episode of Melvyn Bragg's radio programme *The Voices of the Powerless* (2002).

During the period of mid-16th century to mid-17th century Ulster is unique in being the only place to be colonized on a major scale within Europe.

James 1 was closely involved in the planning. The official government sponsored plantation of Ulster (previous plantation schemes had been privately organized) began in 1610, initially with the co-operation of many Irish landowners.

The Ulster Plantation, like earlier 16th century plantations in Leix, Offaly and Munster, was chiefly driven by the English government's desire for financial gain and increased security, pragmatic concerns rather than a political or religious crusade.

The aims were: to replace Gaelic law with English law; protect against future alliances between a Gaelic Ulster and Spain; establish the king's title to confiscated lands and offer land to English servitors and settlers.

Irish chieftains of the 16th century, from the *Encyclopaedia of Costume* by James Planche (1876). The wearing of traditional Irish dress was banned in the plantations.

THINKING HISTORICALLY   Cause and consequence (6c)

Connections

Look at Extracts 2 and 3 and Sources 7 and 8. Work in groups or individually and answer the following questions.

1 Read Extract 2. How might this be seen as similar to problems the British faced in governing the Canadas in the 1820s and 1830s?

2 Read Source 7.

   a) What did Dalhousie believe about the French-Canadians?

   b) How is this similar to James I's ideas about the Irish?

3 Look at Extract 3 and Source 8. What did the British in Lower Canada in the 1820s and 1830s copy from the English methods of subduing the Irish?

4 Make a list of other similarities between Lower Canada and 16th- and 17th-century Ireland. How may their understanding of the Plantation have affected the attitudes and actions of the British in Canada?

5 Why it is important for historians to see these links across time and be able to explain how causal factors can influence situations much later in time?

HOW SIGNIFICANT TO THE DEVELOPMENT OF BRITAIN'S RELATIONSHIP WITH ITS COLONIES WAS THE EARL OF DURHAM'S REPORT ON CANADA PUBLISHED IN 1839?

The citizens of Quebec might have been forgiven for scepticism regarding Lord Durham's ability to solve the crisis in Lower Canada as he pranced through the streets on his arrival in the province on a white charger dressed in the full silver and white regalia of a Knight of the Order of Bath, before installing himself at the Château St Louis. During his months in the colony, visitors to the governors' residence were treated to the use of gold and silver plates as dinnerware and served the vintage champagne Durham was used to imbibing. 'Radical Jack' Durham was after all the man also known as 'jog along Jack', having replied to the question, 'What is a sufficient income for an English gentleman?', by saying that a man might jog along very comfortably on £40,000 per annum (about £4 million in today's money). He was by any standards fabulously wealthy but, more importantly, he was one of the last Whig grandees. The great Whig aristocrats were a unique group. They were completely a product of their time and environment, but their efforts can be credited for preventing a bloody revolution in Britain as they reformed the political system sufficiently to allow the growing middle class a voice in politics. Aristocrats aligned by birth, marriage and wealth, they were nevertheless open to new ideas, willing to consider change to the social order and energetic and powerful enough to effect the changes they envisioned. Their personal lives were colourful and their attitudes high-handed, but it is to their credit that they devoted their time (all of them were in receipt of large inherited incomes based on landed wealth) to public service in British politics rather than solely to the pursuit of pleasure.

By 1837, when Durham was dispatched to Canada, the great reforms of the Whig decade were largely history and they were under the leadership of the detached and cynical Lord Melbourne. Nevertheless, Lord Durham's brief sojourn in Canada in many ways epitomises the strengths and weaknesses of the Whigs in general. Fortunately for Canada and the Empire as a whole, his analysis of the situation in the Canadas was astute and his openness to new intellectual arguments meant that out of the Durham Report the concept of 'responsible self-government' slowly emerged. Lord Durham's report was the first official definition of responsible self-government in British politics and contained recommendations for the immediate unification of the Canadas to solve the issue of the French-Canadian majority in Lower Canada. Responsible self-government, as we understand the term post-Durham, was the system by which settler colonies elected their own legislatures and executives following the Westminster model and were wholly responsible for their own economies and taxes. The report was a policy document for the consideration of the British parliament; Whig infighting and weakness meant that only the unification of the Canadas became law as a direct result. It took ten years before the first British colony was granted responsible self-government (Nova Scotia in 1848). Durham's report was a necessary ingredient in the development of 19th-century colonial policy, but the adoption of self-government in the Empire did not immediately result from his report and was not a foregone conclusion. The eventual granting of self-government to white settler colonies fostered loyalty in the white settler colonies of Canada, New Zealand and Australia by dealing with the issue of executive power.

EXTEND YOUR KNOWLEDGE

Lord Melbourne (1779–1848)

A member of the Whig aristocracy, Melbourne served with distinction as home secretary during the turbulent years 1830–34, which combined acute agricultural hardship and an unstable political situation during the passing of the Reform Act. He became prime minister briefly in 1834 and then from 1834 to 1841 as the best compromise candidate, and from 1837 was devoted to mentoring the young Queen Victoria rather than to reform. He instinctively disliked reform, although in some circumstances accepted it as the least worst option (as in the case of the Great Reform Act 1832).

His private life was colourful. His wife had a public affair with Lord Byron before her early death and he faced an attempted blackmail attempt by the husband of Caroline Norton during his premiership. The Norton separation and subsequent custody battle and Caroline's campaigning helped lead to changes in custody, divorce and property laws for women.

However, Durham's failure to mention native Americans at all in the report must count as a serious omission in a report which considered the future of land settlement and land tenure in the provinces. There was no acknowledgement of the contemporary debate on the future of Aboriginal peoples within the Empire (there was an active Aboriginals Protection Society in Britain) and the preoccupation of the Colonial Office with the question of indigenous peoples at this point in time. Indeed when Durham referred to native citizens in the report he meant French citizens. Furthermore, Durham's solution to the Canadian problem was only ever used by the British in the white settler colonies. No such self-government was ever granted to Jamaica or India and the failure to employ Durham's political solution more widely provides part of the explanation for the growth of late 19th and early 20th-century nationalism in Britain's directly ruled subject colonies.

SOURCE

9

A prisoner's box made by one of the rebels imprisoned after the rebellion in Lower Canada. The box is inscribed with the words 'Liberty' and 'Equality' and 'A present to Mr. Edward Smyth from (words unclear) Elton while a prisoner in Toronto Gaol for High Treason. July 13th 1838'. The photograph was taken for the *Toronto Star* in 1969 after readers wrote in with details of family heirlooms.

The importance of Lord Durham's role as high commissioner

Lord Durham's appointment as high commissioner for the Canadas was highly significant for the history of the two provinces. His actions in his short time in the provinces stabilised the political situation temporarily and he was the focus of considerable popularity within the provinces. Partly as a result of his actions and partly as a result of the fierce military response to the revolts, all but the most extreme Reformers were once more engaged in trying to find a political solution with London and, as a result, the trouble that reignited in Lower Canada following Durham's departure was dealt with quickly and expediently. By consulting widely and speedily with the populations of the province and by publically discounting the views of those who had previously held executive power in a tight grip, Durham proved to be an effective high commissioner in the way that the previous incumbent, Gosford, not endowed with the same sweeping powers, was unable to be. His popularity may have partly derived from London's intervention and his removal before he had time to disappoint his supporters, but it was nevertheless important in turning the tide away from the revolutionary American model and back once again to engagement with Westminster.

Lord Durham's early career

Durham was part of the Whig inner circle: his second wife was the daughter of Earl Grey, the reforming Whig prime minister. Durham was responsible for the passage of the Great Reform Act. His nickname 'Radical Jack' refers to his avocation of utilising whatever means necessary to pass the Reform Act. His lineage, his wealth and his undoubted intelligence all placed him at the heart of the Whig establishment, but he was also regarded as touchy and high-handed. Lord Melbourne, the British prime minister from 1835 to 1841, had no intention of including Radical Jack in his government if he could help it, as he had no wish to embark on the further political reform such as **household suffrage** advocated by Durham. Durham's prominence and abilities necessitated he be given some kind of role and in the summer of 1837, as the Gosford Commission floundered, Melbourne asked Durham to take on the Canadian question. Durham initially refused, but following the revolts and a personal appeal from the queen accepted the mission.

KEY TERM

Household suffrage
A vote in national and local elections for the male head of every household.

SOURCE 10

From Lord Melbourne writing to Lord Durham in the summer of 1837 asking him to travel to Canada to attempt to solve the deadlock which the Gosford mission had reached.

It has long been evident that not only the Government, but the country, is subject to daily increasing embarrassment from the present state of affairs in Lower Canada, and consequently in all of the North American possessions. The final separation of those colonies might possibly not be of material detriment to the interests of the Mother Country, but it is clear that it would be a serious blow to the honour of Great Britain, and certainly would be fatal to the character and existence of the Administration under which it took place...

Now what I wish to ask is, whether you would for a moment entertain the idea of undertaking this duty, and of rendering this great and important service to her Majesty, her Ministers and the country. You are the fittest mean for it, certainly the fittest in my opinion. You have every quality which will enable you to perform such a duty, and your character, your station, your abilities, and your principles, all combine to five you a weight and influence, and to command for you a respect and a confidence, which will attend upon no other individual.

This proposition may be attributed to motives of present political interest and convenience. If you draw this inference, I must submit to it; but I can assure you that I make it in the full conviction that the question is pressing and full of difficulty, pregnant with danger, and what I propose would offer to the country the best chance of a favourable issue. I would make the appointment as high and honourable as it can be made, in order, by giving it weight, to give it a better chance of success.

Durham's choice of advisers led Melbourne to attempt to intervene in the mission before it had even departed. Durham's insistence on taking his chosen advisers in Canada, despite criticism, demonstrates his disregard for convention and for Melbourne's advice, and was entirely in keeping with his personality. The eight advisers he took with him on his mission to Canada included Gibbon Wakefield and Thomas Turton; both had colourful pasts. Wakefield had served time in prison for the attempted abduction of a 15-year-old heiress from boarding school. This was no romantic elopement, but a cold-hearted plan by which a very young girl was lured from her school under false pretences and then persuaded into a nominal marriage with Wakefield. Wakefield had served three years in Newgate as a result. Thomas Turton's past had received almost as much coverage as Wakefield's. His wife had successfully sued him for divorce, citing his adultery with her sister. Durham overruled Melbourne's objections regarding Turton before he left England and his selection of both Turton and Wakefield as advisers left London with deep concerns regarding their ability to control Durham while he was in Canada.

Durham's mission in Canada lasted precisely four and a half months before censure of his actions from London precipitated his resignation. During that time he, and his team of aides-de-camp, met extensively with Canadians, including the moderate Reformers from Upper Canada, compiling the evidence for his report, which was published on 11 February 1839. During his time in Canada, he was also the effective executive power in the province and it was his actions in this capacity, as well as the ongoing controversy surrounding his choice of advisers, that led to his decision to resign over lack of support from the Melbourne government.

Almost his first action on arrival in Lower Canada was the removal of the old executive council and their temporary replacement with his own staff. He then ordered that all the depositions of the rebels be submitted to him for review and the French-Canadian newspapers noted with approbation that the political prisoners had been granted permission to exercise in the prison courtyard. He also issued a proclamation promising to work with all those who sought peaceful reform and asking for their co-operation.

During his time in Canada, he made friendly contact with the government of the USA over the matter of Canadian rebels and American troublemakers seeking re-entry and further revolt in Canada coming over the border and, as a result, the USA instituted patrols of the border. He established Canada's first police force and appointed a Commission of Inquiry on Crown Lands and Emigration for all the British North American provinces, with the aim of improving the system of land tenure in Lower Canada and also recommending a means by which land was no longer freely given to immigrants, as the influx of poor immigrants into the provinces in the 1830s had been a major source of tension in both the Canadas.

In the matter of the political prisoners, he had been instructed to free most of them, but Glenelg, the colonial secretary, had suggested that a token group be permitted (or persuaded) to plead guilty on the condition that they would exile themselves from Canada, probably to the USA. Durham took it upon himself to pardon the majority but instead banished the 'most' guilty to Bermuda, another imperial colony, before embarking on a tour of Upper Canada and making a short visit to America. Durham's ordinance pardoning most rebels and exiling a handful was highly popular in Canada, but stirred up controversy in Britain over the question of its legality in international law. The controversy resulted in the proposal of a **Bill of Indemnity** against Durham by Melbourne's rival Lord Brougham as a method of destabilising the faltering Melbourne government. During the debates on the bill in the House of Commons, Melbourne's government did not defend Durham's ordinance and it was the news of Melbourne's refusal to support his actions that prompted Durham's resignation on 9 October 1838 and his early return to Britain on 1 November 1838. He felt that he had been publicly undermined by Melbourne, who had offered him full support in his role. His failing health may also have played a role in his decision.

KEY TERM

Bill of Indemnity
A bill introduced in the British parliament declaring Lord Durham's actions regarding political prisoners illegal.

Resignation

Durham resigned because he was not prepared to submit to censure from London over his actions in sending the political prisoners to Bermuda and because he was annoyed with Melbourne's criticisms of his choice of advisers when he believed he had been given free reign over such matters. His resignation was greeted with great excitement in Lower Canada in particular and an effigy of Lord Brougham, who had led the parliamentary opposition in the House of Commons to Lord Durham's actions, was burned in Montreal. His sense of betrayal was strong and he published a frank proclamation defending himself and his mission.

In many ways, the ignominious end to the mission can be blamed on the political machinations of Westminster. Conscious of his tenuous grip on power, Melbourne simply could not afford to defend Durham and risk the fall of his ministry. Melbourne can certainly be criticised for double-dealing in his treatment of Durham, but equally it is possible to blame Durham for departing from his instructions and bringing the government under justifiable criticism as a result.

Nevertheless, his time in the Canadas left the provinces stronger than they had been before his arrival. John Colburne, the commander-in-chief, assured Durham that he could depart early from his mission knowing that the provinces were now secure from further rebellion and he dealt with the trouble that broke out in 1838 along the border from rebels based in the USA efficiently and effectively. There was no danger in 1838 that British power would be unseated and in many ways this was the result of Durham's ability to work with those in the provinces who had been advocating reform for years. The mere fact that he was from the highest echelons of the aristocracy and the political ruling class left many Canadians willing to wait for his report, rather than contemplate a return to rebellion, which had little apparent chance of success if the efforts of 1837 were anything to go by.

A Level Exam-Style Question Section B

'A genuine innovator in the changing relationship between Britain and its colonies.'

How far do you agree with this assessment of Lord Durham?
(20 marks)

Tip
Consider the intellectual origins of responsible self-government, as well as the process of compiling and drafting the Durham Report.

ACTIVITY
KNOWLEDGE CHECK

Durham's role as high commissioner

1 What evidence is there to support the view that the British were more concerned with party politics than solving the problems of the Canadas in 1838–41?

2 Explain why Durham's treatment of political prisoners was popular in Canada, but the subject of criticism in Britain.

Influence of Wakefield and Buller

Durham's high-handed approach to choosing his advisers contributed to the short life of his mission, but the inclusion of Gibbon Wakefield and Charles Buller among those who were to travel to Canada with him demonstrated his sharp eye for those with distinct skills to offer. Credit has been given to both of them regarding the drafting of the report. Indeed, Lord Brougham, Durham's political opponent, even quipped that 'Wakefield thought it, Buller wrote and Durham signed it.' However, except for the section on colonisation, Wakefield's direct influence cannot be demonstrated. Although both were obviously highly instrumental in the collection of material for the report, the final document is generally accepted to be Durham's own.

During their time in Canada, both Wakefield and Buller were active in the process of interviewing a wide spectrum of Canadian society, including Robert Baldwin, the first recorded advocate of responsible self-government, for the purposes of completing the report. As such, they served as a conduit for ideas, some of which found their way into the final report.

They also exercised some executive authority. Durham replaced the executive council with a number of commissions to administer the provinces and Buller headed a number of these, delegating some of the responsibility to Wakefield. Wakefield had expected to serve as the commissioner for Crown lands, responsible for the surveying and sale of Crown lands, but was prevented from doing so because of his notoriety. Instead, Buller held the actual position and was supported unofficially by Wakefield. Wakefield concluded that the system of free land grants in Canada was the worst possible system and his work in Canada influenced his subsequent actions in New Zealand, devising a system where land was sold, thereby encouraging more respectable colonists. There was no change to Canadian land policy as an immediate result of their work.

Systematic colonisation
Wakefield proposed that land should be sold to immigrants in colonies at a reasonably high price, rather than given away or sold very cheaply, arguing that doing so would benefit the economies of colonies.

Edward Gibbon Wakefield (1796–1862)

Wakefield's time in Newgate gave him ample opportunity to study and he developed a theory of **systematic colonisation**, which was published anonymously. After his release, he was still too shady a character, despite his wealth, to enter politics officially, but he attempted to influence the land schemes and settlements of a number of colonies. He was involved in the South Australian Association responsible for colonisation in Adelaide and had become close to Lord Durham in connection with the New Zealand Land Scheme, in which he hoped Durham might become prominently involved. He regarded the system of free land grants in Canada to be at the root of the problems in North America and advocated the complete opposite in his theory of colonisation. His theory of imperial settlement was that land must be sold at a sufficient price to encourage worthy settlers rather than being given away.

He had hoped that Durham would appoint him commissioner of lands in Canada, but his notoriety and intervention from Lord Melbourne prevented this. Instead he acted as an unpaid adviser and secretary to Durham and Buller. The only part of the report which is directly attributable to Wakefield is the appendix on Crown lands and emigration, which suggested that there be a tax on wild lands that had been granted but not settled and that the proceeds of this tax should go to public works to encourage further settlement. His recommendations were not acted on. He was, however, a strong advocate, under the influence of Louis-Hippolyte Lafontaine, of the union of the two provinces as the best way forward for their economic future and Durham was probably influenced by his views as the report recommended the union of the provinces as the best way to deal with the problem of the French-Canadian majority in Lower Canada.

Charles Buller (1806–48)

Charles Buller was an able and well-liked young man, untouched by any of the scandal that followed Wakefield and Turton. Although he had been called to the Bar, he took up a career in politics and journalism in the 1830s as a radical and sat on many reforming committees within parliament. He was Durham's official chief secretary and was appointed nominal head of the Commission into Crown Lands, although most of the actual work was done by Wakefield.

He was sympathetic to the French-Canadian rebels and felt that it was British policy that had driven them to revolt. It was his idea to banish a small number of rebels to Bermuda, which proved to be the cause of Durham's resignation from the mission. Buller remained behind in Canada to finish the work of the committees set up to help with the drafting of the report until December 1838 and then returned to London to work on the final draft with Durham. He resumed his political career upon his return and was responsible for the publication of *Responsible Government for Colonies* in 1840, which continued to advocate the principle of responsible self-government in Canada.

SOURCE

11 From a letter to Durham (7 September 1838) signed by Charles Buller but, according to Durham's biographer, the letter, in Buller's handwriting, also shows evidence towards the end of Wakefield's hand. The letter was sent to Durham after Durham had heard the news of Melbourne's failure to defend his actions over the exile of political prisoners and was contemplating resignation.

The people of England gave you despotic power because they thought you had courage, wisdom and justice enough to use it for this people's benefit. And they will hardly believe that such a power has proved inadequate in consequence of the impertinences and slander of one penny and 2 half penny papers. My opinion is that the reasons which you regard as justifying failure or withdrawal from your change will not be considered sufficient...

I report to you the substance of what all your friends, all who have made your interests their own, say in speaking of you; and which it is but just that one of them should say in speaking to you...

For I am convinced that on the course you pursue now depends your own honour and happiness – the welfare of this much injured people – and the preservation of the integrity of the British Empire.

Report on the Affairs of British North America, 1839

Although he might have used the political excitement resulting from his return to Britain to challenge Melbourne, Durham opted instead to complete his report and submit it to the Commons early in February 1838. His health had been affected by his time in Canada and he may simply have lacked the energy and ambition to make a bid for the premiership. His decision to stick to the job in hand resulted in a clear-sighted and analytical response to the problem of governing the two Canadas and the constitutional deadlock which resulted from a governor with executive powers directly appointed by London. The principal recommendations of his report were:

- the unification of Upper and Lower Canada as one province – Durham had initially toyed with the idea of federating all the provinces in Canada. However, in his judgement, the problems in Lower Canada were a result of the French-Canadians and he judged that the best immediate solution would be to ensure that they were placed in a minority position within a united province

- that the freedoms granted to the French-Canadians under the Quebec Act, particularly relating to civil law and land tenure, should be rescinded to improve the economic position of the *habitants* and promote economic growth within the colony

- responsible self-government for the new province, as defined by the moderate Reformer Robert Baldwin – the legislative assembly would be elected, but the party with the majority would hold power and exercise it through cabinet government, following the Westminster model. The governor of the province would therefore be a titular figure only.

SOURCE 12 From Lord Durham's *Report on the Affairs of British North America*, published in February 1839.

It is not difficult to apply the case to our own country. Let it be imagined that at a general election the Opposition were to return 500 out of 658 members of the House of Commons, and that the whole policy of the ministry should be condemned, and every Bill introduced by it rejected by this immense majority. Let it be supposed that the Crown should consider it a point of honour and duty to retain a ministry so condemned and so thwarted;... and, I think, it will not be difficult to imagine the fate of such a system of government. Yet such was the system, such literally was the course of events in Lower Canada, and, at one time or another, in every one of the North American colonies. To suppose that such a system would work well there implies the belief that the French Canadians have enjoyed representative institutions for half a century without acquiring any of the characteristics of free people; that Englishmen renounce every political opinion and feeling when they enter a colony, or that the spirit of Anglo-Saxon freedom is utterly changed and weakened among those who are transplanted across the Atlantic... I know not how it is possible to secure the harmony in any other way than by administering the government on those principles which have been found perfectly efficacious in Great Britain... when a ministry ceases to command a majority in Parliament on great questions of policy its doom is immediately sealed....

I admit that the system which I propose would... place the internal government of the colony in the hands of the colonists themselves; and that we should thus leave to them the execution of the laws, of which we have long entrusted the making solely to them. Perfectly aware of the value of our colonial possessions... I know not in what respect it can be desirable that we should interfere with their internal legislation in matters which do not affect their relations with the Mother Country... The constitution of the form of government – the regulation of foreign relation, and of trade with the Mother Country, the other British colonies, and foreign nations – and the disposal of the public lands, are the only points on which the Mother Country requires control....

The British people of the North American colonies are a people on who we may safely rely, and to whom we must not grudge power.

Importance of the Durham Report

There can be, and were, many criticisms made of the report's treatment of French-Canadians and the ruthless recommendation that Lower Canada be absorbed into a united province with the intention of sweeping away the protection of their institutions and their way of life, but by following this recommendation Britain certainly maintained its power in the territory. Even greater criticism might be made of the report's complete absence of any mention of the indigenous population of the two Canadas.

Nevertheless, the section on self-government is vital in explaining the development of the Empire in the second half of the 19th century. It demonstrates the belief in Britain's parliamentary (not Crown) institutions that one might expect from 'Radical Jack', who had fought so hard for parliamentary reform in Britain. By effectively defining the term 'responsible self-government' within an imperial context, the Durham Report became the intellectual basis of the relationship between Britain and its white settler colonies, which was adopted over the next 20 years.

Results of the report in Canada

The recommendation of the report that both the Canadas should be united was accepted by Melbourne's government and the legislation was introduced into the British parliament in May 1839. Charles Poulett Thomson was sent as governor general to obtain the consent of both the Canadas to the union between the provinces. The Upper Canadians voted cheerfully for union, aware that their debt-ridden province would benefit from union with Lower Canada and secure in the knowledge that British settlers would be in the majority in the new province. The Lower Canadian assembly had been suspended since 1838 and replaced with a special council and, with the principal French-Canadian rebels still in America, the British were able to proceed with union undeterred by significant Lower Canadian opposition. Following the passage of the bill through the British parliament, the Act of Union was proclaimed on 10 February 1841 in Montreal.

Long-term implications of the report

When Lord Durham died in July 1840, his obituary in the *Spectator* was full of praise for his part in the passing of the Great Reform Act and his tenure as governor in the Canadas, and it noted his restraint on his return with regards to those who had attacked his actions. There was no mention in the long article on responsible self-government or even on the union of the Canadas. The significance of his proposal was not immediately recognised by his contemporaries.

Responsible self-government was eventually granted to all the Canadian colonies between 1848 and 1855 and in Australia and New Zealand during the 1850s (with the exception of Western Australia, which was granted self-government in 1890). As the political structure of the Empire changed, so too did the way in which Durham's report was interpreted. It held the distinction of providing the definition of the concept for the first time in Britain and, as such, its importance grew as the policy was adopted in white settler colony after white settler colony. Had the policy not been implemented, which might easily have been the case, and instead the settler colonies departed from the Empire one after another in the mid-19th century, the report would have been little more than a footnote in imperial history.

EXTRACT

4   From Niall Ferguson, *Empire: How Britain Made the Modern World* (2003), discussing the importance of the Durham Report.

'Responsible government', then, was a way of reconciling the practice of empire with the principle of liberty. What the Durham Report meant was that the aspirations of Canadians, Australians, New Zealanders and South Africans – which were to be little different from the aspirations of the Americans in the 1770s – could be and would be answered without the need for wars of independence. From now on, whatever the colonists wanted, they pretty much got. That meant, for example, that when the Australians demanded an end to transportation, London gave in. The last convict ship sailed in 1867.

So there would be no Battle of Lexington in Auckland; no George Washington in Canberra; no declaration of independence in Ottawa. Indeed, it is hard not to feel, when one reads the Durham Report, that its subtext is one of regret. If only the American colonists had been given responsible government when they had first asked for it in the 1770s – if only the British had lived up to their own rhetoric of liberty – there might never have been a War of Independence. Indeed, there might never have been a United States. And millions of British emigrants might have chosen California instead of Canada when they packed their bags to go.

ACTIVITY
KNOWLEDGE CHECK

The results of the Durham Report

1 Write your own definition of the term 'responsible self-government' as you think Durham would have understood it.

2 Why did union of the two provinces take place immediately, but Durham's other recommendations take ten more years to achieve?

ACTIVITY
SUMMARY

Learning from past mistakes: Canada and the Durham Report, 1837–40

1 Using the diagram in Figure 5.2 as a model, complete a similar diagram for the united province in Canada showing the political system of government established by the Canada Act.

2 Compare events in the Canadas in 1837 with those in America in 1774–76. What were the similarities and differences?

3 Do you agree with Extract 4's assessment of the significance of the Durham Report? Might a similar offer to the Americans have prevented revolution or do you think there are important differences in the Canadian situation?

 WIDER READING

Bothwell, R. *The Penguin History of Canada*, Penguin (2008)

Burroughs, P. *The Canadian Crisis and British Colonial Policy*, Edward Arnold (1972)

Carstens, P.R. and Sanford, T.L. *The Republic of Canada – Almost*, Xlibris (2013)

New, C.W. *Lord Durham: A Biography of John George Lambton, First Earl of Durham*, Clarendon (1929)

The Canadian Dictionary of National Biography (www.biographi.ca)

3.6 Nearly losing an empire: the British in India, 1829–58

KEY QUESTIONS

- To what extent did the British control India in 1829?

- What were the causes and significance of the clash of cultures between the British and Indians?

- What were the immediate causes of the outbreak of rebellion in 1857 and why were the British able to retain control of India?

INTRODUCTION

Regular contact between Britain and India had begun in the 1600s after the granting of a trading **charter** to the East India Company by Elizabeth I. The company established fortified trading posts in Bombay, Madras and Calcutta and traded with the **Mughals**, the established power in the subcontinent. As Mughal power declined and was challenged by the native Marathas, the Company was drawn into treaties and military activity to protect its interests.

Britain's relationship with India in the 18th and early 19th centuries was a complicated web of treaties and alliances between local power-holders and the Company. At the same time as the Company was developing a new relationship with India, the British government attempted to regulate and assert its authority over the Company as a result of corruption and financial instability, which threatened British stockholders. By 1829, the British government had asserted its power over the Company but the relationship between the Company and the subcontinent remained fluid and dependent on local alliances which exploited the end of Mughal control.

The British did not conquer India; they collaborated with existing power-holders and benefited enormously from their divisions and weaknesses. By the 1820s, they saw themselves as the dominant power in the region for the foreseeable future, but their early efforts at civil administration of their Indian territories could have lost them their empire in 1857 when the Indian Rebellion took place. This is sometimes known as the Great Rebellion, and was referred to in 19th- and early 20th-century Britain as the Indian Mutiny. The lessons learned by the British from this event were to colour their imperial policies in all the countries under their control for as long as the British Empire lasted.

1757 – June: Battle of Plassey – East India Company forces defeat of the Nawab of Bengal and his French allies

1784 – British parliament passes East India Company Act

1813 – Charter Act renews the East India Company's charter but ends their trading monopolies on everything except tea and trade with China

| 1755 | 1775 | 1780 | 1785 | 1815 | 1825 |

1773 – British parliament passes Regulating Act

1786 – British parliament passes a supplementary Act which strengthens the power of the governor general

1829 – Governor Bentinck makes the practice of *sati* illegal and subject to prosecution in all British territory in India

TO WHAT EXTENT DID THE BRITISH CONTROL INDIA IN 1829?

The subcontinent that was to become the imperial jewel in Britain's crown was a huge and complex melting pot of religions and languages. Broadly speaking, it can be divided into three distinct geographical areas: the Indo-Gangetic Plain, which has been settled since pre-history along the Indus and Ganges rivers; the Himalayas, which protect from invaders from the East; and the Southern Plateau with its important trading ports. The inhabitants' religions were Hindu, Muslim, Sikh and Buddhist. There were six main languages, with over 200 different dialects, reflecting the size and diversity of the subcontinent.

During the late 18th century and early 19th century, the British East India Company emerged as surprise winners in the battles between local power-holders in India. Company power increased and they became responsible for the civil and legal administration of vast amounts of Indian territory and millions of native Indians. Their new role raised thorny questions regarding the way in which these new subjects should be governed and the objectives of the Company and British politicians as imperialists.

The role of the East India Company and the governor general

In the late 18th and early 19th centuries, the system by which the East India Company governed the territory, acquired at the Battle of Plassey and subsequently, was changing. The British parliament passed a series of Acts with the intention of ensuring the financial solvency of the Company and extending the British government's control over the East India Company following its near bankruptcy in the 1770s. Initially they attempted to bring only the political and administrative functions of the Company under parliament's control while leaving the Company in charge of its commercial interests. As it proved impossible in practice to divide the functions, from 1786 the Company acted as a **regularised subsidiary** of the Crown.

Historically, the Company had made money as a result of the monopoly of trade (see page 24) granted in its original charter. This monopoly came under increasing attack in the late 18th and early 19th centuries from politicians influenced by the doctrine of free trade (see page 11). In the **Charter Act** 1813, the British government renewed the Company's charter for another 20 years, but removed its monopoly on Indian trade, with the exception of the trade in tea with China, which was removed in the Charter Act 1833. Seeking new sources of income, the East India Company became increasingly involved in the civil administration and tax collection of Britain's territories in India. The collapse of the Mughal Empire left a power vacuum in the subcontinent into which the East India Company stepped, acting as a self-funding agent of imperialism for the British government.

> **KEY TERMS**
>
> **Regularised subsidiary**
> In this context, the term refers to the fact that the East India Company was no longer autonomous but overseen and regulated by the British Crown and parliament.
>
> **Charter Act**
> Acts of the British parliament in 1813 and 1833 altering the terms and conditions of the East India Company's charter which was their basis of legal authority (from the British perspective) in India.

1833 – Government of India Act ends the Company's commercial activities completely and reorganises the administrative system of the territories

1835-39 – William Sleeman leads and publicises the campaign for the suppression of *thagi*

1857 – 9 May: Mutiny of sepoys at Meerut sparks widespread mutineering within the Bengali army

16 July: Company forces reach Cawnpore and discover the entire garrison including 200 women and children has been massacred

1 July–21 September: British lay siege to the rebels in Delhi, finally retaking the city

27 November: The British finally evacuate Lucknow

| 1830 | 1835 | 1840 | 1850 | 1855 | 1860 |

1835 – Legislative council in India passes the English Education Act

1856 – Awadh is annexed by Dalhousie for the British under the doctrine of lapse

1858 – 2 August: Government of India Act passes, ending Company rule in India and passing control of the Company's territories to the Crown

There was a period of aggressive territorial acquisition by the Company in the early 1800s, which meant that by 1818 the entire Indo-Gangetic Plain, as far as the Sutlej River was under their control. Annexations continued between 1829 and 1857, and by 1857 this control had been extended from the three presidencies across the central plain of India and included the north-eastern and north-western provinces. These new territories were governed and administered by the East India Company through the presidencies with administrative power residing in the Bengal presidency at Calcutta.

The East India Company

The East India Company had begun life as a trading company benefiting from a charter giving it the monopoly of trade with India. During the 18th century, it had put three private armies on the field, one for each of the **company presidencies**, to protect its trading interests and to support its local collaborators. The three company presidencies – the Bengal presidency, the Madras presidency and the Bombay presidency – grew out of territorial expansion from the Company's original trading posts or factories in Calcutta, Madras and Bombay. The great 18th-century power struggle between the British and the French was fought in India by the Company armies and, by the 19th century, Britain was the only serious Western power contender in the subcontinent.

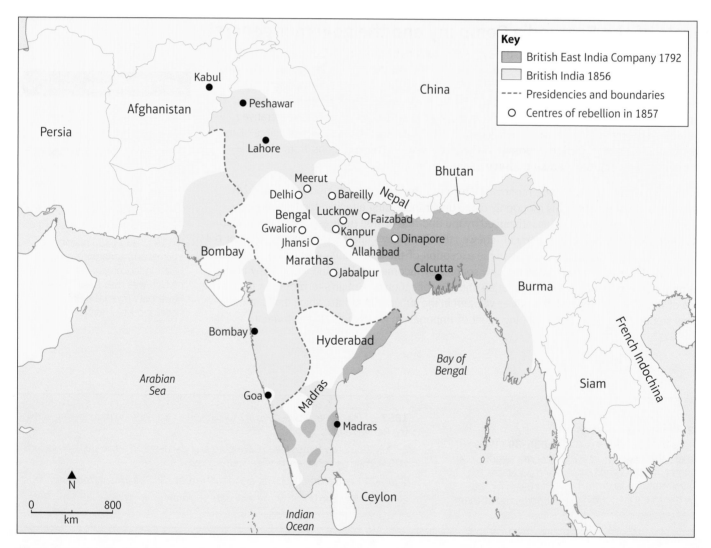

Figure 6.1 British (East India Company) expansion up to 1856, showing centres of rebellion in 1857.

Enormous private fortunes were made by Company **nabobs,** but poor management and corruption precipitated the British government to take control over the Company's structure and Acts of Parliament were passed in 1773, 1784 and 1786 to establish the relationship between the East India Company and parliament. The Regulating Act 1773 created a governing council of five, based in Calcutta, of which two were Company members and three were nominated by parliament, thereby ensuring a parliamentary majority. Furthermore, the appointment of governor generals was made subject to approval by a council of four, who were nominated by the Crown. The 1784 Act made the East India Company subordinate to the Crown in all its political functions and a further regulatory body, the Board of Control, was set up to achieve this. The members of the Board of Control were the Chancellor of the Exchequer, the Secretary of State for India and four **privy councillors** appointed by the king. The 1786 Act enabled the governor general in special cases to override his council. Executive power was therefore exercised by individual governor generals, whose appointments, although nominated by the Company, were ultimately at the discretion of the Crown.

KEY TERMS

Nabob
Originally the name for an official under the Mughal regime, the word was used in Britain in the 18th century to describe the Company employees who made their fortunes in India.

Privy Council
A body of advisers appointed to advise the monarch. In this case, it was the highest court of appeal to which those protesting against the law making *sati* (see page 143) illegal could appeal.

The relationship between the Company and parliament was also altered by the political doctrine of free trade. Although parliament renewed the Company's charter in 1813 and 1833, they drastically reduced and then ended completely the commercial monopoly on trade which the Company had previously enjoyed. The ending of this monopoly, combined with the increased territory the Company now controlled, hastened the already evolving function of the Company.

In the three presidencies, the changes in Company functions resulting in the Charter Acts of 1813 and 1833 caused Company representatives to think seriously about the way in which the territory it controlled should be administered and the ways in which the territories could be 'improved'.

- The Charter Act 1813 ended the Company's commercial monopoly on trade, except for the trade in tea and trade with China, and there were provisions within the Act for the education of Indians. Missionaries were also permitted to preach and teach English within the Company territories under the terms of the Act.

- The 1833 Act ended the Company's commercial activities completely and reorganised the administrative system of the British territories.

The change of function of the East India Company from commerce to administration meant that British representatives in India now saw themselves as ruling the territories, rather than simply engaging in and protecting their commercial interests. Instead of concentrating on trade, they were now more than ever involved in local administration and tax collection. They had been in the business of tax collecting for local princes, both Hindu and Muslim feudal overlords, for many years, but as only one aspect of their commercial activities. However, the Company's ability to put private armies on the field that were at least equal to, and often stronger than, those of indigenous rulers, was central to its increasingly widespread role as tax collector. It made sense for local rulers to ally themselves with the British to ensure protection from other rulers and to ensure the smooth collection of taxes from their subjects. An army of civil servants came into Company employment to oversee the collection of taxes, supported by the Company's armies when necessary.

EXTRACT

1 From *A New History of India* by Stanley Wolpert (2009). Wolpert is an American academic specialising in the political and intellectual history of India and Pakistan. His book was first published in 1977 and has been continuously in print since then.

British success in retaining control over India, after wresting land from indigenous powers on the field of battle, was primarily due to the methodical, evenhanded way in which newly conquered territories were 'settled'. Land revenue demands were no lower than those previously claimed by the Marathas, but peasants soon learned that once their share was paid to the British collector, they were free to live quietly for the rest of the year, unassailed by neighbouring robbers demanding another quarter or third of their wealth. The petty pilfering and princely warfare that had become endemic to the Deccan, and in fact to most of India, during the latter part of the eighteenth century was virtually eliminated by the strong hand of the British Raj in the early nineteenth century. Maratha brahmans would soon be able to tell their families in awed delight that a man could 'carry gold at the top of his walking stick from Poona to Delhi without being molested by robbers.'

The role of the governor

The governor and president of Fort William (a fort in Calcutta, in Bengal) was nominated by the Company's Court of Directors to serve a five-year term, but from 1773 the appointment was subject to the approval by the council of four, who were Crown appointments, thereby bringing the position of governor under the ultimate control of the Crown. Warren Hastings served as the first governor under the newly established system from 1774 to 1785. The other presidents of East Indian Company territory, in Madras, Bombay and Bencoolen, could not make war or accept a peace from an Indian prince without the approval of the governor in Fort William in Bengal. In 1784, parliament passed another India Act strengthening the executive power of the governor and a supplementary Act passed in 1786 enabled governors to override their council if they deemed it necessary.

The first governor appointed with these increased powers was Lord Cornwallis, fresh from the defeat at Yorktown that had effectively ended the American War of Independence. He was also appointed as commander-in-chief of the military forces of India. The 1784 Act also stipulated that the other presidencies could not make war or peace unless directed by Bengal, giving control of foreign policy to the governor of Bengal. As a result of all the India legislation passed between 1774 and 1784, government regulation and control was extended over the East India Company, especially over its political activities. During the same period, there was a centralisation of power within the three presidencies, giving the Bengali governor pre-eminence over those of the other two Company presidencies.

In 1833, as a result of the Government of India Act, the governor general of Fort William became the concurrent governor general of India. The position continued to be filled by the Board of Directors of the East India Company, but the appointment was subject to the approval of the sovereign. The new governor general of India, Sir William Bentinck, was responsible not only for the foreign policy of the territories and their administration, but was given legislative control over all the territory held by the Company. Although the governor general of Bengal and his council were technically overseen by the Board of Control in London, because of slow communications in practice they exercised huge powers and their level of autonomy was comparable to that of other governors in British colonies, who were appointed directly by the Crown. From 1833, power was given to the governor general of the 'superintendence, direction and control of the whole civil and military Government' of the whole of British India. The role of the governor had changed from the co-ordination of treaties and alliances with local rulers to being responsible for the administration and legislation of all the territory under British control. Because of the size of the subcontinent and the historic development of the British presence in India, the administration of the territories was organised within the three presidencies and each presidency retained a separate army.

ACTIVITY
KNOWLEDGE CHECK

British parliament and the East India Company

1 Construct a timeline of the Acts of Parliament from 1773 to 1833 that impacted on the East India Company.

2 Explain the impact of free trade on the changing functions of the East India Company in the early 19th century.

EXTEND YOUR KNOWLEDGE

John Stuart Mill (1806–73)
John Stuart Mill followed his father James Mill, a committed **Utilitarian**, into the East India Company and worked there for 35 years until the Company was finally dissolved. He is also famously the philosopher of classical liberalism, hugely influential as an economic theorist and a tireless campaigner for women's rights.

However, his dispatches regarding the Company's relations with native princes show that, in the case of India, he was willing to temper his doctrine of 'universal liberty' because he shared the 19th-century belief in the hierarchy of races and was therefore willing to support policies such as the doctrine of lapse (see page 146). His view regarding colonial policy was: 'Despotism is a legitimate mode of government in dealing with barbarians, provided the end be their improvement, and the means justified by actually effecting that end. Liberty, as a principle, has no application to any state of things anterior to the time when mankind have become capable of being improved by free and equal discussion.' This view is consistent with his memorandum in defence of the record of the East India Company written in 1858.

KEY TERM

Utilitarianism
The philosophy that the governing principle of rulers should be the effort to secure the greatest happiness for the greatest number. Utilitarian thought was the basis for significant social reform in 19th-century Britain including education, poor law reform, the employment of children and women and the reform of prisons. The original philosopher of utilitarianism was Jeremy Bentham and Governor Bentinck wrote regarding his posting in India 'I shall govern in name, but it will be you who will govern in fact'.

The importance of Bengal and the Company army

The Company had established three private armies in the mid-18th century to protect its commercial interests. By 1820, the troops numbered 200,000, more than in most European states. They were based in the three presidencies of the Company and there were white regiments and local, or **sepoy**, regiments under the command of European officers. Native regiments were recruited en masse in particular areas and villages and the Europeans had clear ideas about which religions and **castes** were the most warlike. From the mid-18th century, there were also a small number of British army regiments dispatched from Britain to serve as backup to the Company armies. By 1857, there were 45,522 European soldiers of all ranks in India out of a total of 277,746 soldiers, the rest being sepoys.

KEY TERMS

Sepoy
An Indian soldier serving under British or European command.

Caste
Each of the hereditary religious groups of Hindu society, distinguished by relative degrees of ritual purity or pollution and of social status. The Bengali army was traditionally recruited from the highest castes, the Brahmins and the Rajputs. These castes were most likely to be concerned about possible pollution and loss of caste.

The Company armies were the force that ensured that local rulers signed treaties with the Company in order to protect themselves against other local rulers or simply as an act of self-preservation in the face of British military superiority. In addition, the armies supported the Company's tax collection and administrative roles. Their strength and increasing professionalisation meant that British territory in India controlled by the Company increased to 243,000 km^2 by 1800 as successive governor generals, notably Sir Richard Wellesley (governor general 1798–1805), sought to increase Company territory and eradicate any pockets of remaining French influence in the subcontinent.

The officers of the East India Company armies were trained from 1809 at the Addiscombe Military Seminary in Surrey, the sister of the college established to train Company civil servants at Haileybury. Service in the presidency armies offered the promise of almost constant military engagement to its recruits, unlike the regular army which was experiencing a period of calm, following the defeat of Napoleon at Waterloo in 1815. The increased focus on the training of both the Company's civil servants and military personnel reflected the changing Company focus to civil administration in India in the 19th century, as it developed beyond being a purely commercial company with hired mercenaries. Recruits shared the values and same sense of cultural superiority as the Company's Civil Service intake.

Between 1829 and 1853, the Company fought a number of campaigns in the north-west in Afghanistan, Sind and the Punjab with varying success. It had successfully annexed Assam, Manipur and Cacher between 1823 and 1826 (although at significant financial cost) and, in the late 1830s, its attention turned to the far more difficult proposition of subduing the north-west frontier.

The British obsession with the north-west frontier was fuelled by their fear of a Russian invasion, either through Afghanistan or, if Russia were to extend its influence in Persia, through Sind. The First Afghan War from 1838 to 1842 was predictably enough a disaster and was nicknamed 'Auckland's folly' after the governor general who was foolish enough to be persuaded by his young secretary to meddle in the internal politics of Afghanistan without the promised support of the local ruler in the Punjab. The utterly futile war cost British India 20,000 lives (one man reached safety in Jallalabad) and more than £15 million. The impact of the disaster was to resonate through the century as the British attempted to bring Afghanistan under its control. Its immediate impact, however, was to make the Company determined to secure Sind and the Punjab in compensatory conquest.

Sind was formally annexed in 1843, following a decisive campaign, but conquering the Punjab took most of the 1840s until it was completely brought under British control by 1849. British soldiers were left with a strong sense of admiration for the warlike Sikhs and their admiration for Sikh soldiers was repaid during the Indian Rebellion when the Sikhs supported the British against the rebellious local soldiers, partly as a result of long-held grievances relating to the Anglo-Sikh wars of annexation, which had been fought in part by sepoy regiments of different religions. The bitterness which the Punjabi soldiers nursed towards the native sepoys of the Bengali Company army illustrates the complicated local tensions that the Company was so successfully able to exploit as it expanded its presence in the subcontinent.

Bengal

Bengal was the most important presidency in the Company in the 19th century and its president was the governor general of all the territory controlled by the East India Company following the passing of the Government of India Act 1833. The Battle of Plassey in 1757 had been followed by the annexation of the province of Bengal by the Company and the start of proper territorial expansion by the British. So Bengal's role as the heart of Company power was unsurprising. The administrative structure of Bengal was developed under the governor generalship of Lord Cornwallis (1786–93) and the system laid down in his Code of Regulations was the framework of Indian government for nearly two centuries. Land was divided into districts under a collector and landholders were settled with rights to land in return for fixed tax liabilities. Collectors were, in turn, supervised by the Board of Revenue at Calcutta. Legal administration was placed in the hands of local judges and magistrates, who were supervised by regional courts of appeal. Until 1911, Calcutta was the capital of British India and the building of the initial British trading factory of Fort William can still be seen in modern-day Kolkata.

Reflecting the central role of Fort William in the life of the Company, the army of the Bengal presidency was twice the size of the other two armies. Traditionally, the Bengali presidency army was recruited largely from among the higher castes, in contrast to the recruitment of the other two Company armies. The caste groups within the Bengal army held particular privileges, which they guarded jealously, and they were extremely sensitive to anything which might pollute their caste. According to Company policy, the sepoys of the Bengali army were not recruited locally but from other provinces, particularly from neighbouring Awadh. As the principal army of the Company, they played a pivotal role in the annexation of the Punjab and the resulting enmity of the Sikhs towards the sepoys was part of the explanation for British survival during the rebellion in 1857.

A Level Exam-Style Question Section B

'The power of the Company army was the most significant cause of the increasing British presence in India in the early 19th century.'

How far do you agree with this statement? Explain your answer. (20 marks)

Tip

Consider the changing function of the East India Company as a result of government intervention.

ACTIVITY
KNOWLEDGE CHECK

Late 18th-century and early 19th-century East India Company rule of India

1 What were the reasons for the increasing territorial presence of the Company in India in the 18th century?

2 Construct a diagram showing the relationship between the British government and the Company, and the structure of the Company in India in 1833.

WHAT WERE THE CAUSES AND SIGNIFICANCE OF THE CLASH OF CULTURES BETWEEN THE BRITISH AND THE INDIANS?

By 1829, although the Company maintained flourishing commercial divisions in China and the Far East, in India it had reinvented itself to concentrate on administration and taxation rather than seeing its function as primarily commercial. Driven by their perception of racial superiority, Company operators were becoming less tolerant of local customs and religions, and increasingly seeking to change the societies which they now governed as a result of the Mughal Empire's disintegration. Its administrators were also governed less by motives of pure profit and increasingly sought to modernise and 'improve' India for the benefit of the native population.

A sense of cultural superiority was emerging in the Company staff, which resulted in the paternalistic desire to change and 'improve' Indians. The early 'white Mughals' had not suffered from the delusion of cultural superiority. The wealth and complexity of Mughal civilisation and the luxury goods that they obtained from the subcontinent in no way gave the early East India Company factors a sense of cultural superiority. Indeed, in many ways, life in Stuart and Georgian England was vastly inferior to the life enjoyed by the Mughal elite in India and many nabobs preferred to adopt a local lifestyle, which was far more pleasant than the one they might enjoy back in Britain.

By the 19th century, this racial harmony was being challenged by the growth of **evangelical** Christianity and the arrival of more British women in India. Committed Christians challenged inequality where they found it, resulting in laudable campaigns like that for the abolition of slavery. However, they also judged other religions, and by extension societies, to be inferior, because they were not Christian. Increasingly, missionaries attempted to convert the Muslims, Hindus, Sikhs and Buddhists whom they found on the subcontinent, and this often destabilised local social systems.

The arrival of more and more British women reinforced a sense of growing cultural division between the Company employees and Indians. Increasingly, British women came out to India to find themselves husbands and, with their arrival, the division between races became fixed. Victor Jacquemont, a French botanist visiting India wrote in 1830: 'Portionless girls who have not succeeded in getting married in England arrive here in cargoes for sale on honourable terms, I mean to young civil and military officers.'

The impact of the arrival of British women in India was that the racial intermingling that had been commonplace in the 18th century now became socially taboo. Mixed-race children were not accepted in the developing white 'society' in India and, while an English man could visit the home of another English man with an Indian wife or partner, no English woman would do so. William Dalrymple, in his book *White Mughals*, found that in 1780, one-third of Company men left wills making provision for native spouses or cohabitees and their children. By 1850, the wills of Company men show that only a tiny proportion of men were involved in relationships with Indian women.

As a result of the modernising agenda of the East India Company between 1829 and 1857, partially derived from the changing perceptions of race and partly from the changing functions of the Company, a number of grievances built up in the native populations under British rule. These tensions found their ultimate expression in the Indian Rebellion which resulted in the end of Company rule and the establishment of the British Raj. The rebellion was fundamentally a reaction to the challenge the British presented to traditional religious and social structures. Discontent rumbled throughout the modernising decades, which meant that, when a mutiny broke out in the Bengali army in 1857, it quickly became a much wider uprising as different social groups were inspired to raise their own local rebellions in response to the news of the army mutiny.

Historians, and indeed the Victorians themselves, identified a number of changes made by the British as the cause of the deep undercurrents of discontent that were ignited by the actions of the sepoys in Meerut in May 1857. Between 1833 and 1857, the Governors Bentinck and Dalhousie, both heavily influenced by Jeremy Bentham and Utilitarianism, instituted significant civil reform. Their reforms demonstrate the new Company preoccupation with the 'modernisation' of India and were controversial and, in the case of Dalhousie, nearly disastrous. Bentinck's actions included the

KEY TERM

Evangelical
In this context, it denotes a member of a new tradition within the Protestant churches interested not only in individual salvation but the salvation of others through missionary efforts.

abolition of *thagi* and *sati* and the decision to allocate Company funds for education to only English-speaking institutions and to make English the official language of government and the higher legal courts. Dalhousie's actions were less altruistically driven than Bentinck's and were characterised by considerable impatience with the social structures and 'inefficiency' of the princely states which he sought to annex to be run by the British whenever possible.

SOURCE 1

Major William Palmer with his second wife, the Mughal princess Bibi Faiz Bakhsh (1785). The painting was originally attributed to Johann Zoffany and later to Francesco Renaldi. Major Palmer served in the Bengali Artillery and as military secretary under Governor Warren Hastings.

SOURCE 2

From Macaulay's *Minute on Indian Education* (1835). Thomas Babington Macaulay was a British historian and Whig politician. He served as secretary to the Board of Control and in 1833 was appointed as the first law member of the Governor General's Council, travelling to India and serving on the Supreme Court from 1834 to 1838. His Minute (a policy document) was formative in Governor William Bentinck's decisions regarding the public funding of Indian education.

Whoever knows [English] has ready access to all the vast intellectual wealth, which all the wisest nations of the earth have created and hoarded in the course of ninety generations. It may be safely said, that the literature now extant in that language is of far greater value than all the literature which three hundred years ago was extant in all the languages of the world together. The question now before us is simply whether, when it is in our power to teach this language, we shall teach languages, by which, by universal confession, there are not books on any subject which deserve to be compared to our own; whether, when we can teach European science, we shall teach systems which, by universal confession, whenever they differ from those of Europe, differ for the worse; and whether, when we can patronise sound Philosophy and true History, we shall countenance, at the public expense, medical doctrines, which would disgrace an English farrier, –Astronomy, which would move laughter in girls at an English boarding school,–History, abounding with kings thirty feet high, and reigns thirty thousand years long,–and Geography, made up of seas of treacle and seas of butter.

Thagi
An Urdu word for those who practised highway robbery and ritual murder by strangling in the service of the Hindu mother goddess, Kali. Common variants of the word include *thugi* and *thuggee*. The English word 'thug' comes from the same source. In Urdu, it is written *t̤hagī*.

William Sleeman's campaign against *thagi*

Legal assaults began under Bentinck in the 1830s on the practice of ***thagi*** (highway robbery and ritual murder). Between 1836 and 1848, a number of legal Acts were passed outlawing *thagi* and *dacoity* (a form of banditry) and the suppression of the *thagi* became a justification for further 'modernisation' by the British. The campaign, led by Colonel William Sleeman, began in 1835, following his capture of a *thagi*, Feringhea (also known as Syeed Amir Ali), on whose life the 1839 novel, *Confessions of a Thug* was based. Feringhea confessed and described the practices of the secret network to Sleeman, who then energetically devoted himself to its eradication. The Thugge and Dacoity Department was created in 1835, with Sleeman as its first superintendent, and a vigorous and highly publicised campaign ensued during which more than 1,000 *thagi* were transported or hanged for their crimes and around 3,000 tried and punished in total. The campaign was based on capturing *thagi* and then using their confessions to track down and capture others. The campaign and the suppression of *thagi*, documented in no small part by Sleeman's three books on the subject, created a sensation throughout the Empire. The action against *thagi* led to significant amounts of self-congratulation on the part of the British as the *thagi* only attacked other Indians, so the suppression of the cult was depicted as a wholly altruistic act.

SOURCE

Two *thagi* point to the sky to distract their victim as another thagi creeps up behind to strangle him. From a drawing by an unknown Indian artist for Captain James Paton, Assistant Resident at Lucknow 1829–40. Paton was personally involved in the campaign to eradicate *thagi*.

The *thagi* activity was most prevalent in central and northern India. Bands of up to 400 *thagi* existed; they acted in small groups preying on travellers by befriending and accompanying them on their journeys, before stealing from them and garrotting them. Their practices were obscure, but their criminality was based on worship of the Hindu goddess Kali and the belief that they were predetermined to kill their victims (and steal their money) thereby releasing their victims into their next life. Sleeman's activities in the suppression of the *thagi* led to his identification as a true imperial hero in Britain. His tales of adventures among the thugs were of intrepid adventure, laced with exciting descriptions of Orientalist religion and with a strong moral tone, as the entire campaign was intended to protect native Indians from the 'menace'. Queen Victoria requested proof copies and *thagi* stories persisted throughout the century, with Sleeman's nephew claiming in the 1890s that they had been responsible for up to a million deaths.

Actual *thagi* activity seems to have been largely dealt with by Sleeman's efforts in the 1830s. Although there has been some revisionism regarding Sleeman's presentation of the *thagi* campaign by historians, its suppression does not seem to have been widely resented by Indians at the time, unlike other campaigns resulting from the 'modernising' agenda. Of far greater significance was its impact on the British in India and the lessons they drew from the campaign for other 'necessary' social reforms.

The drive against *sati* and female infanticide

If the campaign against *thagi* was accepted and even welcomed by Indians at the time, the Act of Abolition in 1829 against *sati* was not. *Sati* was the tradition of self-immolation by Hindu widows on the funeral pyres of their husbands. The tradition reflected the Hindu belief in the sanctity of the marriage bond which meant that remarriage was not an option for widows. The custom was most common among higher castes and the caste of those involved suggests that the motivation was primarily religious belief rather than economic necessity. *Sati* occurred most commonly in the Bengal presidency and the Sikh Punjabi kingdom, which was outside British jurisdiction in 1829. The British estimated that around 600 deaths a year in their territories were taking place as a result of the custom and, in 1829, driven by a campaign by evangelical Christians such as Wilberforce (see page 13) and Governor Bentinck's own strongly held personal views, *sati* was abolished. Anyone assisting with a *sati* was deemed to be guilty of culpable homicide and prosecuted accordingly.

British Company officials disliked the practice and had tried to discourage it for years, but there were serious concerns about the impact of such a ban on the local population. Without the personal agenda of Bentinck, it is unlikely that abolition would have been implemented as early as 1829 and his long and detailed minute from which Source 4 is taken, shows that he even gave serious thought to the possible consequences of introducing the ban.

SOURCE 4

From Sir William Bentinck's Minute on *sati*, November 1829. This Minute, or policy note, was circulated by the governor general to Company officials shortly before Bentinck and the council made the practice illegal by law.

Whether the question be to continue or to discontinue the practice of *sati*, the decision is equally surrounded by an awful responsibility. To consent to the consignment year after year of hundreds of innocent victims to a cruel and untimely end, when the power exists of preventing it, is a predicament which no conscience can contemplate without horror. But, on the other hand, if heretofore received opinions are to be considered of any value, to put to hazard by a contrary course the very safety of the British Empire in India, and to extinguish at once all hopes of those great improvements—affecting the condition not of hundreds and thousands but of millions—which can only be expected from the continuance of our supremacy, is an alternative which even in the light of humanity itself may be considered as a still greater evil....

When we had powerful neighbours and had greater reason to doubt our own security, expediency might recommend an indirect and more cautious proceeding, but now that we are supreme my opinion is decidedly in favour of an open, avowed, and general prohibition, resting altogether upon the moral goodness of the act and our power to enforce it; and so decided is my feeling against any half measure that, were I not convinced of the safety of total abolition, I certainly should have advised the cessation of all interference.

The first and primary object of my heart is the benefit of the Hindus. I know nothing so important to the improvement of their future condition as the establishment of a purer morality, whatever their belief, and a more just conception of the will of God. The first step to this better understanding will be dissociation of religious belief and practice from blood and murder... I disown in these remarks, or in this measure, any view whatever to conversion to our own faith. I write and feel as a legislator for the Hindus, and as I believe many enlightened Hindus think and feel.

Descending from these higher considerations, it cannot be a dishonest ambition that the Government of which I form a part should have the credit of an act which is to wash out a foul stain upon British rule....

A Level Exam-Style Question Section A

Study Source 4 before you answer this question.

Assess the value of the source for revealing the attitude of Lord Bentinck towards Indian customs and to his understanding of the nature and purpose of British rule in India.

Explain your answer, using the source, the information given about its origin and your own knowledge about the historical context. (20 marks)

Tip

Use the text and the source to help you discuss the impact of Utilitarianism on the British government of India in the 1820s and 1830s.

The Company banned the practice in Calcutta itself in 1798 and in 1813 William Wilberforce had forced amendment to the 1813 Charter Law to allow missionaries to preach against *sati* and other Hindu practices. The Company initiated the collection of statistics relating to *sati* in the remainder of their territories from 1815 and a vigorous campaign for abolition was also waged by the Hindu religious philosopher and polymath, Ram Mohan Roy. He began to campaign against the practice in 1818, following the death of his sister-in-law, who was forced to commit *sati*. Roy did, however, counsel Bentinck against the ban in 1829, judging it to be too contentious and preferring instead to try to persuade people to change their minds by reasoning with them. Once the ban was in place, however, he supported Bentinck against efforts made to reverse the law and presented evidence to the Privy Council in Britain, arguing that the law should remain in force. The Privy Council upheld Bentinck's law against the petitioners in 1832 and dismissed their appeal.

The law only applied in territory under the control of the Company, although with British encouragement many of the **princely states** followed the example of the British in the 1830s and 1840s. Most *sati* that continued occurred in the Punjab, until the Sikh kingdom finally came under British control. The practice was outlawed in the totality of India in 1861, although cases continued throughout the 19th century and occasionally occur today. For higher caste Indians who practised *sati*, the interference by the British was a deliberate attack on caste purity and the presumption of cultural superiority inherent in the new law rankled.

KEY TERM

Princely state
A state in the subcontinent that had not yet been conquered by the British and was ruled by local rulers, either Hindu or Muslim. Also known as a native state.

SOURCE

From Sir Charles Napier, commander-in-chief 1849–51, cited in his brother William Napier's book *History of General Sir Charles Napier's Administration of Scinde* (1851). Napier summed up the position of many of the British officials when he replied to Hindu priests complaining about the abolition of *sati* with the following response.

'This burning of widows is your custom; prepare the funeral pile. But my nation has also a custom. When men burn women alive we hang them, and confiscate all their property. My carpenters shall therefore erect gibbets on which to hang all concerned when the widow is consumed. Let us all act according to national customs.'

In addition to the banning of *sati*, Bentinck enforced the laws that had been passed in 1795 and 1802 against female infanticide. The practice of killing girl babies at birth was common in Rajputana, Maharashtra and some parts of northern India. It stemmed from the difficulty of providing dowries for female children and the shame attached to having unmarried daughters.

Bentinck's efforts materially improved the lot of women in India and, as such, are worthy of celebration. However, they did represent a new departure in terms of government intervention in Indian society, and in the case of *sati* of ritual religious practice, and both interventions contributed to the rumbling discontent towards British rule which existed in the 1830s and 1840s.

The impact of missionaries

British missionaries began to arrive in India in the late 18th century, despite the opposition of many Company officials to them. The East India Company officials were nothing if not pragmatic and were anxious to avoid trouble in the territory they controlled as a result of a clash of belief systems.

The first missionaries to arrive in Bengal before the end of the 18th century, the Baptists, Joshua Marsham, William Carey and William Ward, were banned from Calcutta and forced to settle in the nearby Danish territory of Serampore. The Baptist mission concentrated on education and translation of the Bible into Bengali. In 1818, they set up a college for the training of indigenous ministers for the growing local church.

Baptists were not the only evangelicals active in seeking a foothold in India. Charles Grant, an Anglican and member of the Clapham Sect, having worked for the Company in India from 1767 to 1790, campaigned with William Wilberforce to remove the Company's ban on missionaries. By the Charter Act 1813, their influence in London was powerful enough to insist on the removal of the Company's blanket ban on missionaries and the first missionaries arrived in the Bengal presidency. From the Charter Act onwards, Protestant missionaries arrived in increasing number in India.

Both the Anglicans (the London Missionary Society and the Church Missionary Society) and Baptists (Baptist Missionary Society) were primarily engaged in the education of Indians in their native languages, but they also exercised their influence in campaigns against traditions like *sati*. In 1830, Alexander Duff, a missionary from the Church of Scotland, arrived in Bengal and he promoted the teaching of English in schools with the intention of attracting higher caste Hindus to Christianity, as he believed that the teaching of English was attractive to Indians ambitious for their children's futures and that Bible studies taught by English schools would naturally convince students that Christianity was superior to Hinduism. His work was very influential in the development of Bentinck's educational policy, the principles of which were described by Macaulay in his Minute on Indian Education in 1835 (see Source 2).

SOURCE

6

From Charles Grant, member of the Clapham Sect and superintendent of the Board of Trade under Cornwallis, in the pamphlet *Observations on the State of Society among the Asiatic Subjects of Great Britain*, written in 1792 and placed before the Company's Board of Directors in 1797. In 1813, on the orders of the House of Commons, it was published. It was a plea for the toleration of the educational and missionary work of evangelicals in India in the 1790s.

It is not... the introduction of a new set of ceremonies, not even a new creed, that is the ultimate object here. Those who conceive religion to be conversant merely about forms and speculative notions, may well think that the world need not be much troubled concerning it. No, the ultimate object is moral improvement. The preeminent excellence of the morality which the Gospel teaches, and the superior efficacy of this divine system, taken in all its parts, in meliorating the condition of human society, cannot be denied by those who are unwilling to admit its higher claims; and on this ground only, the dissemination of it must be beneficial to mankind.

A fundamental aspect of missionary work was education and missionaries were generally very competent linguists in vernacular languages to enable them to preach and convert native peoples. However, they also made a significant contribution to the debate that raged from 1813 until 1835 on the allocation of Company funding for higher education for Indians. The evangelical voice was strongly in favour of higher education for Indians being in English, hoping that a new 'educated' class of Indians would rise up and weaken the traditional dominance of the **Brahmin** caste, translating the new ideas they had learned back into their native languages and disseminating Western ideas and thought. The Education Act 1835 and Bentinck's decision to make English, not Persian, the language of government and the higher legal courts partially resulted from this evangelical pressure.

In some ways, the activities of early missionaries can be credited with stimulating the **Bengal Renaissance,** of which Ram Mohan Roy was such a notable exponent. He articulated a complex response to Western philosophy and learning, which attempted to adapt elements of all that he considered best in Indian and Western learning. Other responses to the missionaries were more conservative and resistant to any Western influence. The outcome of this philosophical debate by Indians in response to Western influences was to make Bengal the centre of Indian cultural thought and learning. Indian interest in their own religious traditions and philosophy was in many ways vitalised by missionary influence and in no way did Western ideas sweep the ancient languages and philosophies away.

KEY TERMS

Brahmin
Varna or caste within Hinduism specialising as priests and protectors of sacred learning across generations.

Bengal Renaissance
An Indian social reform movement which grew out of reinterpreting Indian religious philosophy. The thinkers who founded the movement were familiar with both Western and Eastern philosophies and created a complex fusion of the two traditions.

The arrival of missionaries threw yet another group into India's complex social mix and added to the undercurrents of opposition that Company officials faced in trying to tax and administer their territories. Although administrators often shared the cultural prejudices and perceptions of missionaries, their appetite for sweeping change was always tempered by the realities of having to govern successfully and continue to collect taxes. Missionaries were often the bugbear of local officials as they were driven to carry out what they believed to be God's work, regardless of the trouble they might stir up by their actions. They were physically much closer to the Indians and, as they were poor and insisted on living alongside the Indians, this proximity was often the cause of specific local tensions. Their presence was another long-term destabilising factor and, at a local level, Indian society was alive with different strands of opposition to Company consolidation of power. Throughout the 1830s and 1840s, there was resistance to the British in all the regions they governed and across caste and social groups. The British, a tiny minority in the subcontinent, were able to maintain their control on power because resistance to them was localised and sprang up at different times in reaction to particular sets of events.

EXTRACT

2

From *A New History of India*, by Stanley Wolport (2009). The academic describes the uneasy relationship between British administrators and missionaries in his well-respected general history of India.

The struggle between British officials, whose primary concern was survival through stability, and British preachers or lay reformers, who were preoccupied with salvation through conversion or reform, was to remain a source of tension in the superstructure of the new Raj throughout the nineteenth century. It would in fact, never be fully resolved until the end of British rule, for Britons were no more united on how to handle and rule their Indian Empire than Indians were in their responses to the consolidation of British rule. The simple motivating force of greed that had nurtured British factors through the hardships of the seventeenth century, mixed as it was with a lust for power that helped them to survive the rigors of Mughal collapse and French antipathy in the eighteenth was suddenly thrown into a state of confusion by such complex questions as international conscience and concern for "civilising" India's "poor, benighted native souls".

ACTIVITY
KNOWLEDGE CHECK

Changing Company policy in 19th-century India

1 How did attitudes to Indians change in the 19th century, and why?

2 What was the impact of Utilitarianism on Company policy in the 1830s?

WHAT WERE THE IMMEDIATE CAUSES OF THE OUTBREAK OF REBELLION IN 1857 AND WHY WERE THE BRITISH ABLE TO RETAIN CONTROL OF INDIA?

The reforms of Dalhousie

James Andrew Broun-Ramsay, 1st Marquess of Dalhousie, was one of India's most energetic governor generals. To his critics, he was the man responsible for ending Company rule in India through his reckless policies. He served as governor general from 1848 to 1856, during which time the Punjab was pacified and locked into Company rule, its fertile soil yielding a substantial revenue surplus for the Company, the first Indian railroads were constructed, the first telegraph line was laid and the Penny Post was introduced. Dalhousie was an energetic moderniser and committed Utilitarian, devoted to his vision of an improved India. Having subdued the Punjab, he turned his attention to the princely states of central India. He saw no reason to continue with alliances with the princely states which had been agreed when the Company was a less powerful entity in the subcontinent, especially as he viewed the princes as conservative forces getting in the way of his vital modernisations.

His solution, to the annoyance of dilettante native rulers, who had previously been treated by the Company as foreign or semi-independent powers, was to simply redefine them as being under the ultimate British authority. By assuming British **paramountcy**, he drew up the conditions in which it was stated that the British would and should intervene in the affairs of a native state. The first condition for British interference was in the case of the death of a native ruler without a legitimate heir. In such cases, under the **doctrine of lapse**, the princely line was deemed to have 'lapsed' and therefore the state passed directly into British control. This was in direct conflict with Hindu law, which allowed for the succession of an adopted son in such cases. The second condition for British interference was the misgovernment of a state. The third condition, in which intervention was judged to be legal, was created by the redefinition of a number of ruler's titles and powers as non-hereditary and therefore also subject to the doctrine of lapse.

The annexation of Awadh

Dalhousie's annexation of Awadh in 1856 occurred under the doctrine of lapse and was Dalhousie's worst blunder and a primary cause of the rebellion the following year that ended Company rule and whose echoes were to reverberate throughout the rest of the British Empire until it was dismantled in the 20th century. Nwab Wajid Ali Shah was deposed after being accused of maladministration. In his personal life, Shah certainly conformed to British prejudices regarding debouched and extravagant princes. More importantly, Awadh was a prosperous province and one which it would benefit the Company to control. It was taken by the British on 7 February 1856, the seventh annexation to occur under the new Dalhousie policy.

The annexation was widely resented in Awadh, the traditional recruiting ground of the sepoys of the Company's Bengali army. Determined to reform the state, the British announced that land would be taken from all *talukdars* (landowners) unable to prove legal title to their estates. As each landowner was responsible for large retinues of relations and servants living with them, the British attack on the established social order was deeply destabilising. In 1857, Awadh was one of the areas which saw widespread participation in the uprising against the British, as what began as a mutiny became a rebellion.

Outbreak of rebellion and events in Meerut

The immediate cause of the Indian Rebellion were rumours amongst the sepoys that new cartridges were about to be issued, lubricated with animal fat, placing both Hindus and Muslims at risk of defilement, as beef fat was repugnant to Hindus and pork to Muslims. To many sepoys, it seemed to prove Britain's dark plan for the Christianisation of India and the rumour proved to be the spark that ignited all the simmering resentments held against missionaries, for interference in religious practices and the choice of English as the official language and finally for the upheaval and disturbance to the pattern of rural landownership in Awadh.

KEY TERMS

Doctrine of lapse and paramountcy
An annexation policy devised by Dalhousie which stated that any princely state under direct influence of the British should be annexed if the ruler was incompetent or died without an heir. Paramountcy over Indian states had been claimed by the British since 1813, but Dalhousie's policies of intervention were an extension of this principle. After 1857, the British supported the incumbents of the princely states rather than attempting to remove them and annex their territories.

Talukdar
An Indian landholder in Mughal and British times with responsibility for tax collection.

SOURCE

From a letter written on the eve of the Indian Rebellion in 1857, from a British captain, Captain Martineau, commander of the Ambala musketry depot at the headquarters of the Bengali army to Captain Septimus Becher in Simla.

Feeling... is as bad as can be and matters have gone so far that I can hardly devise any suitable remedy. We make a grand mistake in supposing that because we dress, arm and drill Hindustani soldiers as Europeans, they become one bit European in their feelings and ideas. I see them on parade for say two hours a day, but what do I know of them in the other 22? What do they talk about in their lines, what do they plot? For all I can tell I might as well be in Siberia. I know that at the present moment an unusual agitation is pervading the ranks of the entire native army, but what it will exactly result in, I am afraid to say. I can detect the new approach of the storm, I can hear the moaning of the hurricane, but I can't say how, when, or where it will break forth... If a flare up from any cause takes place at one station it will spread and become universal.

The Bengal army was already in a state of unrest following the General Service Enlistment Act 1856, which broke the long-held tradition by which soldiers of the Bengali army did not serve where they were unable to march, as travel over water would pollute their caste status. Canning, the new governor general, wanted to rectify what he saw as an anomaly so that he could use the army alongside the other two company armies in Burma. The Act only applied to new recruits, but the sepoys feared that eventually they too would be forced to serve abroad. As recruitment in the Bengal army traditionally drew very largely from the higher caste Hindus, this was a very contentious issue.

Following the court martial of 85 sepoys for refusing to load the new rifles in Meerut on 9 May 1857, all three sepoy regiments rose in revolt while the British were at church, freeing the original mutineers and then proceeding to massacre all the local Europeans, including women and children.

Cawnpore and Delhi

The mutiny spread rapidly throughout the rest of the Bengal army, and the fact that the British had only a single European regiment between Calcutta and Agra meant that virtually nothing could be done to stop the mutineers. The army mutiny rapidly became a more general revolt spreading through the Indo-Gangetic Plain and the British temporarily lost control of Awadh, the old Mughal capital Delhi and some centres within the Punjab. In Awadh, the mutiny proved to be the spark which ignited a wider revolt as the discontented *talukdars* were joined in opposition to the British by those with familial links to the sepoys of the Bengali army. The situation was complicated by peasant uprisings, whose grievances were centred on local issues around changing land structures and excessive tax collection. Local leaders emerged as the head of anti-British forces, including the surprising female, the Rani of Jhansi, who died in battle.

EXTEND YOUR KNOWLEDGE

The Rani of Jhansi

The Rani of Jhansi is famous for her participation in the rebellion in 1857 and her death in battle, defending her claim against the British. Examination of her story illustrates several important aspects of the rebellion resulting from the breakdown in British authority. These include the fighting which was common between Indians in 1857 and the weakness of the British at the onset of the unrest.

The Rani's husband, the Raja of Jhansi, had left the walled city and hereditary title to her and their adopted son, and she was then removed by the British under the doctrine of lapse. Nevertheless, she raised an army for her own protection at the beginning of the rebellion, reasserting some of the power that she had lost and she agreed to hold the area for the British authorities

The British suspected the Rani of playing a double game and alleged that she was involved in the massacre of Europeans and their wives following the rising of the 12th native Bengali army. During the chaos of the rebellion, Jhansi was attacked by two native allies of the British who wished to seize power themselves. The Rani appealed to the British for help. This was not forthcoming, but the Rani successfully repelled the invaders and the region remained peaceful under her rule throughout 1857.

When the British finally arrived in Jhansi in March 1858, they demanded the surrender of the city and the Rani refused saying, 'We fight for independence'. Her escape before the surrender of the city was popularly believed to have taken place by jumping the walls of the city on her horse with her son tied to her back. It took a further two months for the British to defeat her and kill her. She became a symbol of the 'nationalist' resistance to the British.

On 11 May, Bahadur Shah II, the last of the Mughal dynasty, was 'restored', reluctantly, to his imperial position in Delhi as the mutineering regiments arrived at the ancient capital. Had he been younger or more ambitious, he could have presented a serious threat to the British by attempting to rally the ancient Mughal heartlands in his support. However, the initial blow struck by the Meerut sepoys stagnated in Delhi and he and his sons did not emerge as national leaders against the British.

Nevertheless, the Rebellion dealt some stinging blows to the British. In Cawnpore, Sir Hugh Wheeler had not been careful enough in his preparations and the British held out for only 18 days before surrendering on 27 June, having been promised safe conduct in boats down the river to Allahabad. During the transfer onto the boats, fighting broke out and 400 were killed on the riverbanks and in the boats. The remaining British, mostly women and children, numbering around 200 people, were held, possibly for use as hostages, but were massacred on 15 July, the day before relief arrived.

SOURCE

8 An illustration by A.D. McCormick (1860-1943) depicting the massacre that took place at Cawnpore during the Indian Rebellion. McCormick was a notable British illustrator of historical and naval scenes. The illustration appeared in *India*, by Victor Surridge, as part of the Romance of Empire series. Its exact publication date is not known.

Siege and relief of Lucknow

If Cawnpore was the British at their most vulnerable, Lucknow emerged as an enduring symbol of British resistance. The governor (also known as the resident), Sir Henry Lawrence, had read the situation accurately and shepherded his Europeans into the fortified residency from the end of May, with enough food and ammunition that Lucknow was able to hold out against attack for five months. The siege of Lucknow commenced at the end of June and Lawrence died on 4 July having been hit by an exploding shell. (The epitaph on his tomb reads, 'Here lies Henry Lawrence who tried to do his duty'.) Successful relief eventually reached Lucknow, with a force numbering over 3,000, made up of six British infantry battalions and one Sikh battalion; previous efforts had failed to penetrate through Awadh, which was in full rebellion. The first relief reached Lucknow on 25 September, 87 days after the siege had begun.

It was not possible to evacuate Lucknow immediately due to the casualties that the relief effort had sustained, but the defended area was extended and their decision to remain in the Residency rather than fight their way out was influenced by the discovery of buried stores of which Lawrence's second-in-command was unaware, which were sufficient to provide for both those who had entered the Residency in May and the new arrivals for the next two months. The second relief was led by the new commander-in-chief, Sir Colin Campbell, and fought their way into the Residency between 14 and 17 November. Twenty-four Victoria Crosses were awarded for actions which took place on 16 November, the highest number ever awarded in a single day. Because Campbell deemed the area to be so volatile and was conscious of his stretched supply lines, Lucknow was evacuated and abandoned and the area was not retaken by the British until March 1858.

ACTIVITY
KNOWLEDGE CHECK

The Indian Rebellion

1 Complete a mind map of the causes of the rebellion. Highlight the causes that resulted from changing policies in British rule in one colour and those that resulted from the structure of British rule in another.

2 Explain why the rebellion was most serious in Awadh.

A Level Exam-Style Question Section B

How accurate is it to say that the Indian Rebellion occurred because of the attack on Indian religion and customs by the British in the years leading up the 1857? (20 marks)

Tip
Consider all the factors that led Indians to rebel.

SOURCE
9

SOURCE
9 The Lucknow flag flew over the ruined Residency, as it had continued to fly during the siege, until it was finally lowered at Indian Independence in 1947. This photograph originally appeared in the *Illustrated London News* in 1947, shortly after Indian Independence.

Reasons why the British retained control

Although the rebellion was shattering in its impact, the survival of the British on the subcontinent was assured for two reasons.

- The rebels were not a cohesive force. There were mutineers, aggrieved landowners in Awadh, peasants expressing their resentment against local land and taxation policies and local leaders unwilling to co-operate together to forge a national revolt. The centres of the revolt in Delhi, Lucknow and Cawnpore each had their own centres of power converged around rebel leaders, two Muslim rulers and one Hindu Maratha, so once the British had regrouped they simply needed to eliminate one centre of resistance after another. Awadh came closest to representing a unified challenge from all social levels to the British because of British actions in the province and the familial links to the mutineering sepoys of the Bengali army, but this was not replicated anywhere else in India.

- The other two presidency armies remained loyal to the British and the area around Calcutta itself remained unaffected by the unrest. Indeed, the Punjabi sepoys, still nursing a grudge against the sepoys of the Bengali army, proved key in suppressing the rebellion. Even in Lucknow, the centre of disaffected Awadh, about half of the 7,000 soldiers who sought refuge in the Residency were Indian soldiers and camp followers. When Delhi was retaken by the British, 82 percent of the soldiers killed in the action were native sepoys.

The British had gained a foothold, and then ascendency, in the subcontinent because they were able to exploit local religious and political divisions. This was a key reason for their continued survival after the rebellion, always referred to by the British as the 'Indian Mutiny' to reduce its importance. The competing rebel power blocs were unable to forget their differences to unify against the British and drive them out, and in many cases the alliances forged between the British and local allies proved enduring. Ultimately too, there were many good things attached to British rule in India. Indians in many areas had originally been prepared to pay taxes to the Company because they were better than the local alternative on offer and this remained the case. British rule remained acceptable to many Indians because of their record and this local support ensured their continuing presence in the subcontinent.

EXTRACT

 From Judith Brown, a British academic specialising in Indian history in her seminal work, *Modern India: The Origins of an Asian Democracy* (1994).

The complexities of 1857 may disconcert those who look for simple patterns of grievance and revolt: but they are a rich source of insight into the nature and results of interaction between Indian society and influences stemming from British rule. At the simplest level, 1857 demonstrated that in the century since Plassey the erstwhile merchants had successfully consolidated a new political dominion over the subcontinent. They might lose control over a limited area, but there were no other contenders for the role of continental rulers. They proved in the months of local but bitter conflict, and painful re-consolidation following May 1857, that if rebellion was geographically confined and their military strength was reinforced from Britain, they could re-establish their authority. But the breakdown of their authority in parts of northern India also demonstrated their fundamental reliance on a network of Indian subordinates and sympathizers prepared to collaborate with their regime. Where that network held firm, as in Bengal or in the princely allies from Punjab, their dominion was secure. It was extremely vulnerable when these layers of loyalty proved untrustworthy. The British collapse in Oudh and part of the North-West Provinces was presaged by the mutiny of their military collaborators, the sepoys. It was total and catastrophic where this defection was followed by the non-co-operation or active hostility of the rural elites and those Indians recruited into the administrative and revenue services.

Results of rebellion

Punishment of rebels

British retribution was terrible, with entire villages massacred. At Cawnpore, mutineers were forced to try to lick clean blood-stained buildings, before being forced to eat pork or beef and then publicly hanged. In Peshawar, 40 men were strapped to the barrels of cannon and blown apart, the old Mughal punishment for mutiny. In Delhi, the British retaking of the city was accompanied by terrible slaughter and Bahadur Shah's three sons were arrested, stripped and shot by William Hodson.

SOURCE

 From William Hodson, son of a clergyman, writing to his brother in England, also a clergyman. In the letter, dated 24 September 1857, he describes his actions in the battle to retake Delhi. Hodson gave the order that the King of Delhi's three sons should be killed during the slaughter.

I appealed to the crowd, saying that these were butchers who had murdered and brutally used helpless women and children, and that the government had now sent their punishment: seizing a carbine from one of my men I deliberately shot them one after the other… the bodies were taken into the city, and thrown out on to the Chiboutra (midden)… I intended to have them hung, but when it came to the question of 'They' or 'Us', I had no time for deliberation.

The lessons drawn from the rebellion by London were that the creaky machinery of the Company and its presidency armies was to blame for the crisis. In future, the British were determined to reorganise the method of ruling India and to place it directly under the control and scrutiny of parliament.

End of Company rule

The Government of India Act 1858 was passed on 2 August and ended Company rule in India and, from this point, until Indian Independence, British India was ruled directly by Britain, through the medium of a viceroy. The viceroy was accountable to parliament and there was a secretary of state for India and an India Council. A royal proclamation was issued and published in India setting out the future rights of Her Majesty's new subjects in the subcontinent. The whole tone of the proclamation was conciliatory and benevolent; Indians were promised religious toleration, equal protection under the law and the rights of native princes to their lands were protected.

The princely states were brought under indirect control by a series of treaties which left the indigenous rulers in no doubt that their privileged existence was preserved by British dominance and should not be challenged. Bahadur Shah II, who had survived the retaking of Delhi (he was 82) was sent into exile in Burma, effectively ending the Mughal dynasty for good. Annexation of territory ceased and, instead of seeking to take control of the princely states, the British now assiduously cultivated the princes as bastions of conservatism and collaborators. In many ways, this policy was successful as the 560 autonomous princely states remained loyal to the British Raj until the very end of the British Empire in India. In Awadh, accommodation was made with the rebellious *talukdars* and from then on the British steered clear of land reform which challenged feudal ties. This was in many ways a retrograde step as it resulted in the stagnation of much of rural India in feudal poverty.

The cost of ending the rebellion had been a staggering £50 million and, with the winding up of the Company, the debt was transferred to the new Raj. The taxation system was revamped, although with a wary eye to the impact of restructuring landownership and taxation in Awadh before the rebellion. Instead of the wholesale reform of landownership and taxation that Dalhousie had instigated, the British relied on their old collaborators in the countryside and instead introduced an income tax on wealthier urban groups.

The official mind drew a clear link between the activities of missionaries and the outbreak of the rebellion. Officials could not prevent missionary activity, but they could, and did, keep proselytising (attempting conversion) out of official policy as much as possible and, when they sought to move against religious customs and rituals, they proceeded with extreme caution. The laws on *sati* and female infanticide remained in place, but it was only in 1891 that the age of consent for girls for marriage was raised from ten to 12. Unsurprisingly perhaps, the evangelicals themselves were unrepentant about their role in causing the rebellion and, in 1858, the London Missionary Society resolved to send an additional 20 missionaries to India within the next two years, earmarking £5,000 for their passage and outfit and another £6,000 for their maintenance. While the London Missionary Society's response to the events of 1857 was a belief that efforts must be redoubled in India, this was not the view shared by the administrators on the ground. Religious toleration, as laid down in the 1858 proclamation, and increasingly the view that all religious groups must be represented politically, shaped much of the 20th-century policy response to Indian nationalism.

The impact on Empire more widely was a convulsive reaction to the stories of atrocities suffered by white men, and more particularly white women and children, at the hands of 'brown men'. The massacre at Cawnpore and the resistance at Lucknow became the stuff of imperial legend. The shock waves radiating from the events of the rebellion were felt by British administrators in the furthest reaches of the Empire and the lesson learned was that the events of 1857 could occur again without continued caution. Racial prejudice, segregation and racial hatred grew among the white imperialists of the British Empire as the memory of the rebellion cast its long shadow until the flags eventually came down. For the 2,000 white men in India, governing some 200 to 300 million, the Mutiny meant withdrawing into a tight enclave, resistant to both growing nationalism among Indians and to more liberal policies from Britain. Over the Empire as a whole, this pattern was to be repeated again and again.

Changes to the Indian army

The proportion of Indian sepoys in the army was reduced by 40 percent and British troops were increased by 50 percent so that the ratio became 3:1 rather than 9:1. Recruitment was switched from the Brahmin and Rajput Hindu castes, who had formed the backbone of the Bengali army and whose wholesale recruitment in Awadh had contributed so disastrously to events in the province. From 1858 onwards, sepoys were recruited from areas deemed to be more loyal to the British, principally the Sikh Punjab and the Muslim north-west. Army policy and planning ensured that from then on adjacent regiments had different ethnic and religious backgrounds to prevent the spread of mutiny from regiment to regiment, and within regiments sepoys were to come from a mix of geographical areas and ethnicities. Troops were allowed to use whatever grease they preferred for their rifles and the introduction of the breech-loading rifle in 1867 made this type of cartridge obsolete anyway.

Longer-term lessons of the rebellion

The longer-term lessons drawn from the rebellion were that the modernising agenda of Bentinck and Macaulay had been misjudged. Modernisation had certainly stemmed from a sense of cultural superiority. But the modernisation that sprang from Utilitarianism also sprang from a positive belief that Indians, if they adopted Christianity and received Western education, would eventually be ready for democratic self-government on the Westminster model. When Macaulay had written his introduction to the Charter Act 1833, he had signalled a possible future whereby India would demand European institutions and stated that if this occurred this would be the proudest day in English history.

Following the rebellion, the attitudes of British imperialists were no longer imbued with the self-confidence and optimism which characterised the modernising agenda of the pre-rebellion British in India. From then on, policy was to become far more pragmatic and cautious.

SOURCE 11

From Queen Victoria's proclamation, announcing the Government of India Act 'to the Princes, Chiefs and People of India' and published by the governor general on 1 November 1858 in Allahabad.

We desire no extension of our present territorial Possessions; and while we will permit no aggression upon Our Dominions or Our Rights, to be attempted with impunity, we shall sanction no encroachment on the rights of others. We shall respect the Rights, Dignity and Honour of Native Princes, as Our own; and We desire that they, as well as Our own Subjects, should enjoy that prosperity and that social advancement which can only be secured by internal Peace and good Government.

We hold ourselves bound to the Natives of our Indian Territories by the same obligations of Duty which bind Us to all Our other Subjects; and these Obligations, by the blessings of Almighty God, We shall faithfully and conscientiously fulfil.

Firmly relying Ourselves on the truth of Christ, and acknowledging with gratitude the solace of Religion, We disclaim alike the Right and Desire to impose our Convictions on any of our Subjects. We declare it to be our Royal Will and Pleasure that none be in any way favoured, none molested or disquieted, by reason of their Religious Faith or Observances; but that all alike shall enjoy the equal and impartial protection of the law: and We do strictly charge and enjoin all those who may be in authority under us that they abstain from all interference with the Religious Belief or Worship of any of our subjects on pain of Our highest Displeasure.

We know, and respect the feelings of attachment with which the Natives of India regard the Lands inherited from their Ancestors; and We desire to protect them in all Rights connected therewith, subject to the equitable demands of the State; and We will that generally, in framing and administering the Law, due regard be paid to the ancient Rights, Usages and Customs of India.

We deeply lament the evils and misery which have been brought upon India by the action of ambitious Men, who have deceived their Countrymen, by false reports, and led them into Open Rebellion. Our Power has been shown by the Suppression of that Rebellion in the field; We desire to shew Our Mercy, by pardoning the Offences of those who have been thus misled, but who desire to return to the path of Duty.

A Level Exam-Style Question Section A

Study Source 11 before you answer this question.

Assess the value of the source for revealing the attitude of the British parliament towards religious policy and landownership by native princes in India in the wake of the Indian Rebellion.

Explain your answer, using the source, the information given about its origin and your own knowledge about the historical context. (20 marks)

Tip

Consider the extent of the rebellion in Awadh and the impact of annexation under Dalhousie.

The British were determined to hold India as an important source of wealth and for its strategic value, but they were far less inclined to educate or 'develop' Indian society. The alliance with the conservative forces in the princely states was once again upheld and, in their own territory, the British turned to infrastructure and railways, a far less controversial field of endeavour. By 1861, the rail network had 1,588 miles of track open compared to 288 miles in 1857 and, by the turn of the century, 24,760 miles had been built. Irrigation projects, the telegraph and postal network, sanitation and lighting projects all made steady progress. Avoiding famine was judged to be the key to keeping the native population content and the officials in India liked to see themselves as taking up the 'white man's burden' for the benefit of the voiceless masses. Expressions of nationalism or discontent by the educated middle class, in many ways created by Macaulay and Bentinck, were disregarded, arguing that these 'Westernised' Indians did not understand the true India of the rural poor and its traditional landowners. Late 19th-century British imperialists believed that the removal of British rule would result in famine and chaos in the subcontinent and they applied themselves to the task of ruling India for the benefit of the poorest Indians by improving their material state. There was the added benefit that the telegraph, the railway and the opening of the Suez Canal meant that, in the case of a future emergency, backup could be moved swiftly into position and never again did an official of the Indian Civil Service discount rumblings of discontent from the native population.

THINKING HISTORICALLY   Interpretations (6a)

Ever-changing history

Our interpretations of the past change as we change. This may be because our social attitudes have changed over time or perhaps a historian has constructed a new theory or perhaps technology has allowed archaeologists to discover something new.

Work in pairs.

1 Make a timeline that starts with the Indian Rebellion and ends 50 years in the future. Construct reactions that illustrate the point that time changes history. In the future box, you can speculate how people might react to the event in 50 years' time. Here is an example:

1857	1858	1942	2007	2066
Event: The Indian Rebellion	British government: 'The policies of the Company almost lost us India.' Landowner from Awadh: 'A disaster.'	British administrator in the Indian Civil Service during the Quit India campaign: 'A sepoy mutiny that got out of hand. We must exercise constant vigilance.' Indian nationalist seeking independence from the British: 'A pan-Indian nationalist struggle against the British.'	British politician visiting India on the sixtieth anniversary of Indian Independence: 'Dark days in our common pasts.' Indian politician: 'The first step towards independence from Britain.' An Indian historian: 'The convulsive last gasp of local princes asserting their rights against the British.'	?

2 Answer the following questions:

  a) Identify three factors that have affected how the Indian Rebellion is interpreted over time, or might affect it in the future.

  b) If a historian was to write a book proposing a radically new interpretation of the Indian Rebellion, how might other historians react? What would affect their reaction?

  c) How will the future change the past?

ACTIVITY
KNOWLEDGE CHECK

British reaction to the Indian Rebellion

1 How useful is the image of Cawnpore (Source 8) in explaining the attitudes of the British towards the Indians as they retook rebellious territory?

2 What were the changes made to recruitment for the Indian army resulting from the rebellion?

ACTIVITY
SUMMARY

1 Explain why each of the following dates was a turning point in the nature of British rule in India.

   a) 1773

   b) 1813

   c) 1833

2 What were the results of the rebellion in terms of British rule in India?

WIDER READING

Bose, S. and Jalal, A. *Modern South Asia: History, Culture, Political Economy*, Routledge (1998)

Brown, J. *Modern India: The Origins of an Asian Democracy*, 2nd edition, Oxford University Press (1994)

Farrell, J.G. *The Siege of Krishnapur*, Weidenfield and Nicolson (1973)

Leadbeater, T. *Britain and India 1845-1947*, Hodder Education (2008)

Wolpert, S. *A New History of India*, 8th edition, Oxford University Press (2009)

3.7 The Nile valley, 1882–98

KEY QUESTIONS

- Why did the British intervene in Egypt in 1882?
- Why was Egypt controlled by the British from 1882?
- Why were the British drawn further into the Nile valley?

INTRODUCTION

Following a wave of Arab nationalism in Egypt directed against the ailing Ottoman Empire, the British government, under Prime Minister William Gladstone, ordered the occupation of Egypt and took control of the country. They insisted it was a temporary measure to restore calm and protect British interests. The occupation was to last until 1922. Historians have studied the period assiduously for two reasons.

- The occupation appeared to be a complete U-turn in policy for Gladstone, the champion of cheap government with low taxation and efficient spending, and an anti-imperialist to boot.

- The occupation was followed by what became known as the scramble for Africa (see page 11) and the partition of the interior of the continent by the European powers.

The historical interpretations and theories developed regarding the occupation of Egypt are used by historians to explain the swift colonisation of the rest of Africa, Britain's later interventions in the Nile valley and to explain Gladstone's dramatic change in policy.

SOURCE

As part of a spirited election campaign in 1879, Gladstone attacked the Conservative prime minister, Disraeli, for his decision to purchase shares in the Suez Canal. Disraeli had argued that the action was necessary to safeguard Britain's route to India.

What is the meaning of safeguarding the road to India? It seems to mean this; that a little island at the end of the world, having possession of an enormous territory at the other end of the world, is entitled to say with respect to every land and every sea lying between its shores and any part of that enormous possession, that it has a preferential right to the possession of control of that intermediate territory, in order, as it is called, to safe-guard the road to India. That, gentlemen, is a monstrous claim.

1869 – Suez Canal is opened

1874 – Disraeli acquires a 45 percent share in the Suez Canal

1878 – Dual Control by the British and French established in Egypt

1879 – 26 June: Khedive Ismail receives a telegram from the sultan addressing him as the ex-khedive following pressure on the sultan by the British and French to remove him

1881 – Radical Islamic leader, the mahdi, emerges in Sudan intent on driving out the Egyptian/Ottoman overlords

1882 – 11 June: British warships begin the bombardment of Alexandria following French withdrawal from joint action

1883 – Sir Evelyn Baring arrives in Egypt as consul general

November: An Egyptian army led by an Englishman, Sir William Hicks, is wiped out by mahdist forces

1884 – January: General Charles Gordon is dispatched to evacuate Egyptian garrisons and foreign nationals from the Sudan

| 1869 | 1874 | 1878 | 1879 | 1880 | 1881 | 1882 | 1883 | 1884 |

WHY DID THE BRITISH INTERVENE IN EGYPT IN 1882?
The problem of the Ottoman Empire

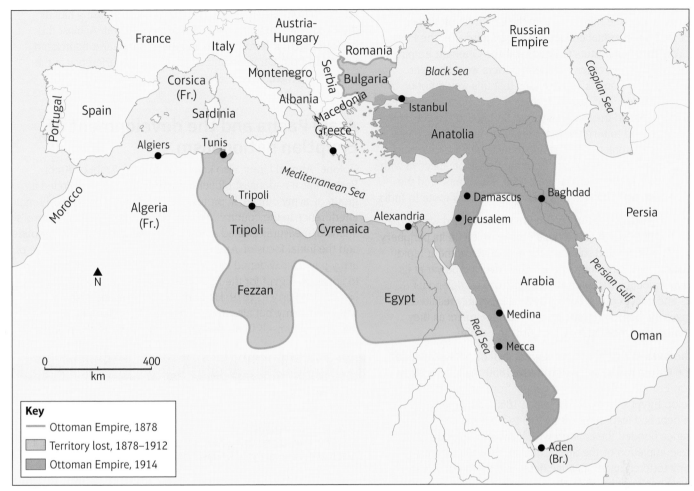

Figure 7.1 The decline of the Ottoman Empire in the late 19th century. Territory in North Africa was lost to the French, the Italians and the British.

1885 – 26 January: General Gordon is besieged in Khartoum by mahdist forces and dies with the entire garrison

1887 – 22 May: Agreement for British withdrawal is reached with the Constantinople Convention between the Great Powers, but French and Russian threats against the sultan convince the British that their strategic interests are not best served by withdrawing; there is no withdrawal

1892 – 8 January: Abbas II becomes khedive of Egypt

1898 – 2 September: Battle of Omdurman

18 September: British and French forces meet at Fashoda in an incident that could have led to war between the British and French

| 1885 | 1886 | 1887 | 1890 | 1891 | 1892 | 1896 | 1897 | 1898 |

1886 – July: Lord Salisbury, a Conservative, becomes prime minister

1890 – British declare the whole of the Nile valley under their sphere of influence

1896 – Salisbury orders an expedition to be led by Kitchener to secure the source of the Nile and pacify the mahdists

The Ottoman Empire had captured Egypt in 1517 and expanded its hold along the North African coast, controlling the ancient cities of Tripoli and Tunis, along with Algeria and Morocco. By the 19th century, the hierarchical and highly bureaucratic Ottoman Empire was in decline, something which worried British foreign secretaries and prime ministers from the Congress of Vienna in 1815 until the eventual collapse of the Empire after the First World War. British ministers feared that if the Ottoman Empire collapsed completely, other European powers would benefit and gain territory from its collapse and that this would not be to Britain's advantage. The Austro-Hungarian and Russian Empires were keen to extend their influence into Serbia and Greece, and the French wished to turn the Mediterranean into a French lake if possible. The problem of what line to take with the Ottoman Empire had become more acute from the British perspective with the completion of the Suez Canal in 1869. This connected the Mediterranean with the Red Sea and opened a new route to India.

The way in which the Ottoman Empire was governed was at the heart of the problem. It was a huge empire, ruled on its periphery by powerful princes and sultans. Like all empires without rapid methods of communication, the Empire devolved power at its periphery to local lords to ensure the rule of law, defend its borders and collect taxes. Such a system inevitably resulted in challenges for Constantinople from its satellite rulers as they sought more and more autonomy from the Empire.

The **khedives** in Egypt enjoyed a great deal of political freedom from the Ottoman Empire and from the 1850s had increasingly relied on European financial investment from Britain and France to develop Egypt's economy. Between 1863 and 1870, Egypt's foreign debt had leapt from £3 million to £100 million as Britain and France flooded the country with loans and investment. Despite completion of the Suez Canal in 1869, the Egyptian economy tottered under its huge debts and the khedive was effectively bankrupt by 1875–76.

KEY TERM

Khedive
A title, similar to 'lord' or 'viceroy', used by the ruling family of Egypt and Sudan during the 19th century.

Britain and France established a system of financial control for the country, known as the Dual Control, and acted in a fashion similar to the way in which the International Monetary Fund acts in the present day in cases of heavily indebted governments. They forced Ismail Pasha, the khedive, to introduce stringent financial reforms, including cutting the pay of the army and introducing sales taxes on food and goods to increase revenue. At the same time, they reduced the interest the Egyptians were forced to pay on foreign debt (held mostly by themselves) to a more manageable five percent. Egyptian actions were supervised by an international commission, the *Caisse de la Dette,* and France and Britain were represented by separate controller generals. The economic rashness of the khedive had bankrupted Egypt in 1876 and three years later he was deposed by the sultan of the Ottoman Empire.

The sultan was persuaded by the British to replace him with Khedive Ismail's son, Tewfik Pasha, who was much more willing to compromise.

British and French interference meant that Ismail received a telegram from the sultan on 26 June 1879, addressing him as the ex-khedive and informing him of his removal. Against this background, it is hardly surprising that a nationalist figurehead critical of both Ottoman and Anglo-French interference in the country emerged.

Arabi Pasha and the development of Egyptian nationalism

Colonel Ahmed Urabi, also known as Ahmad Arabi or Arabi Pasha, was a nationalist officer in the Egyptian army who led a group of army officers in protest against Tewfik and Anglo-French interference in the country. Dissatisfaction with the Dual Control's financial measures existed among all of the Egyptian **bourgeoisie** and the initial focus of Arabi's protests from 1876 was the issue of army pay. This widened into a nationalist platform and he began to speak of 'Egypt for the Egyptians' and formed the Egyptian Nationalist Party in 1879. He commanded considerable support within the army, but also appealed to the Egyptian peasants referring to himself in his proclamations as one of the *fellahin.*

KEY TERMS

Bourgeoisie
The middle class.

Fellah, plural *fellahin*
An Arabic word that literally means 'ploughman'. In its plural form, it is used as a term for Egypt's peasant class.

In 1879, Arabi led a coup following the attempt to dismiss 2,500 officers from the army and halve the salaries of those who remained, and he successfully forced Khedive Tewfik to appoint a nationalist ministry, including himself. The new nationalist cabinet reversed this policy, borrowing another £400,000 from the Rothschilds to avoid the disputed cuts. The British and French feared that he would next force Tewfik to repudiate the loans and ignore the financial measures the Dual Control had insisted on. The British were deeply concerned by the volatility of the situation and in no way disposed to look kindly on the development of a distinct Egyptian nationalism which ran counter to their interests.

Protecting European loans and people

British intervention in Egypt took place in 1882 for a number of reasons. Strategically and economically, the area was too important to them to allow Egyptian nationalists to depose the khedive. As the situation deteriorated and the lives of Europeans were threatened in anti-Christian riots, the British also argued that intervention was morally necessary to prevent further loss of life.

Strategic

The opening of the route to India through the Suez Canal was of paramount importance to the British. It dramatically shortened the journey to India and 80 percent of shipping that travelled through the canal was carried on British ships. The main shareholders in the canal were the French, who had pushed through its investment and building, but in 1875 Disraeli had purchased the remaining 45 percent of shares from the bankrupt khedive. There was clear Anglo-French rivalry in this period, as well as co-operation over the protection of their investments, and Britain was not prepared to let France become too powerful in North Africa and the Middle East as the Ottoman Empire tottered.

Trade

The Egyptians provided an important and growing market for British exports during its period of modernisation under the khedives, and Khedive Ishmail's railway and harbour building projects had provided attractive contracts for British businesses. By 1880, Britain purchased 80 percent of Egypt's exports (largely cotton) and supplied 44 percent of Egypt's imports. British exports to Egypt in the 1880s were about five percent of its total exports. During the **American Civil War**, Britain had imported substantial amounts of Egyptian cotton to make up for the loss of American cotton from the blockaded Southern states. Once the war ended in 1865, British mills reverted once again to American cotton, which had exacerbated Egyptian economic difficulties.

> **KEY TERM**
>
> **American Civil War**
> A war fought between the northern non-slave states of the American Union and the Southern slave states between 1861 and 1865. The naval blockade of the South prevented Southern cotton being exported to Britain for manufacture in the cotton mills. It caused severe economic hardship in the areas of Britain dependent on the textile industry.

Financial

British **bond-holders** in the City of London were heavily exposed to any failure by Egypt to pay its debts. Britain and France had already reacted to the bankruptcy of the khedive in 1875 by establishing financial control on the country through the Dual Control, and the British government was responsive to the demands of the City of London that Egypt must continue to pay its debts to bond-holders whatever that entailed. As much as 37 percent of Gladstone's personal fortune was invested in Egyptian loans.

> **KEY TERM**
>
> **Bond-holder**
> Governments and companies can raise money by selling (or 'issuing') bonds. These are certificates that are sold at a face value. The issuer agrees to pay back that money plus a set amount of interest at a later, set date. If the issuer goes bankrupt, the bonds become worthless and investors lose their money. Government bonds are usually considered safe investments.

People

In the short term, Britain could claim that intervention in Egypt was necessary to prevent European loss of life. On 11 June 1882, with the British and French expedition fleet anchored off Alexandria, a city of 232,000 where every fifth person was European, tensions in the city boiled over and a row between an Egyptian donkey boy and a Maltese man escalated into violent anti-Christian riots across the city. At least 50 Europeans were killed and perhaps 250 Egyptians. Britain blamed the riots on Arabi Pasha's supporters, almost certainly incorrectly.

French withdrawal

In 1882, the British and French responded to the increasing tensions in Egypt by issuing the **Gambetta Note**. The note, which stated that the two powers regarded the maintenance of the khedive's power as the best guarantee for the order and development of prosperity in Egypt, was primarily issued at the insistence of the French. It was intended to warn the nationalists under Arabi Pasha that the powers were minded to intervene militarily in Egypt should they deem the powers of the khedive to be under threat.

The nationalists responded by forcing a nationalist cabinet on the khedive and threatened to depose him. France and Britain, fearing that Arabi would repudiate Egyptian debt payments and determined to protect their bond-holders, sent warships in May to Alexandria to threaten the nationalists and restore the authority of the khedive.

> **KEY TERM**
>
> **Gambetta Note**
> A diplomatic note presented by the French and British to the Egyptian government in 1882. Such diplomatic notes are often presented as the last official communication before military intervention in another state.

However, the French commitment to joint action did not result in actual participation in military action in Egypt or the subsequent occupation. When the bombardment of Alexandria began in July, French warships did not participate and they did not offer support for British military action on the ground. The two reasons for their sudden change of policy and withdrawal from any intervention in Egypt were as follows.

- The actions of Bismarck, the maverick chancellor of Germany, indicated that Germany had changed its position on Egypt and was no longer willing to support dual action by France and Britain in Egypt. France was in no position to argue with Germany, having been defeated by them in 1870 and forced to surrender territory to the powerful military state that Bismarck was developing. Bismarck and the other Great Powers, Russia, Italy and Austria, had delivered notes to the sultan stating that there should be no changes in Egypt without the consent of the Great Powers. This note left the French in no doubt that the Germans were opposed to intervention by France and Britain without Bismarck's agreement.

- French internal politics meant that, on 30 January 1882, Léon Gambetta fell from power in France and was replaced by Charles de Freycinet, who was personally less inclined to intervene in Egypt than Gambetta. He was supported in this by the French parliament, who feared Germany more than any losses to bond-holders and who refused to back military intervention.

However, the decision of the French not to participate in the military campaign in Egypt and the subsequent occupation did not represent a total French withdrawal from the region. They were frustrated by growing British control in Egypt and saw themselves as having a strategic interest in North Africa generally. Between 1882 and 1898, they challenged British dominance in the region on a number of occasions.

The British military campaign, 1882

The British had followed the French lead, both politically and in agreeing to the joint expedition, for the usual reason that they were unwilling for France to have more influence than Britain in the region. Having launched the expedition, they then found themselves in the uneasy position of acting unilaterally when the French parliament refused to sanction bombardment of Alexandria.

TIMELINE: THE OCCUPATION OF EGYPT BY THE BRITISH IN 1882

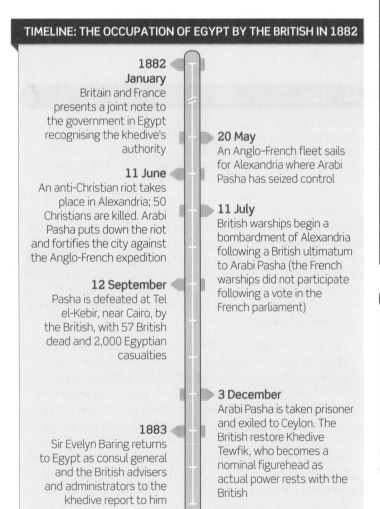

1882
January
Britain and France presents a joint note to the government in Egypt recognising the khedive's authority

11 June
An anti-Christian riot takes place in Alexandria; 50 Christians are killed. Arabi Pasha puts down the riot and fortifies the city against the Anglo-French expedition

12 September
Pasha is defeated at Tel el-Kebir, near Cairo, by the British, with 57 British dead and 2,000 Egyptian casualties

1883
Sir Evelyn Baring returns to Egypt as consul general and the British advisers and administrators to the khedive report to him

20 May
An Anglo–French fleet sails for Alexandria where Arabi Pasha has seized control

11 July
British warships begin a bombardment of Alexandria following a British ultimatum to Arabi Pasha (the French warships did not participate following a vote in the French parliament)

3 December
Arabi Pasha is taken prisoner and exiled to Ceylon. The British restore Khedive Tewfik, who becomes a nominal figurehead as actual power rests with the British

The consequences of Anglo-French rivalry in Egypt

1 Complete a timeline of the events from the issuing of the Gambetta note until the establishment of Sir Evelyn Baring as consul general in Egypt, highlighting joint actions in one colour, French actions in another and British in a third colour.

2 Explain the impact of Germany's changing position on Egyptian action on the French.

SOURCE

Gladstone explaining his government's aims in Egypt in response to hostile questioning in the House of Commons, from *Hansard,* 14 June 1882. *Hansard* is the official record of all speeches and debates in the House of Commons.

Now, the hon. Gentleman who has just sat down complained of us, in the first instance, because he says we have not answered a number of questions which have been put to us by himself and others. He asks—Is there to be an Anglo-French intervention in Egypt? Is there to be a Turkish military intervention in Egypt? and many other questions, to which he thinks we ought to have given categorical answers. My reply is, that to no one of these questions was it our duty to have given a categorical answer; on the contrary, we should have departed from our duty if we had given categorical answers to any of them; for, had we done so, we should have been merely limiting and curtailing liberty of action, not only on our own part, but on the part of all other Governments, and especially on the part of the Government of Turkey. Our business is to preserve that liberty of action; our business is to indicate the ends we have in view, and not the means by which those ends are to be attained. Those ends have been most distinctly and repeatedly stated by my hon. Friend the Under Secretary of State for Foreign Affairs. They are well known to consist in the general maintenance of all established rights in Egypt, whether they be those of the Sultan, those of the Khedive, those of the people of Egypt, or those of the foreign bondholders, or whatever they may be—that, in fact, the single phrase, that we seek the maintenance of all established rights, and the provision of due guarantees for those rights, is the description of the policy by which the Government is directed. With regard to the means to be adopted for carrying out those ends, I say that the specific measures ought not to be indicated, and that it would be a gross error and dereliction of duty on our part either to affirm what they are, or to exclude any specific measures that may be adopted.

A Level Exam-Style Question Section A

Study Source 2 before you answer this question.

Assess the value of the source for revealing the reasons for the decision of Gladstone's government to occupy Egypt in 1882, and the opposition to this occupation.

Explain your answer, using the source, the information given about its origin and your own knowledge about the historical context. (20 marks)

Tip
Consider the context of the source carefully when assessing Gladstone's position on the occupation.

SOURCE

3

Following the defeat at Tel el-Kebir, Arabi Pasha surrendered peacefully to General Drury Curzon Drury-Lowe in Cairo. Drury-Lowe was publicly thanked in the House of Commons and knighted on 18 November 1882.

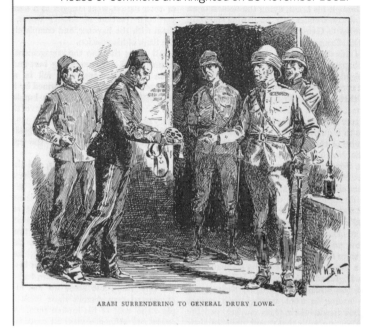

ARABI SURRENDERING TO GENERAL DRURY LOWE.

Historical interpretations of the occupation

Historians of Britain's imperial past agree that the occupation of Egypt in 1882 and Britain's subsequent involvement in the partition of Africa was due to a mixture of power politics and economic motivation. The occupation of Egypt has received particularly detailed scrutiny by historians as its formal occupation kickstarted the process of the extremely swift colonisation of the rest of Africa. Once the British were in control in Egypt, no matter how often they asserted that this was a merely a temporary measure, the other Great Powers began to seize territory in Africa in what became the greatest land grab in history. The emphasis that the many interpretations place on events differs greatly and there is certainly no definitive explanation for the occupation of Egypt or subsequent events in the scramble for Africa. When considering the occupation of Egypt by the British in 1882, three clear interpretations exist.

- Robinson and Gallagher described the 'pull factors' in their book *Africa and the Victorians: The Official Mind of Imperialism* (1961). They argued that there was no period of anti-imperialism in the 19th century and that the British pursued a policy of imperialism through informal empire when possible and formal when necessary. They identified local crises as drawing the British into Empire in Africa. In Egypt, they highlighted the crucial importance of the Suez Canal and the route to India as the pull factor that led Britain in Egypt.

- Cain and Hopkins (1993) placed the importance of bond-holders and capital investment by the City of London at the centre of their explanation into the occupation of Egypt. They pointed to Gladstone's explanation of events and his

personal financial holdings in Egyptian loans to help frame their explanation. For Cain and Hopkins, the national interest was determined by the City of London as the politicians defining the national interest were the investors in Egyptian loans and, therefore, the City's interests and what were defined as national interests were inextricably linked.

- The national historians of Egypt, such as Al-Sayyid Marsot, explore the social and economic tensions caused by the modernisation of the khedives and the birth of a distinctive national voice in Egypt to provide an interpretation of events which is not eurocentric.

EXTRACT

1

Historian Bernard Porter discussing the official mind-set of the British politicians responsible for the occupation of Egypt and subsequent imperial colonisation. From *The Lion's Share: A Short History of British Imperialism 1850–1995* (1996).

'It is not the habit of the English people to set out with their eyes open on a career of conquest and annexation. The conquests which we make are forced upon us'. This was how the Manchester Guardian explained the Liberal government's colonial acquisitions of the 1880s, which must have bewildered many Liberals who thought Gladstone had originally been voted into power to stop this kind of thing. The plea of 'self-defence' was a common one. There was no aggression: Britain was only protecting what was hers already, under pressure from other European powers; so went the argument. For the native inhabitants of the countries she took this could carry very little comfort or even conviction. It sounded cynical, especially when Britain's rivals were making exactly the same claims. It was the kind of thing all of them would say whether it were true or not, because no country ever liked to admit to aggression. Britain was certainly the aggressor on them, the natives, whose land it was, and who had done little themselves to offend her. But of course natives were not taken much into account when Britain talked of her 'rights' and 'interests' in Africa.....

When she took a country, she said, it was only when she had good cause to fear that someone else would take it if she did not, and stop her doing whatever it was she did there before – trade or preach or travel through. She would have preferred not to have to do this kind of thing, but to carry on as she had in the past, picking the world's commercial apples wherever she wanted without owning the orchards, because this way had served her well until now: but others were not going to let her. There was a note of resentment in it. Britain certainly regarded herself throughout this period as more under attack than attacking, and most of her colonial exploits had more the character of salvage operations than movements of genuine aggrandisement.

A Level Exam-Style Question Section B

How far can British strategic interests be regarded as the most significant cause of the occupation of Egypt in 1882? (20 marks)

Tip

Remember to consider factors for the occupation other than strategic interests.

ACTIVITY
KNOWLEDGE CHECK

Causes of formal British occupation of Egypt

1 Explain the strategic, trading, financial and humanitarian causes of the British occupation of Egypt in 1882.

2 Which cause do you believe to have been the main driver for the occupation? Support your answer from the text and sources.

3 Read Source 2. How useful do you consider Gladstone's explanation of the reasons for the occupation to be?

THINKING HISTORICALLY Cause and consequence (7a & b)

Questions and answers

Questions that historians ask vary depending on what they think is important. It is the questions that interest us that define the history that is written. These questions change with time and place. Different historians will also come up with different answers to the same questions, depending on their perspectives and methods of interpretation, as well as the evidence they use.

Below are several historians who have different areas of interest:

Robinson and Gallagher	Cain and Hopkins	Al-Sayyid Marsot
They published *Africa and the Victorians* in 1961 changing the accepted interpretation of the scramble for Africa. They identified local crises as drawing the British into Empire in Africa. In Egypt, they highlighted the crucial importance of the Suez Canal and the route to India as the pull factor that led Britain in Egypt.	They published their controversial revisionist argument in the 1990s. They placed the importance of bond-holders and capital investment by the City of London at the centre of their explanation of the occupation of Egypt. They pointed to Gladstone's explanation of events and his personal financial holdings in Egyptian loans to help frame their explanation.	An Egyptian-born historian who has been writing on Egyptian history since the 1960s. She explores the social and economic tensions caused by the modernisation of the khedives and the birth of a distinctive national voice in Egypt to provide an interpretation of events which is not eurocentric.

These are some key events in the Nile valley, 1882–98:

The financial collapse of the khedive	Gladstone's decision to occupy Egypt	The establishment of the 'veiled protectorate'
The emergence of the mahdi of Sudan	The Baring reforms in Egypt	The death of Gordon at Khartoum
Salisbury's decision to subdue the Sudan	The Battle of Omdurman	The Fashoda incident

Work in groups of between three and six.

1 Which of these events would have been of most interest to each historian? Explain your answer.

2 Each take the role of one historian and devise a question that would interest them about each of the events.

3 Discuss each event in turn. Present the questions that have been devised for each historian and offer some ideas about how they would have answered them.

4 For each event, decide as a group which question is the most interesting and worthwhile of the three.

Answer the following questions in pairs.

5 Identify the different ways that each historian would approach writing an account of the occupation of Egypt.

6 In what ways would Robinson and Gallagher and Cain and Hopkins differ in their explanations of the significance of the interests of British bond-holders and the importance of strategic interests? What would be the focus of their arguments?

Answer the following questions individually.

7 All three historians may produce very different accounts and explanations of the same piece of history. Of the three historians, whose account would you prefer to read first? Explain your answer.

8 Do the differences in these accounts mean that one is more valid than the others?

9 Explain why different historical explanations are written by different historians.

10 Explain why different explanations of the same event can be equally valid.

WHY WAS EGYPT CONTROLLED BY THE BRITISH FROM 1882?

The British occupation of Egypt, the result of Britain's actions in 1882, was never intended at the outset to be permanent, and Gladstone reiterated endlessly that, as soon as financial stability was assured, the British advisers to the khedive would withdraw. This would leave Egypt as an autonomous country, nominally under the control of the Ottoman Empire. However, there was no retreat from Egypt and, consequently, the country remained under the control of the British for the next 32 years in what is commonly referred to as the **veiled protectorate,** as the fiction of the British being there merely to assist the khedive was maintained during this period. The reasons for continuing British involvement were:

- the defeat in November 1883 of the Egyptian army under the leadership of Sir William Hicks, who had entered the khedive's service following the occupation of 1882, by radical **jihadist** forces under the leadership of the mahdi in Sudan, Muhammad Ahmad

- the nature of the British administrator Sir Evelyn Baring and his agenda for Egypt

- the defeat of Gladstone over the question of Irish **Home Rule** in 1886 and the dominance of the Tory Lord Salisbury for the last years of the century.

EXTEND YOUR KNOWLEDGE

Muhammad Ahmad bin a-Sayyid Abd Allah, the mahdi of Sudan (1843–85)
The mahdi was a Sudanese religious and military leader who created a huge Islamic state that extended from the Red Sea to central Africa. The high-watermark of his campaign was his capture of Khartoum in 1885, defeating the British general, Gordon of Khartoum. Gordon died during the battle. Following the battle, the mahdi created a theocratic state in Sudan with Omdurman as its capital. Later that year, the mahdi became ill, possibly with typhus, and died aged 41. Successor mahdis emerged to lead the Sudanese movement following his death.

The veiled protectorate

The veiled protectorate is the name given to the years between 1882 and 1914 when London effectively controlled Egypt, with no legal basis for their presence other than the fiction that they were there at the request of the khedive. Although Gladstone, and even Salisbury, initially worked for a British departure, this never occurred, partly as a result of the way in which the consul general acted in Egypt and partly as a result of the continuing strategic importance of the region to the British.

Baring's 'Mission in Egypt'

The occupation was always intended by London to be a temporary expedient, at least at the outset and, between 1882 and 1914, the British government announced its intention of withdrawing from Egypt on no fewer than 66 separate occasions. The fiction was maintained that Egypt was a province of the Ottoman Empire, ruled by its own khedive. However, the khedive was unable to make political decisions without the agreement of the British consul general and there were increasingly large numbers of British appointees in the Egyptian army and administration. The nationalists in the Egyptian army had been crushed and the British set about reforming the finances of the country to assure its continuing stability. Perhaps a different consul general might have simply ensured that the country was subject to financial controls and worked towards the departure of British officials, but Baring was not that man.

Sir Evelyn Baring, later Lord Cromer, was the British consul general in Egypt from 1883 until 1907. He was a key factor in the continuation of the occupation, as he believed that there needed to be fundamental changes made in the agricultural infrastructure and governmental institutions of the country and that he was the man to deliver the necessary changes. Wholesale participation in infrastructure projects could never have been achieved in the short term and, if Sir Evelyn was extending his brief more than London might have wished, they did nothing to restrain him.

The emergence of radical Islam in the Sudan

The emergence of radical Islam in the Sudan convinced Baring and the British that it would be dangerous for the British to withdraw and it became a further justification for their continuing presence. Unsurprisingly, considering its own internal problems, Egyptian control of Sudan (the Ottoman Empire placed Sudan under Egypt's control) had faltered by the 1870s. In 1873, Khedive Ismail had appointed, with London's support, Charles George Gordon (later to become famous as Gordon of Khartoum) as governor general of Sudan. He had put down a series of revolts against the khedive and taken action to suppress the slave trade, in line with his strong Christian principles. He resigned and returned to England when Ismail was deposed and his successors failed to maintain order in the country or prevent a resurgence of the slave trade.

As Egyptian control slipped further and further away, the situation in the Sudan was complicated by the appearance in 1881 of a radical jihadist leader, the mahdi, intent on driving out their Egyptian–Ottoman overlords and establishing a purer form of Islam. Mahdist forces had a number of victories against the Egyptian army, but the wiping out of all but 300 of an original 7,000 troops under the command of Sir William Hicks in November 1883 convinced London that Egypt no longer exercised any level of control over the province.

Sudan was of little interest to British politicians, with Gladstone, and later Salisbury, determined not to become involved in the affairs of the country. However, London had no intention of allowing similar forces to take control of Cairo and Alexandria, places which really mattered in the maintenance of British interests. As they had no confidence in the khedive's ability to control the mahdi in Sudan or prevent the spread of the mahdi's brand of militant Islam into Egypt, the chances of British withdrawal from Egypt were extremely reduced by the emergence of the mahdi.

The collapse of liberalism in Britain

Gladstone's commitment to Home Rule in Ireland resulted in the splitting of the **Liberal Party** and the dominance of the Conservatives for most of the last decade of the century. Their leader, Lord Salisbury was too subtle and clever a politician to be carried away by imperial rhetoric and jingoism (see page 59), and he began his premiership frustrated by Britain's presence (of dubious legality) in Egypt. However, he was not prepared to give the French any potential strategic advantage in North Africa by withdrawal from Egypt and he was aware of the patriotic sentiments stirred up by the actions of the mahdi.

Although he agreed with Baring's assessment that full reform of Egypt would take at least 15 years, Salisbury was prepared to sacrifice building projects in Egypt in the interests of withdrawal if he could protect Britain's interests in the region.

Between 1887 and 1889, Salisbury worked with Turkey, France and Germany to hammer out an agreement by which the British could re-enter the country if necessary. Agreement for withdrawal was actually reached with the sultan in Constantinople on 22 May 1887 with the Constantinople Convention, only to be blown out of the water by the French and the Russians, who threatened the sultan with the invasion of Syria by the French and of Armenia by the Russians if the British were granted ongoing rights to re-enter Egypt. The sultan immediately buckled under the pressure and, if their threats were designed to convince Salisbury he should withdraw, they had the opposite effect as Salisbury drew the conclusion that the French remained the greatest threat to the British Empire. The combination of the threat Russia posed to India's borders and French aggression in the Mediterranean led Salisbury to conclude that Britain's strategic interests could only be guaranteed by maintaining Britain's presence in Egypt. He could hardly have taken any other position given the power politics of the 1890s and his own understanding of Britain's position in the world.

EXTEND YOUR KNOWLEDGE

Lord Salisbury (1830–1904)
Lord Salisbury was Conservative prime minister for 13 years in three different terms in the 1880s and 1890s. He combined the roles of prime minister and foreign secretary and was in power during the period of the scramble for Africa.

During his stewardship, he managed to steer British foreign policy successfully during the partition of Africa and during a period of intense international competition between the Great Powers, which was to culminate in the First World War.

His foreign policy is often described as one of 'splendid isolation' (i.e. refusing to engage in European conflicts and alliances), but was more subtle than that and he always showed a keen understanding of Britain's interests in any given set of circumstances. Although he had a keen interest in empire, he was not a fervent imperialist, disliking and distrusting popular jingoism and always taking the time to assess whether British interests would really be served by a forward imperial policy by the men on the ground.

He famously said of British foreign policy in the 1860s that 'English policy is to float lazily downstream, occasionally putting out a diplomatic boathook to avoid collisions', but this does not accurately reflect his acute analysis of foreign affairs and the skills he showed in pursuing British interests so effectively.

The work of Sir Evelyn Baring

Lord Baring, a descendant of the great banking dynasty, had his early imperial experience in India and much of his work in Egypt reflects the lessons learned at the outset of his career. He was convinced of the superiority of the Anglo-Saxon and had little patience with what he believed to be the 'oriental' mind. He was convinced that the future of Egypt rested on developing its agriculture and a large proportion of his time in Egypt was devoted to improving drainage for agriculture. He was convinced of his own righteousness, convinced of the need for Britain to remain in Egypt and convinced that he knew what Egyptians needed to keep them happy.

He was in many ways a classic example of a late Victorian imperialist. A product of a public school education and the Indian Civil Service, he was fair, hardworking, paternalistic, incorruptible, patriotic, an imperialist and confident both in himself and in Britain's place in the world. In addition to implementing yet more financial controls on Egypt, he set out to reform the administrative and agricultural systems to place the economy on a firm future footing. He believed not only that Britain had the right to intervene in Egypt, but that as it was there it should reform the country for the benefit of its poorest subjects.

This was clearly incompatible with both Gladstone and Salisbury's attempts to withdraw from an occupation of dubious legality and with the risk of further involvement in Africa and destabilising the fragile peace between the Great Powers.

Achievements of Baring's reforms

- By instituting stringent financial controls and making cuts in public spending, Baring restored the government of Egypt to solvency by 1887. This was the stated British objective for the occupation in the first place. The London Convention of 1885 agreed a loan of £9 million to Egypt and £8 million was spent on stabilising the debt situation of the country. Debt repayment constituted half of the money raised in tax during the Baring years.

- Baring spent the remaining £1 million of the Convention loan on irrigation and clearing the silted drainage canals of the Nile's flood plains to improve agriculture. He was firmly convinced that the ongoing stability of the country rested on proper drainage to improve the agricultural output of the country, thereby improving the lot of the peasant farmers or *fellahin*. Between 1882 and 1902, eight percent of government revenue was devoted to agriculture and hydraulic improvements under the Public Works Department of the Baring years.

The weaknesses of the Baring reforms are attributable to two factors: budgetary constraints, and the inevitable results of the Baring mind-set.

Baring's annual budget was largely allocated to debt repayments, to military spending to protect the population against the mahdi and to irrigation. This meant that other spending was limited and that progress was slow or non-existent. An 1884 survey of the land taxation system demonstrated that tax was paid on **kharaj** land (held by peasant farmers) at a rate or £1 6s 4d per **fedden** (roughly an acre) compared to 10s 7d paid on **ushr** land (that held by large landowners). British land and tax officials argued that the tax system should be immediately equalised to prevent rebellion and to promote agricultural investment by peasant farmers, ultimately improving output. However, Baring, constrained by other budgetary demands and cautious of upsetting the large landowners, put off fundamental taxation reform until a full land survey was completed early in the 20th century, and the inequality in the taxation system was not addressed until then, despite its glaring inequality. This meant that although agriculture was boosted by improved irrigation, its development was held back by the inequality of the land tax system.

Investment in education was also limited. Baring believed that increased secondary education in particular was not the responsibility of government. He refused to fund secondary education, thus limiting the upward mobility of the *fellahin* and, in 1901, he raised tuition fees in existing primary schools to decrease enrolment. He believed that too much progress, too quickly would destabilise society and that the responsibility of the governing class was to ensure material prosperity and not to get involved with the state provision of education.

KEY TERMS

Kharaj
Land tax paid on land held by peasants in Egypt under the Ottoman Empire.

Fedden
An Egyptian measurement unit for land, roughly equal to an acre.

Ushr
Land tax paid on land held by large landowners in Egypt under the Ottoman Empire.

EXTRACT

2 From Ronald Hyam discussing the limits of Baring's reforms in Egypt and Baring's perception of Egyptians, in *Britain's Imperial Century 1815–1914* (2002).

To ensure material prosperity and contentment was the only real good that could be done. An aggressive reforming policy would only result in undermining the fabric on which the whole society rested. To do too much might lose the trust of the conservative masses. Thus, he concluded, 'there may be even worse evils than the continuance for a while of insanitary conditions and ignorance of illiteracy'. His unwillingness to support a more active reform policy was determined to a considerable extent by his belief that the East could not be reformed. : 'it will probably never be possible to make a Western purse out of an Eastern sow's ear; ignorance was too widespread, despotism too ingrained, Muslim religious influence too crushing and reactionary for reform ever to have any chance of success. Why then disrupt society futilely.

Baring's greatest weakness, however, was his complete underestimation of the strength of developing nationalism in Egypt at the end of the 19th century. Nationalism lay dormant in the early years of the veiled protectorate, but the death of Tewfik in 1892 and the succession of his son, Abbas Hilami (a far less compliant figure), saw the return of Egyptian nationalism amongst the ruling classes. Abbas, the new khedive, intrigued against the protectorate with young intellectuals including Mustafa Kamil, financing his journey to France where he hoped he would influence foreign opinion against British rule. Baring was hugely irritated by the plots and intrigues at the khedive's court and tended to lay the blame for any displays of nationalism at the door of the khedive.

Baring remained oblivious to the significance of the growth of *fellahin* nationalism at the end of the 19th century, remaining firmly convinced that all nationalistic feeling emanated from the new khedive and completely underestimated its existence among the *fellahin*. He believed that his reforms had brought warm gratitude from the masses towards the British, conveniently forgetting the limits to *fellahin* mobility caused in part by the restrictions placed on the extension of education, and the long delay in reforming the land tax.

Baring left Egypt for retirement in England in 1907. The country was solvent and there had been some important agricultural and economic reforms made. Nationalism was present at every level of society from the khedive, to the middle-class journalist writing inflammatory articles, to the *fellahin* class frustrated by their lack of opportunity for upward mobility in Baring-controlled Egypt.

ACTIVITY
KNOWLEDGE CHECK

The veiled protectorate

1 How significant do you consider Baring to be in the continuing British occupation of Egypt?

2 List the achievements and limitations of British rule in Egypt under Baring.

3 Read Extract 2. How far does this extract help explain the growth of nationalism in Egypt?

WHY WERE THE BRITISH DRAWN FURTHER INTO THE NILE VALLEY?

The problem of the Sudan

The problems emerging in Sudan in the late 19th century were a result of changes within the relationship between the Egyptians and the Ottoman Empire earlier in the century. As the Ottoman Empire declined, Egyptian rulers had become more and more powerful and, from 1821, Egyptian control over the Sudan had changed from charging the Sudanese leader a tribute to formal occupation and administrative control. In 1873, Khedive Ismail, as part of his modernisation programme, had appointed the British General Gordon as governor of the Equatorial Provinces of Sudan to end the slave trade, which was embedded in Sudanese society. Gordon made significant progress in this area, but the impact of his work proved destabilising to both the economy and the control of society through traditional groups (the slave traders were generally some of the most powerful members of the society). Gordon resigned in 1880, exhausted, and subsequent governors had limited control over a rapidly fracturing society.

The mahdi of Sudan

The rise of a militant Islam under the leadership of Muhammad Ahmad, who proclaimed himself the mahdi (promised redeemer of the Islamic world) in 1881, was a further factor in the rapid destabilisation of the area. The charismatic leader capitalised on Sudanese resentment about Egyptian taxes and authority, and his support grew rapidly. An inadvertent result of the attack on the slave traders by Gordon was that it left an important gap in traditional society by removing the only local leaders who might have provided effective opposition to mahdist forces.

The Egyptian army launched a number of operations against the mahdi, which were conspicuously unsuccessful and culminated in the wiping out of the 1883 expedition, led by the British Sir William Hicks, at Kashgil. Sir William Hicks had entered the khedive's service after the occupation in 1882 and was leading an Egyptian force of 7,000 infantry and 1,000 cavalry. All but 300 were killed by mahdist forces.

Gladstone's concerns and policy

Gladstone and Baring feared that the problems of the Sudan would destabilise their programme of financial consolidation in Egypt and they judged the Egyptians to be unable to rule the Sudan effectively. Although they did not like the mahdi's ideas, they were prepared to cut Sudan loose in the interests of maintaining stability and control in Egypt. Indeed, the British government came to the conclusion that evacuation of Egyptian garrisons in the Sudan (often under the command of Englishmen) was necessary, as Egypt could not fund the continuing cost of attempting to keep order in the province.

Gladstone could see no reason for Britain to be drawn into the problems of the Sudan. Unlike in Egypt, Britain had no strategic interests (other than protecting Egypt) or economic interests in the area. Sudan was largely desert, inhabited with warlike tribes, and its main economic basis was the slave trade, which Britain was committed to stamping out. The rise of radical Islam and growing support for the mahdi made Gladstone even more cautious about the possibility of being drawn into a long and expensive campaign.

In 1884, General Gordon, who had governed the Sudan for the khedive in the 1870s, was dispatched to the Sudan to organise the evacuation, with instructions from both London and Baring in Cairo. In the light of later events at Khartoum, historians have studied Gordon's instructions assiduously to identify any room for misinterpretation of them by Gordon. Almost exactly a year later on 26 January, the mahdi broke through British fortifications at Khartoum and the entire unevacuated garrison was wiped out.

SOURCE 4

From General Gordon's instructions of 18 January 1884 from the foreign secretary, Lord Greville, regarding his role in Khartoum, as he left for Sudan to evacuate the Egyptian garrisons and any Europeans remaining in the Sudan.

Her Majesty's Government are desirous that you should proceed at once to Egypt to report to them on the military situation in the Soudan, and on the measures which it may be advisable to take for the security of the Egyptian garrisons still holding positions in that country, and for the safety of the European population in Khartoum. You are also desired to consider and report upon the best mode of effecting the evacuation of the interior of the Soudan, and upon the manner in which the safety and the good administration by the Egyptian Government of the sea coast can best be secured.

In connection with this subject you shall pay especial consideration to the question of the steps that may usefully be taken to counteract the stimulus which it is feared may possibly be given to the Slave Trade by the present insurrectionary movement and by the withdrawal of the Egyptian authority from the interior.

Your will be under the instructions of Her Majesty's Agent and Consul Genl at Cairo...

You will consider yourself authorised and instructed to perform such other duties as the Egyptian Government may desire to instruct to you and as may be communicated to you by Sir E Baring.

SOURCE 5

From Baring's instructions to General Gordon, 25 January 1884. Its strong emphasis on the evacuation of the province as the priority reflects official anxiety regarding Gordon's possible actions in the Sudan. Unfortunately for the government, he was the only real candidate for the job, based on his experience in the province in the 1870s.

You will bear in mind that the main end to be pursued is the Evacuation of the Soudan...

I understand also that you entirely concur in the desirability of adopting this policy, and that you think that it should on no account be changed.

General Charles Gordon's mission in Sudan, 1884–85

If Sir Evelyn Baring was an example of the classic Indian-trained colonial administrator, Major General Charles George Gordon was a notable example of the kind of imperialist who existed on the very edges of the Empire, the 'man on the spot' adventurer. He was regarded by the establishment back in London as half mad, and with some reason. Niall Ferguson, a notable imperial historian, notes that, early in his career, Gordon had resigned the private secretaryship to the viceroy of India after three days because he was asked to write a letter to the effect that the viceroy had read something with interest, declaring that he couldn't possibly write this as the viceroy had done nothing of the sort. He spent most of his time on the fringes of the Empire, in China and the Sudan, acting first for the Chinese imperial dynasty and then for the khedive. He mapped the Nile as far as Uganda and was hugely energetic in efforts to end the slave trade in Sudan in the 1870s. He was used to running his own show, a fervent Christian and by no means a safe pair of hands. Unfortunately for Gladstone, he was also the obvious choice to organise the evacuation as he had commanded the Egyptian garrisons and knew the area and its people well.

What Gordon was trying to achieve in Sudan in 1884–85 has been a subject of debate ever since his death. Historians have examined all the documentary evidence available to try to establish at what point Gordon decided to depart from his orders. His dispatches and extracts from his time in Khartoum in many ways suggest that his intention was to try to generate enough publicity to change government policy from one of evacuation to one of intervention, but it is equally possible to argue that the orders themselves were impossible to carry out without adequate reinforcement, which Baring and London refused to sanction.

Certainly Gordon was his own worst enemy. Instead of concentrating on withdrawing the garrison in Khartoum, he spent his early time in the city wiring plans to London for handing over authority to an anti-mahdist popular figure (including a notable ex-slave trader) and sending messages to Baring asking for more troops. When the mahdi drew close, instead of withdrawal by river, Gordon refused to leave on the grounds that there were still more people to be evacuated from outlying areas and fortified the city, necessitating the dispatch of a relief operation. His diary, written with an eye to posterity, shows a man with strong Christian principles prepared for the worst if necessary, with contempt for the politicians, especially Baring, whom he blamed for the predicament and indulging in long flights of fantasy. When things had almost reached their worst, Gordon arranged for copies of the journal to be smuggled out of Khartoum, demonstrating a sharp appreciation of the value of publicity as they were intended for publication.

The siege of Khartoum was followed exhaustively in the newspapers and there was a vociferous campaign for a relief expedition to be organised. One was in fact eventually dispatched by the reluctant Gladstone, but it arrived two days too late to rescue Gordon. The mahdi broke through the fortifications at Khartoum on 26 January and the entire garrison was killed, with Gordon's decapitated head being presented to the mahdi as a prize. The news that reached London on 5 February 1885 was first of the fall of Khartoum, followed by confirmation of the death of Gordon and the rest of the garrison.

The public blamed Gladstone for dragging his feet in dispatching the rescue expedition to rescue Gordon, and the uncoded telegram sent from the queen rebuking him for Gordon's death became public knowledge. Instead of the 'GOM' (Grand Old Man of politics), Gladstone was nicknamed the 'MOG' (Murderer of Gordon) by the press, and events in Sudan contributed to the defeat of Gladstone and the Liberals in the general election of 1885.

SOURCE 6

Queen Victoria sent the following telegram to Gladstone on 5 February 1886. All such communications were usually sent in code to prevent their contents being passed on by telegram operators. Victoria chose to send this telegram uncoded in the full knowledge that it would become public knowledge.

These news from Khartoum are frightful, and to think that all this might have been prevented and many precious lives saved by earlier action is too frightful.

Express to Lord Wolseley [who was in charge of the relief expedition] my great sorrow and anxiety at this news and my sympathy with Lord Wolseley in this great anxiety; pray, but have little hope, brave Gordon may yet be alive.

SOURCE 7

Queen Victoria writing to Sir Henry Ponsonby in 1886. Victorians commonly wrote about themselves in the third person. This is not Ponsonby recounting a conversation with the queen, but Victoria writing about her feelings to Ponsonby. He must have been grateful that her public telegram to Gladstone was not more inflamed.

She meant that Mr G (Gladstone) should remember what SHE suffers when the British name is humiliated... & he can go away and resign but she MUST REMAIN and she has suffered so cruelly from humiliation and annoyance from the present Govt. since the unlucky day when Mr Gladstone came in - that she was boiling over with the indignation & horror which everyone in this country felt and feels! Mr G never minds loss of life etc. and wraps himself up in his own incomprehensible delusions and illusions....

In the Queen's heart (& that of many others she knows) she holds Mr Gladstone responsible by imprudence, neglect, violent language for the lives of many 1000ds tho' unwittingly... Look at our relations abroad! No one trusts or relies on us & from '74 to '80, especially the 1st three of four years... England stood very high...

Sir Heny must speak very seriously to Ld Hartington [minister in Gladstone cabinet] as to eventualities but without making him think that he is certain to be Mr Gladstone's successor.

If Gordon was hoping to prevent withdrawal from Sudan in the short term, he failed. Gladstone's cabinet were deeply divided among themselves on a number of issues, but found it very easy to agree that Sudan was to be left to the mahdi, whatever public demands there were to the contrary. Their considered assessment of the difficulties inherent in trying to annex the area, combined with the threat they were facing from Russia, meant they were prepared to ride out the considerable public disapprobation that resulted from Gordon's death.

In the long term, the desire to avenge Gordon made a deep impact on important decision-makers like General Kitchener, sent by the British to quell the mahdi in the 1890s, and played a part in the way in which the reconquest of the Sudan was conducted in 1896. Culturally, Gordon's last stand in Khartoum became one of the central parts of the imperial story, akin to Nelson putting his telescope to his blind eye or the charge of the Light Brigade. A national day of mourning was declared for Gordon and books, paintings and school books depicted his last hours (as gleaned from survivors of the garrison). It was possible to buy busts, jugs and bookmarks of the 'hero' and Alfred, Lord Tennyson, wrote a poetic epitaph for the hero of Khartoum. His statues stood in Trafalgar Square (later moved to the Embankment), Aberdeen, Rochester and across the Empire, and he has memorials in Westminster Abbey and St Paul's Cathedral.

ACTIVITY
KNOWLEDGE CHECK

The impact of General Gordon

1 Read Sources 4 and 5 carefully. What do you understand General Gordon's instructions to have been?

2 Consider the provenance of the sources. How far do you think it is fair to say that the British government had concerns regarding Gordon's possible actions?

3 Use the text and the sources to explain why Gladstone's government was forced to send a relief expedition to rescue General Gordon.

The conquest of the Sudan, 1898

In 1896, Lord Salisbury ordered a campaign in Sudan to secure the source of the Nile. The campaign, led by Kitchener, was to result in the annexation of Sudan and the crushing of mahdist forces. Salisbury was not a 'new imperialist' hell-bent on expanding the British Empire at every opportunity, but a wily player of great power politics. In the early 1880s, the partition of Africa had not yet taken place and British interests were served best by the occupation of Egypt only. By the 1890s, the map of Africa looked very different and there was a considerable body of opinion that held that, in order to protect British interests in Egypt (which secured the vital route to India), it was necessary to control the source of the Nile. Forward policy in the Sudan by the British was dictated by two threats to British interests in the region.

- The first was the centuries-old Anglo-French rivalry, which found its latest expression in control of the headwaters of the Nile.

- The second was driven by fears of the newly emergent mahdist forces in the region and the problems that further pan-Islamic nationalism might cause in Egypt.

In 1896, an expedition was launched under the leadership of Lord Kitchener to try to address the two threats to British interests posed by the French and the mahdi. The defeat of the Italians by mahdist forces at the Battle of Adowa in 1896 convinced Salisbury that the time was now right for a show of force against the jihadists to reassert European superiority and prevent the spread of pan-Islamism into Egypt.

Its scope and nature were cautious at the outset and the British objective was set initially as Dongola, about half way between Egypt and Khartoum if one follows the Nile. The expedition was to proceed with care, ensuring supply lines remained intact at all times. It was to culminate in the conquest of the Sudan and the defeat of the mahdi at Omdurman, one of the bloodiest and most unequal battles of all time.

The fear of French occupation

In 1890, the British declared that the whole of the Nile valley was its 'sphere of influence'. London was successful in its diplomatic efforts with Italy, Germany and Belgium to achieve recognition of their sphere of influence, but not with the French. In 1894, Sir Edward Grey, the under-secretary of state for foreign affairs, told the Commons that French interference in the Nile valley would be interpreted by the British as an unfriendly act, a statement which was no doubt intended as much for French consumption as English. As the partition of Africa continued, it became clear to Salisbury that at some point Britain's interests must move forward from declaring a sphere of influence to a more visible presence in the Sudan. Such a move would thwart French expansion and protect the amount of water available to irrigate the cotton fields in Egypt, thus securing Egyptian stability by preventing a competitor Great Power from controlling the Nile.

The ultimate French ambition in Africa in the partition was to link its western colonies with its port in Djibouti, on the Horn of Africa, following first the Niger and then the Blue Nile. British interests were almost exactly the reverse. Apart from the occupied territory in Egypt, Britain's territorial interests lay in South Africa and British East Africa. The White Nile linked Egypt with Britain's colonies in East Africa.

In 1898, two armed forces met at Fashoda, at almost the exact point at which British and French interests intersected (see Figure 7.2). It was one of the great set piece stand-offs in the history of Anglo-French relations. A tiny French force of about 120 men under the leadership of Major Marchand had reached Fashoda after a long 14-month journey from Brazzaville. They were waiting there in vain for another French expedition travelling from Djibouti, when Kitchener's 1,500 strong force, accompanied by five gunboats and fresh from his victory over the mahdi at Omdurman, arrived at the oasis on 18 September, having travelled on the White Nile. Kitchener had opened his sealed envelope from Salisbury instructing him to establish a British claim over the whole of the Upper Nile, repudiating any rival claims.

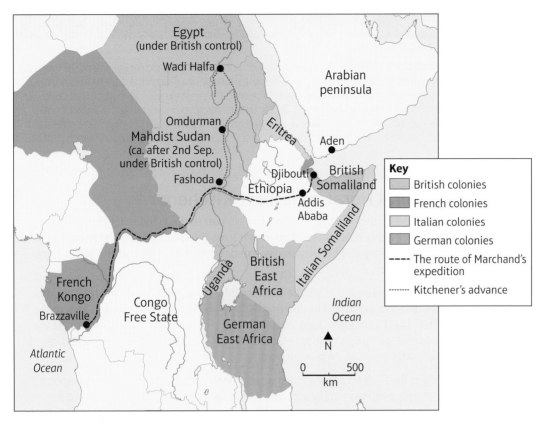

Figure 7.2 The political situation in eastern and central Africa in 1898 at the time of the Fashoda incident.

SOURCE

From Thomas Pakenham, in *Scramble for Africa* (1991), describing the meeting at Fashoda between the British and the French. No exact transcript of the meeting exists, but enough evidence remained from the participants for Pakenham to reconstruct the dialogue.

Kitchener: 'My instructions are to regain possession of Fashoda in the name of the Sublime Porte (Sultan of the Ottoman Empire) and His Highness the Khedive.'

Marchand: 'My orders are to occupy Fashoda and other parts of the upper Nile abandoned by Egypt and therefore without a legal owner....'

Kitchener: 'I cannot argue these points, but I would suggest you consider the preponderance of the force at my disposal...'

Marchand: 'Until we receive orders to retire we shall not haul down our flag but are ready to die at our posts...'.

Kitchener: 'But this situation could lead to war...'

At which Marchand gave what his companion called *une profonde inclinaison de la tête*, to confirm that this was indeed so.

In fact, the tact on Kitchener's part in allowing the French flag to remain flying, the overwhelming British force, the restraint shown by Marchand and the general relief on the part of the French that they were dealing with a British force rather than trying to repel mahdists meant that both sides agreed to refer the matter to London and Paris, and a rather bizarre party took place, complete with warm whisky and soda (supplied by the English) and champagne (supplied by the French).

Back in Europe, the press and public of both nations wound themselves up into a frenzy of jingoist imperial sentiment and the navies were mobilised. However, the French government, aware of Britain's naval superiority and caught up in its own internal crisis sparked by the Dreyfus Affair, were prepared to back down. On 3 November, the French quietly dropped their claim to Fashoda and one of the most bizarre sideshows in imperial history was over.

EXTEND YOUR KNOWLEDGE

Dreyfus Affair
In 1894, Captain Alfred Dreyfus of Jewish descent was tried for treason in France for leaking military secrets to the Germans and imprisoned on Devil's Island. In 1896, the real culprit emerged, but there was an army cover-up, which protected him and additional charges were made against Dreyfus as part of that cover-up. In 1898, Emile Zola, a famous writer, wrote an open letter to the newspapers accusing the army of anti-Semitism and of falsely accusing Dreyfus. The case dragged on until 1906, when Dreyfus was exonerated, but it exposed the anti-Semitism which was common in French society and bitterly divided French politics.

The role of General Horatio Herbert Kitchener

Although heavily influenced by the death of Gordon and his part in the failed relief mission to Khartoum, Kitchener was a vastly different kind of soldier from the fanatical and highly individualistic Gordon. Kitchener was pure army and his personality exhibited, to a high degree, the self-control which Gordon so notably lacked.

Kitchener's early career took place in the Middle East and Mediterranean basin, and he was part of the relief effort that failed to extricate Gordon from Khartoum. He had met Gordon as a young man and the evangelical Gordon made a deep impression on him. Kitchener had also learned the lessons of the original relief campaign to rescue Gordon, led by General Wolseley, of which several criticisms can be made in terms of its organisation and planning.

Kitchener's campaigns in the Sudan were methodical, equipped with the most modern weapons and supported by light-gauge railways and gunboats. The initial objective was Dongola, but the positive reports of the expedition and wiping out of the mahdist garrison at Ferkeh in 1896 meant that Salisbury was happy to expand the objective to include the retaking of the whole of Sudan. The campaign was successful and Kitchener won a further victory against the mahdi at Atbara before proceeding to the mahdist capital at Omdurman, where his forces destroyed those of the mahdi.

When Khartoum was finally retaken, Kitchener's actions demonstrated his deep hatred of the mahdi and veneration of Gordon. There was a memorial service for the dead Gordon, which Kitchener watched in tears as the army bands played a selection of inspiring music. He then ordered that the tomb of the mahdi be opened to prevent it becoming a place of pilgrimage. Not content with disposing of the remains secretly, the mahdi's head was decapitated from his corpse, something that outraged the young Winston Churchill, serving with the expedition but also commissioned to write reports of the campaign for the *Morning Post*. The news of the desecration of the tomb was debated in parliament and Baring, who was no friend of Kitchener, had to intervene to ensure the mahdi's head was buried and the ancient enemy was treated with decency.

Kitchener's actions in the Sudan, and his later use of concentration camps in the Boer War, outraged anti-imperialists in Britain and he had powerful critics. However, he was hugely popular with the public and was secretary of war from the outset of the First World War until his death.

A Level Exam-Style Question Section B

'Kitchener's veneration of Gordon is key in explaining his savagery towards the mahdist forces in the Sudan.'

How far do you agree with this opinion? Explain your answer. (20 marks)

Tip
Consider the wider impact among British soldiers of the death of Gordon when reaching your conclusion.

The significance of Omdurman, 2 September 1898

Salisbury had always held the destruction of the mahdi to be a desirable long-term goal, although he accepted it might not be achieved in his lifetime and had spoken of 'our desire to extirpate from the earth one of the vilest despotisms ever seen'. Kitchener's careful advance and the vast advantage the new weapon the British troops carried, the **Maxim gun**, meant that this objective was achieved at the Battle of Omdurman. The numbers speak for themselves:

- of the mahdist forces c10,000 dead, 13,000 taken prisoner and 5,000 wounded

- of the British forces 47 dead and 382 wounded.

The young Winston Churchill wrote a detailed account of the entire campaign and the destruction that took place at Omdurman, as the mahdists were mown down by the new guns. He recorded in his controversial book, *The River War* (1899), that atrocities were committed against mahdist wounded, criticising Kitchener for not reissuing the order issued before the Battle of Atbara that wounded soldiers be spared, and in private he went even further, writing in letters to a number of his influential friends and relations that he believed that Kitchener was responsible for the atrocities.

KEY TERM

Maxim gun
Invented by American inventor, Hiram Maxim, in 1884, this was the first fully-automated machine gun. Maxim, an engineer, invented it while living in London. The gun was used by every major power. Its exceptionally swift rate of fire made it a devastating weapon, and it was used to great effect during the colonial wars of the late 19th century.

SOURCE 9

From *The River War*, by Winston Churchill, published in 1899. Churchill's comments in the book regarding Kitchener were highly controversial at the time and subsequent editions were edited to remove the comments. The bad feeling between Kitchener and Churchill continued up to and including the First World War, when Kitchener was commander-in-chief of the army and Churchill was First Lord of the Admiralty.

Too much has been said and written about the treatment of the Dervish wounded for anyone who attempts to write a comprehensive account to avoid the discussion. I shall not hesitate to pronounce, though the question is one about which everyone is a partisan. The reader may recall that before the attack on the Mahmud's zerbia the Sirdar (Kitchener) issued orders that the wounded were to be spared. It is scarcely possible to believe that he wished otherwise at Omdurman. It is nevertheless a pity that his former order was not republished to the troops; for I must personally record that there was a very general impression that the fewer the prisoners the greater would be the satisfaction of the commander. The sentiment that the British soldier is incapable of cruelty is one which never fails to win the meed of popular applause; but there is in fact a considerable proportion of cruel men in every army. The mistaken impression I have alluded to encouraged this class. The unmeasured terms in which the Dervishes had been described in the newspapers, and the idea which had been laboriously circulated of 'avenging Gordon' had inflamed their (the soldiers) passions and had led them to believe that it was quite correct to regard their enemy as vermin and unfit to live. The result was that there were many wounded Dervishes killed. Many atrocious acts were also perpetrated by the camp followers; but their intervention was a factor which no General could have foreseen before the battle, and all were busy while it lasted. Such are what I believe to be the actual facts and I also record in contradistinction, that thousands of wounded Dervishes survived that day, that many were succoured by the soldiers, and that upwards of 5,000 prisoners were taken....

But, when all this has been said, the mind turns in disgust from the spectacle of unequal slaughter. The name of the battle, blazoned on the colours, preserves for future generations the memory of a successful expedition. Regiments may exult in the part they played. Military experts may draw instructions from the surprising demonstration of the power of modern weapons. But the individual soldier will carry from the field only a very transient satisfaction, and 'the glory of Omdurman' will seem to any who may five years hence read this book a very absurd expression.

A Level Exam-Style Question Section A

Study Source 9 before you answer this question.

Assess the value of the source for revealing the attitudes of the British public and Kitchener's army to the Battle of Omdurman in 1898.

Explain your answer, using the source, the information given about its origin and your own knowledge about the historical context. (20 marks)

Tip
Think carefully about how generally Churchill's criticisms were accepted and the precise publication date and nature of the source.

The behaviour of the British towards the French at Fashoda and towards the mahdi forces at Omdurman could hardly stand in starker contrast. Following the defeat of mahdist forces at Omdurman, the British had effective control of the whole of the Nile valley and Sudan became part of the British Empire, although the fiction that Sudan was ruled by Egypt was maintained during the veiled protectorate.

SOURCE 10 This picture of dead dervishes around their leader's standard at Omdurman was published in the *London Evening News* on 24 September 1898. In late 19th-century Britain, the term 'dervish' was used as a descriptive term for mahdist supporters rather than in its exact sense.

THE END OF MAHDISM: THE DEAD YAKUB AND HIS FOLLOWERS BESIDE THE KHALIFA'S BLACK FLAG.

The finest heroic display in the Dervish ranks was made by the Khalifa's brother, the Emir Yakub, who with his followers gathered in a dense mass round their standard and proudly faced the leaden hail. As Yakub expired, several of his wounded bodyguard raised themselves and fired at our men. They were promptly despatched. Slatin Pasha witnessed the death of his old enemy and captor, Yakub, who recognised him.

ACTIVITY
KNOWLEDGE CHECK

Omdurman and Fashoda

1 Why could Fashoda have precipitated an Anglo-French war?

2 Compare Kitchener's treatment of a European enemy as described in Source 8 with the slaughter illustrated in Source 10. What reasons can you suggest for the differences?

ACTIVITY
SUMMARY

1 Define British interests in Egypt and the Sudan at the following dates:

a) 1882

b) 1885

c) 1887

d) 1898.

Make sure at each point you assess Britain's financial interests, the potential threat from the French, the instability of the region and impact of Egyptian nationalism and Sudanese mahdism.

2 How far would you agree that British imperialism in Egypt and the Sudan was defensive rather than offensive in its origin?

WIDER READING

Baring, E., Earl of Cromer *Modern Egypt*, 1st edition in 2 volumes, Macmillan (1908) – reissued by Cambridge University Press in the Cambridge Library Collection (2010) and individual chapters available online from http://ebooks.cambridge.org/ebook.jsf?bid=CBO9780511792649

Churchill, W.S. *The River War: An Historical Account of the Reconquest of the Sudan*, 1st edition in 2 volumes, Longman, Green & Co. (1899) – available online at https://archive.org/details/1899RiverWarVol1

Dunett, R.E. *Gentlemanly Capitalism and British Imperialism: The New Debate on Empire*, Routledge (1999)

Hyam, R. *Britain's Imperial Century*, 3rd edition, Macmillan (2002)

Oliver, R. and Sanderson, G.N. (eds) *The Cambridge History of Africa*, Vol. 6, 1870–1905, Cambridge University Press (1985)

Pakenham, T. *The Scramble for Africa: White Man's Conquest of the Dark Continent from 1876 to 1912*, Abacus (1992)

Robinson, R., Gallagher, J. and Denny, A. *Africa and the Victorians: The Official Mind of Imperialism*, 2nd edition, Palgrave Macmillan (1982)

Preparing for your A Level Paper 3 exam

Advance planning

Draw up a timetable for your revision and try to keep to it. Spend longer on topics which you have found difficult, and revise them several times. Aim to be confident about all aspects of your Paper 3 work, because this will ensure that you have a choice of questions in Sections B and C.

Paper 3 Overview

Paper 3	Time: 2 hours 15 minutes	
Section A	Answer one compulsory question for the option studied, assessing source analysis and evaluation skills.	20 marks
Section B	Answer one question from a choice of two on an aspect in depth for the option studied.	20 marks
Section C	Answer one question from a choice of two on an aspect in breadth for the option studied.	20 marks
	Total marks =	60 marks

Section A questions

There is no choice of question in Section A. You will be referred to a source of about 350 words long, printed in a Sources Booklet. The source will be a primary source or one that is contemporary to the period you have studied, and will relate to one of the key topics in the Aspect in Depth. You will be expected to analyse and evaluate the source in its historical context. The question will ask you to assess the value of the source for revealing something specific about the period, and will expect you to explain your answer, using the source, the information given about its origin and your own knowledge about the historical context.

Section B questions

You will have a choice of one from two questions in Section B. They will aim to assess your understanding of one or more of the key topics in the Aspect in Depth you have studied. Questions may relate to a single, momentous year, but will normally cover longer periods. You will be required to write an essay evaluating an aspect of the period. You may be asked about change and continuity, similarity and difference, consequences, significance or causation, or you may be given a quotation and asked to explain how far you agree with it. All questions will require you to reach a substantiated judgement.

Section C questions

You will have a choice of one from two questions in Section C. Questions will relate to the themes of the Aspects in Breadth you have studied, and will aim to assess your understanding of change over time. They will cover a period of not less than 100 years and will relate either to the factors that brought about change, the extent of change over the period or patterns of change as demonstrated by turning points.

Use of time

- Do not write solidly for 45 minutes on each question. For Section B and C answers, you should spend a few minutes working out what the question is asking you to do, and drawing up a plan of your answer. This is especially important for Section C answers, which cover an extended period of time.
- For Section A, it is essential that you have a clear understanding of the content of the source and its historical context. Pay particular attention to the provenance: was the author in a position to know what he or she was writing about? Read it carefully and underline important points. You might decide to spend up to ten minutes reading the source and drawing up your plan, and 35 minutes writing your answer.

Preparing for your A Level exams

Paper 3: A Level sample answer with comments

Section A

These questions require you to analyse and evaluate source material with respect to its historical context. For these questions, remember to:

- look at the evidence given in the source and consider how the source could be used in differing ways to provide historical understanding
- use your knowledge of the historical context to discuss any limitations the source may have
- use your historical understanding to evaluate the source, considering how much weight you would give to its argument
- come to a judgement on the overall value of the source in respect to the question.

Study Source 1 (Chapter 4, page 88) before you answer this question.

Assess the value of Source 1 for revealing the reasons for the choice of Botany Bay as Britain's first settlement in Australia and the hopes the government had for the colony.

Explain your answer, using the source, the information given about its origin and your own knowledge about the historical context. (20 marks)

Average student response

This source reveals quite a lot about the reasons for the choice of Botany Bay as a colony for the British in Australia, but not as much about the hopes the government had for the colony. There is more evidence about why Joseph Banks thought it was a good place to place a colony (it wasn't) and not much about what the government was hoping for.

The source clearly shows that Joseph Banks believed that Botany Bay would be a good place for a settlement because he states that 'from the Fertility of the Soil' the convicts 'might be able to maintain themselves after the fifth year' and that the 'Weather was mild' and like Toulouse with more rich soil than barren soil. I can infer that this was important in the reason that Botany Bay was chosen as a colony as Joseph Banks was an 'expert witness' and was one of the very few people who had actually been to Australia so his opinion would have been listened to. Joseph Banks had been to Australia many years before with Captain Cook and people would have assumed that the climate in Australia would have been the same.

> This introduction addresses both parts of the enquiry, but comments are solely derived from the content of source and the sentences repeat the same point. To improve the introduction, the student needs to evaluate the nature of the source to assess its use to a historian.

> This paragraph has selected relevant evidence for the choice of Botany Bay and made an inference regarding the importance of Banks' evidence in the decision to place the colony in Botany Bay. To improve the paragraph, the student needs to comment on the validity of Banks' claim (he had visited for a few days 17 years before), but explain why his conclusions about the fertility and climate were not possible to challenge.

The source also discusses whether the colony would be safe from attack and how it would be impossible for convicts to escape, meaning it would solve the problem of convicts coming back. He says that 'he had Reason to believe that the Country was very thinly populated' and that the Aboriginal people were 'naked, treacherous and armed with lances but very cowardly'. To be honest, Banks probably had no idea how many Aboriginal people there were in the area, but he was accurate in his observation regarding their weapons so could be pretty confident that with guns British settlers would be able to overcome any resistance. He would also have noticed that the Aboriginal people did not farm the land so this would have made him think that the land was freely available for settlers.

The student has made some inferences here regarding Banks' attitudes to the Aboriginal people, but these should be developed further with more contextual knowledge. The student also refers to the impossibility of convict escape, but the reference is not specific enough. This forms part of the Select Committee's question to Banks and a better answer would connect this question with the second part of the enquiry regarding the government's hopes.

The source says much less about the hopes of the government for the future, but Banks tells them that the colony would 'find occasion for many European Commodities' so suggests that part of the interest in starting up a colony was to develop a new trading partner. The date of the source is 1779 and I know that the American War of Independence was going on at this time, so can infer that the government would have been interested in new trade as British trade was very disrupted at this time, not just with America but with Europe. Banks says there will be 'an advantageous Return' which means that they will make money despite all the costs of sending out convicts.

The student makes a sensible inference here based on the provenance of the source and their knowledge of the historical context, but the answer is weakened by their reliance on Banks' evidence. The answer would be far stronger if it analysed the questions of the committee rather than Banks' answers to address the second part of the enquiry.

The source is quite valuable for revealing why Botany Bay was chosen as a place of settlement by the British because, after all, Joseph Banks had been to Australia so the government would have been impressed by his answers. It is less valuable for understanding about the government's hopes as it is really more based on Banks and his evidence than on that of the government, although I can infer what his answers might have made them think and why they would have been keen to develop trade.

The conclusion deals with both enquiries and reaches a conclusion, but further consideration of the nature and purpose of the source would help the student evaluate the source successfully.

Verdict

This is an average response because:

- it is largely based on the content of the source, not its nature and purpose
- the points made do not display a great deal of contextual knowledge
- the evaluation of the source is limited to a discussion of Banks.

Use the feedback on this answer to rewrite it, making as many improvements as you can.

Paper 3: A Level sample answer with comments

Section A

These questions require you to analyse and evaluate source material with respect to its historical context. For these questions, remember to:

- look at the evidence given in the source and consider how the source could be used in differing ways to provide historical understanding
- use your knowledge of the historical context to discuss any limitations the source may have
- use your historical understanding to evaluate the source, considering how much weight you would give to its argument
- come to a judgement on the overall value of the source in respect to the question.

Study Source 1 (Chapter 4, page 88) before you answer this question.

Assess the value of Source 1 for revealing the reasons for the choice of Botany Bay as Britain's first settlement in Australia and the hopes the government had for the colony.

Explain your answer, using the source, the information given about its origin and your own knowledge about the historical context. (20 marks)

Strong student response

Source 1 is very valuable for revealing the choice of Botany Bay as Britain's first settlement in Australia and the nature and purpose of the source reveal a considerable amount about the hopes the government had for the new colony.

Joseph Banks' answers to the Bunbury Committee on Transportation are highly significant in the choice of Botany Bay as the destination for the first convict settlement in Australia. He was one of the very few people who had actually been to Australia as he was a member of the expedition that Captain Cook had commanded 17 years before. He was one of the few possible expert witnesses that the government could ask for advice when considering transportation and settlement, and his views on Botany Bay were very positive. He commented on the 'proportion of rich soil' and the mildness of the climate, which were clearly key to the long-term survival of a colony as they would need to grow their own crops. In his view, the colony would become self-supporting quickly 'after the fifth year' and fertility was 'sufficient to support a very large number of people'. This evidence would have weighed very favourably with the committee as they would have relied on Banks' expert knowledge of the otherwise unknown continent.

Banks' evidence would also have been very reassuring to the committee regarding any potential problem with native resistance. The British were familiar with the cost of protecting their American colonies from the native Americans during the Indian Wars and they would have wanted to assess how likely this was to be a problem in Australia. Banks emphasises the small number of Aboriginal people, as well as their lack of weapons 'armed with lances' and their behaviour to the British 'cowardly' and 'retired from our People'. The Aboriginal people did not farm the land but lived in harmony with nature, but to British people like Banks this meant that they had no obvious claim to the land. If he had seen farms in Australia, he would have reported this to the committee as he would have perceived the settled farmers as having a greater claim to the land. Captain Cook had declared Australia to be Terra Nullis which meant he did not recognise that the native people had any claim to the continent.

> The introduction suggests an evaluative answer to both enquiries in the question, based on the nature and purpose of the source, as well as the content.

> The student explains why Banks' evidence would have weighed so strongly with the committee.

> Good use of contextual knowledge to support the points made regarding the claim of Aboriginal peoples to the land.

The nature and purpose of this source are very useful in explaining the hopes the British government had for the colony. The source is the record of a parliamentary committee which would have interviewed expert witnesses to help them make a policy recommendation or decision. The committee's name is the Bunbury Committee on Transportation and in 1779 they were reviewing Britain's options for transporting criminals as they were no longer able to transport any to America due to the War of Independence. Britain's gaols were full to overflowing and they had to find some solution to the problem. The first question they ask Banks is where he would recommend a colony 'in case it be thought expedient to establish a colony of convicted felons in any part of the Globe, from whence their escape might be difficult', which suggests that the main hope and purpose of the committee was to find somewhere to send convicts from where they would never come back.

> The student illuminates their comments on the source in relation to the second enquiry by their understanding of the nature and purpose of the parliamentary committee.

Further questions from the committee reveal the other main hope for the colony. 'And being asked, whether he concurred the Mother Country was liable to reap any Benefit from a Colony established in Botany Bay' clearly shows that at the forefront of the committee's mind were any possible benefits to establishing a colony in Australia. At the very least, the government was determined that the colony should be self-sufficient as the first question reveals: 'From whence their escape might be difficult, and where from the Fertility of the Soil, they might be able to maintain themselves, after the fifth year.' It is clear from these questions that before they fitted out an expensive expedition and provided guards for the prisoners, the British were concerned that there would be no ongoing costs and that there might even be possible trade benefits. Britain was spending a fortune fighting the American War of Independence and its trade was severely disrupted by the war (exports fell by 18 percent between 1775 and 1778, so the potential of new markets would have been enticing).

> This is a sophisticated interrogation of the content of the source, showing contextual understanding and building on the paragraph above, which clearly demonstrates the student's understanding of the nature and purpose of the source.

In many ways, this source is extremely useful, explaining both the hopes of the British government for the new colony and the reasons that the First Fleet set out for Botany Bay, even though it was in fact a terrible place for a settlement. The nature of the source and the questions asked by the committee members are highly revealing as to the priorities of the British government in 1779, the committee was not convened to discuss exploration to Australia, but to discuss the issue of transportation which had been interrupted by the American War. The questions that the committee asks reveal their priorities and hopes. Banks' answers, which were in fact in many ways wrong as Botany Bay was not by any means fertile, were obviously key in the decision to base the colony at Botany Bay as he was so positive about the area and he was practically the only person in Britain who had actually been there. The committee had no choice but to believe his evidence, mistaken though it was.

> Clearly evaluative and reflective of the precise nature of the questions posed to Banks and the circumstances that governed the committee's enquiry.

Verdict

This is a strong response because:

- the student understands the nature and purpose of the source and uses this knowledge to illuminate their comments
- the response uses precisely selected contextual knowledge to support their interrogation of the source and develop inferences
- the answer is well organised and logically presented to help create an effective answer.

Paper 3: A Level sample answer with comments

Section B

These questions require you to show your understanding of a period in depth. They will ask you about a quite specific period of time and will ask you to make a substantiated judgement about a specific aspect you have studied. For these questions, remember to:

- organise your essay and communicate it in a manner that is clear and comprehensible
- use historical knowledge to analyse and evaluate the key aspect of the question
- make a balanced argument that weighs up differing opinions
- make a substantiated overall judgement on the question.

How far do you agree that the Indian Rebellion (also referred to as the Indian Mutiny) occurred because of the nature of Company rule up until 1857? (20 marks)

Average student response

The East India Company was responsible for Britain being in India in the first place. It started off as a trading company and gradually ended up ruling over large parts of India. I think the Company was responsible for the Indian Rebellion in 1857 to a great extent because of the mistakes it made in ruling the British Empire. If you examine long-term and short-term causes of the rebellion, it is possible to see that Company administrators did not understand the concerns of the Indians because they were trying to 'modernise' India and make it more like Britain.

The Indian Rebellion occurred partly because of the changes to Company rule following the Charter Act 1813. The Charter Act ended the East India Company's trading monopoly on many things and the Company got involved in tax collection and administration in India more as a result. They were now ruling large parts of India in the three presidencies and this meant that they began to think about the way they should rule India. They began to bring in changes influenced by the Utilitarians which made changes to Indian society in a way the Company had never done before. Governor Bentinck banned sati and authorised the campaign against thagi. Of course, Indians were not too upset about the prosecution of thagi, but they minded very much the ban on sati as it was seen as an attack on their religious practices.

The way in which the East India Company army was organised led directly to the outbreak of the rebellion. The Bengal army, which was the army which mutinied, recruited mostly from high caste Hindus. In the run up to the rebellion, the Company announced that in the future these Hindu soldiers might have to travel, possibly over sea, which the Hindus did not want to do as it meant that they would lose their high caste status. Because soldiers came from particular villages and families, when the rebellion started news travelled very quickly and the trouble got worse and worse. The Company policy of recruitment led to the outbreak of the Indian Rebellion.

This introduction shows clear direction and is attempting to focus on the question. However, the response is focused on the Company rather than the 'nature of Company rule', which means that the essay may not be sufficiently analytically focused on the question set. A definition of what the student understands to be the nature of Company rule would improve this introduction.

The response attempts to focus on the changes that occurred in the 1830s under Company rule, but in the paragraph there is not sufficient analytical focus on the question. Each paragraph should begin with an explicit link to the question which is analytical rather than descriptive. To improve this response, there needs to be analysis at the beginning of the question, which explains the changing nature of Company rule after 1813 and in which ways this laid the seeds of the 1857 rebellion.

This is better focused on the nature of the East India Company rule, or at least the way in which the Company army was recruited, but is weak in its supporting knowledge. A better answer would be far more specific about when changes to conditions of service were proposed and the castes and localities from which the Company recruited.

The cause of the Indian Rebellion was mutiny in the Bengal army. This was caused by the rumour that cartridges for rifles, which had to be bitten off, were to be greased with a new grease which was a mixture of pig and beef fat. For the high caste Hindus of the Bengal army, this was too much and they mutinied. The mutiny quickly spread especially in Awadh where Indians were unhappy with changes that the Company's governor had made. The East India Company had no idea that the rebellion was coming and they were not prepared for it. It took months of fighting and the intervention of the British government to quell the rebellion and afterwards the British government took control of British India.

The Indian Rebellion was caused not only by short-term actions by the East India Company, but by a rejection by Indians of the British entirely. Indians were not very united or organised, but the widespread nature of the rebellion shows that they were not happy with having the British rule over them. The British were becoming more and more racially dividing and Indians felt insulted by things like Macaulay's Minute on Education, which said their culture was worthless, and the laws that were passed by the Company against sati. They also did not like the spread of missionaries in India which happened after 1813 and William Wilberforce's campaign to get them into the presidencies.

I do agree that the East India Company was responsible for the Indian Rebellion in 1857 by the mistakes it made in the way it ruled India. It viewed Indians as inferior to the British and was trying to modernise India. Some of the things it did, like abolishing sati, were good and necessary, but in the short term they caused widespread resentment against British rule.

This is more focused on the Indian Rebellion than on the nature of Company rule, although the paragraph has indirect focus on the question. The response needs explicit analytical focus on the question at the beginning of the paragraph, which shows how decisions taken by the Company army, resulting from insufficient appreciation of Indian religious beliefs, sparked the army mutiny in Meerut. Some mention is made of Company rule in Awadh, but this needs far more focus on the question and specific supporting evidence.

This paragraph is too generalised and not sufficiently focused on the question, but the response shows that the student understands something of the reasons for the anger that many Indians felt against British rule. Macaulay's Minute on Education would not have been common knowledge among most Indians subject to Company rule, but the belief in British superiority and Indian inferiority, which guided the Minute, would have been apparent to Indians and therefore the paragraph could be made relevant to the question set.

The conclusion addresses the question, but by agreeing completely with the question set the student is not demonstrating that they have really evaluated it.

Verdict

This is an average response because:

- the focus on the question is not sufficiently analytical
- the nature of the supporting evidence is too generalised

- there is no attempt made to show the connections between the different problems of Company rule that have been identified.

Use the feedback on this answer to rewrite it, making as many improvements as you can.

Paper 3: A Level sample answer with comments

Section B

These questions require you to show your understanding of a period in depth. They will ask you about a quite specific period of time and will ask you to make a substantiated judgement about a specific aspect you have studied. For these questions, remember to:

- organise your essay and communicate it in a manner that is clear and comprehensible
- use historical knowledge to analyse and evaluate the key aspect of the question
- make a balanced argument that weighs up differing opinions
- make a substantiated overall judgement on the question.

How far do you agree that the Indian Rebellion (also referred to as the Indian Mutiny) occurred because of the nature of Company rule up until 1857? (20 marks)

Strong student response

In some ways, the Indian Rebellion occurred because of the nature of Company rule up to 1857. The Company's function had changed from commerce to administration and tax collection and this combined with specific actions by Governors Bentinck and Dalhousie led to more conflict with Indians. The actions of governors, combined with the historic recruitment policy of the Bengal presidency army, meant that the mutiny in Meerut fanned out to become a more general rebellion very quickly. However, the widespread nature of the rebellion shows that this was something more than just a protest against Company rule and had roots in a clash of cultures between the British and the Indians.

The nature of Company rule was changing during the first half of the 19th century and the change in Company function from commerce to administration and tax collection was a long-term cause of dissatisfaction with British rule, which contributed to the outbreak of the Great Rebellion. The Charter Act 1813 renewed the Company's charter, but removed its trading monopolies on goods, apart from tea and trade with China and these monopolies ended in 1833. The Company became far more involved in administration and tax collection over their increasing territory. During the 1830s, the Punjab and Sind came under Company rule and Dalhousie pursued an aggressive policy of annexation from local princes under his doctrine of lapse. Although the British were fair when it came to tax collection, they were now involved more and more in the system of landownership and tax collection and this caused opposition to their rule. There were particular issues relating to changes in landownership and collection in Awadh, which was one of the most serious centres of the rebellion, and the fact that people flocked to support the Mughals in Delhi and Hindu princes as well shows that there was opposition to the social changes which replaced local rulers with British administrators.

Changes in the structure of the Company and proposals for the Bengal army contributed to the outbreak of the rebellion in 1857. The doctrine of lapse introduced by Dalhousie and the annexation of Awadh under Dalhousie were important preconditions for the Great Rebellion. Acts of Parliament passed in the 1770s and 1780s had made the governor of Bengal effective governor over all the British territories and, although there was a governing council, the governor could overrule this. This meant that a governor like Dalhousie could institute sweeping changes without being checked easily. There was a Board of Control in London, but with slow communication it meant that executive power was basically in the hands of governors. In Awadh, Dalhousie's actions threatened the traditional fabric of society by threatening to remove all land from the traditional landowner class, the talukdars, if they could not prove legally with documents their ownership of land. Then, in 1856, Canning, the new governor general proposed

This introduction shows direction and purpose. The response is clearly focused on the question and the nature of Company rule. The last sentence suggests that the student is aware of the more complex nature of the rebellion than simply a revolt against the British.

The response is analytical in focus and supported with specific knowledge regarding the changes in the nature of Company rule during the first half of the 19th century.

Analytical and focused on the question, this paragraph uses knowledge from across the whole timespan of the depth study to support the point made.

changes to the conditions of service of the Bengali army meaning that sepoys thought that they could be forced to travel over sea, causing them to lose their caste. As many sepoys in the Bengali presidency army were recruited from the province of Awadh, it is clear that changes instituted in their home province, combined with changes to their conditions of service, made a revolt in the Bengali army highly likely. Although London tried to oversee what governors did, distance and issues with communication meant that executive power rested with individual governors.

However, the Indian Rebellion was more than a simple revolt against the changing structure of Company rule. It was the result of a clash of cultures and values too. As the British became more involved in ruling India, they made changes to the law, which could be seen as attacks on Indian religion and culture, and the spark which led to the army mutiny in Meerut was caused by the rumoured introduction of grease made with pork and beef fat which was abhorrent to both Hindus and Muslims. The British had passed laws to abolish sati in the 1830s and missionaries, who were key in the promotion of Christianity through the medium of teaching in English, flowed into the presidencies from 1813. For the high-caste Hindus, who were so prominent in the Bengali army, the introduction of the new grease in 1857 was the final straw in what must have felt like a slow undermining of their traditions and religious beliefs. British governors like Bentinck and Dalhousie believed they were modernising India and improving it by making it more Western, but their changes led to widespread anger at what was seen as interference by the British.

> An analytical focus, with evidential support drawing on the entire period.

In conclusion, it is clear that in many ways the changes to the function of Company rule combined with structural changes, which gave effective executive power to the governor general, were long-term causes of the Great Rebellion. Specific changes in Awadh, the province from which the Bengal army was drawn, and to the terms of service for the sepoys, sparked the army mutiny which began the rebellion. However, the rebellion was not just a revolt against the Company and its methods of ruling the territories, but an expression of a clash of cultures between British values and religion and Indian values and religion.

> An effective conclusion that reflects the arguments made throughout the essay and focuses on the precise question set.

Verdict

This is a strong response because:

- it is analytical throughout, demonstrating a sophisticated understanding of the terms of the question

- it is well supported with good knowledge deployed from across the depth study
- the writing shows direction and purpose throughout the essay.

Paper 3: A Level sample answer with comments

Section C

These questions require you to show your understanding of a subject over a considerable period of time. They will ask you to assess a long-term historical topic and its development over a period of at least 100 years, and they require you to make a substantiated judgement in relation to the question. For these questions remember to:

- organise your essay and communicate it in a manner that is clear and comprehensible
- use historical knowledge to analyse and evaluate the key aspect of the question covering the entire period
- make a balanced argument that weighs up differing opinions
- make a substantiated overall judgement on the question.

To what extent did the role of the Royal Navy change as a result of Britain's expanding imperial interests in the years 1763–1914? (20 marks)

Average student response

The role of the Royal Navy certainly changed during the years 1763–1914 and this was mostly because of the expanding British Empire, which therefore demanded greater protection from its warships. While there are other reasons for its changing role, such as the actions of other countries, it is the imperial interests of Britain that were the main influence.

> This introduction offers a general argument and acknowledges some debate. However, it could be more focused in terms of how the debate relates to the argument presented. This would sharpen the argument and allow for a better sense of direction in the essay.

Foremost, it is appropriate to suggest that imperial demands were crucial to the changing role of the navy. This is because during the mid-18th century as Britain was developing its Empire, so too were other nations – France, for example – and therefore in order to remain in a dominant position the navy played an important role defending British interests – particularly during the wars with revolutionary France at the end of the century. In this respect, the navy arguably performed the classic role of a defensive force. However, by the turn of the century, it had also adopted other roles, including policeman and also protecting British shipping. That the role of the navy was expanded to include these new demands demonstrates that as the Empire became more complex, the navy had to adapt to support these new pressures and therefore was clearly influenced by them.

> This paragraph offers some good ideas and there is an argument presented, which is generally analytical. It does not develop this analysis very far and includes only general information as supporting evidence. A tangible example would help to strengthen this paragraph.

Evidence to support the idea of imperial demands reshaping the role of the navy is supplied by the way that it became the policeman of the seas during the 19th century, notably patrolling the Atlantic and Africa's 5,000 km coastline to enforce the British government's decision to abolish the slave trade in 1807. In this regard, the navy was not simply a military force acting against enemy ships, it adopted a more interventionist role and targeted merchant vessels and any other ships suspected of trading slaves. This was a thankless task for the navy as often their ships were not fast enough to catch the smaller, more agile cutters that the traders sailed. Indeed, it was not until the navy was able to acquire faster ships for themselves that they had any real impact upon the trade they were trying to interrupt. In addition to faster ships, the navy also benefited from new technologies such as paddle steamers, which allowed them to follow slave traders down the rivers in to hidden ports – HMS Hydra, for example, was able capture four slave ships this way between the years 1844 and 1846. In this sense, therefore, although the role of the Royal Navy changed, it was able to adapt successfully and therefore enforce the imperial demands of the country.

> This paragraph has some focus, but it drifts into narrative quite quickly. Once again, the analysis is generally undeveloped and in places it only implicitly relates its point to the question demand. The strength to this paragraph, however, is the precise evidence on display.

Although clearly the role of the navy was forced to change to suit the imperial demands of the British government, it is also reasonable to suggest that this was not entirely the direct result of these demands. Rather, it is equally valid to say that much of its role changed in response to the actions of other powers, such as Russia and France. This could be said to still be ultimately down to imperial interest, but also simply trying to keep up with the modernising world. In this regard, the adoption of new roles such as mapping the oceans and acquiring new bases across the globe was simply a reaction to the growing interest among the leading powers to increase their position and trading opportunities. On this basis, the navy was arguably just another means for finding out more about the new worlds and was the main way of creating such new opportunities in the hope of matching fellow powers in the changing world of the 19th and early 20th centuries.

Therefore, although it is reasonable to suggest that the role of the Royal Navy did change, it was not entirely the result of the imperial demands, since there were additional factors, such as the desire to keep up with other powers in the changing world. Despite this influence, however, the general role of the navy continued to be that of the British government's policing tool and therefore it was ultimately the servant of imperialism.

This paragraph offers some debate, but it does not fully or clearly develop the ideas in terms of the question demand. The focus of this paragraph is rather implicit and is not entirely successful in distinguishing between 'imperial demands' and 'creating opportunities' in the changing world. It would also be useful to elaborate upon what kinds of opportunities are being developed.

This conclusion has a judgement which is generally supported by the main body. It is related to the question demand, but the overall focus could be sharper which in turn would enhance the evaluation.

Verdict

This is an average response because:

- it is quite narrative throughout and does not cover the breadth of the timeframe asked for
- the points made are developed in a general way, albeit with some good own knowledge
- it does not evenly consider a counterargument.

Use the feedback on this essay to rewrite it, making as many improvements as you can.

Paper 3: A Level sample answer with comments

Section C

These questions require you to show your understanding of a subject over a considerable period of time. They will ask you to assess a long-term historical topic and its development over a period of at least 100 years, and they require you to make a substantiated judgement in relation to the question. For these questions remember to:

- organise your essay and communicate it in a manner that is clear and comprehensible
- use historical knowledge to analyse and evaluate the key aspect of the question covering the entire period
- make a balanced argument that weighs up differing opinions
- make a substantiated overall judgement on the question.

To what extent did the role of the Royal Navy change as a result of Britain's expanding imperial interests in the years 1763–1914? (20 marks)

Strong student response

To a great extent, the role of the Royal Navy is to serve the governments of Britain and its people and as such it is, therefore, in any guise, always going to be motivated by imperial demands since it was governed by the interests of the country during the years 1763–1914. While it could be argued that economic and explorative interests certainly influenced its changing role, these were either directly or indirectly motivated by imperialism, which was the dominant theme of the period.

> In this introduction, there is a clear argument being developed that integrates an awareness of debate and uses this to inform the overall idea being presented.

Given the overriding imperial concerns of the late 18th and 19th centuries, which saw most European nations expand dramatically, it is reasonable to suggest that the role of the Royal Navy was foremost to facilitate that interest. This is clearly illustrated by its primary function as a first line of defence against aggression – notably the 1793 war against revolutionary France and the earlier Seven Years' War (1756–63) against the same nation. In both of these examples, the role of the navy was to defend British interests and in each case it served across the globe, including America and India, both possessions of the Empire. That the navy fulfilled this role is indicative of imperial motivation, since each conflict was arguably sparked by the perception of threat towards national interests. Indeed, such is the importance of imperial defence that the navy was granted substantial funds to reinforce its fleets and it ended the Napoleonic Wars with 792 frigates and 214 ships of the line. Such investment in the navy would only have taken place if it was felt necessary and, given the expanding empire which increasingly included lucrative, far-flung, regions of the world, a strong navy was the only way to protect these interests.

> This paragraph is clearly analytical and starts to build the argument presented in the introduction. There is some supporting evidence and clear direction.

Reinforcing the notion of imperial demand, the navy was arguably a 'multi-tool' for the British government, serving as a defensive barrier, but also as policeman and an exploration company. In the case of law enforcement, the British abolition of the slave trade in 1807 presented the navy with a new role to enforce the Act. This involved patrolling the 5,000 km-long African coastline seeking out slave trading vessels and preventing their activities. It is fair to say that, initially, the navy struggled with this role. However, it quickly adapted and in the years 1844–46 was successful in capturing four slave ships. At first glance, it might be reasonable to suggest that this was not necessarily motivated by imperial demand but rather humanitarian interest. However, upon closer inspection, it must be noted that the decision to end the slave trade, and later slavery itself in 1833, was because of a changing economic environment that arguably undermined imperial interests to the extent that abolition was the best course of action. In this sense, therefore, it would be fair to suggest that by fulfilling this function, the navy was indirectly serving imperial needs.

> Like the previous paragraph, this is nicely analytical and continues to build a clear argument that is consistent and well focused. There is more supporting evidence here, which enhances the points being made.

Reinforcing this argument is also the role the navy played in mapping the world. On one level, this might be viewed as an innocent information-gathering exercise – wanting to understand the world better. This interpretation is supported by the fact that Captain Cook undertook to circumnavigate the globe in the interest of extending geographical knowledge. However, Cook also sought to claim the lands he found for Britain, before being killed in Hawaii in 1779. Furthermore, it could also be suggested that in undertaking these investigative voyages, Cook was also collecting nautical data that would be invaluable for giving the Royal Navy an advantage over rival fleets, thus maintaining the pre-eminent position of that navy and therefore ensuring the Empire remained safe in the increasingly combative 19th century, which saw rival powers vying for greater control of new continents – the 'scramble for Africa', for example, during the mid-century and later the arms race that resulted in the outbreak of the First World War in 1914.

In conclusion, imperial demands were arguably the contextual backdrop of British activities during the years 1763–1914 and therefore any role that the Royal Navy performed was influenced by this concern. This is perhaps most effectively evidenced by the multiplicity of its roles: policeman, navigator and defender – individually all different but still bound by imperial undertones – a fact clearly demonstrated by the outbreak of world war in 1914. In this case, even though the navy had adopted new functions, it was always ready to defend imperial interests against aggressors.

This paragraph introduces some debate, but maintains focus by effectively relating it to the overall argument using logical development and a reasonable range of evidence in support.

A clear judgement is made here, which is well supported in the body of the essay.

Verdict

This is a strong response because:

- it is clearly analytical and offers a well-defined argument
- throughout the response, there is good use of precise and well-selected evidence to support the points made
- it considers a counterargument and includes this as part of an overall developed evaluation.

Index

Acknowledgements

The authors and publisher would like to thank the following individuals and organisations for permission to reproduce photographs and text in this book.

(Key: b-bottom; c-centre; l-left; r-right; t-top)

Alamy Images: Alamy/National Geographic Image Collection 6, David Bigwood 98, GL Archive 43, Select Images 38; **Bridgeman Art Library Ltd:** Private Collection/The Stapleton Collection 47, British Library, London, UK 141, Mitchell Library, State Library of New South Wales 91, Pictures from History 102; **British Library Images Online:** 158; **Getty Images:** Aaron Lynett/Toronto Star 127, Arkivi 42, DEA/G. Dagli Orti 55, Henry Guttmann 13, Print Collector 123, Stock Montage 28, Ullstein Bild 24, Wynnter 125; **Mary Evans Picture Library:** 59, 148, Classic Stock/H. Armstrong Roberts 77, Everett Collection 65, Illustrated London News Ltd 31, 149, 172; **The Art Archive:** British Library 142; **TopFoto:** The Granger Collection 9; **W.L. Crowther Library, Tasmanian Archive and Heritage Office:** 105

Cover image: Bridgeman Art Library Ltd: Leeds Museums and Galleries (Leeds Art Gallery) UK

All other images © Pearson Education

Text

Extract 1 p.33 from *Britain's Imperial Century, 1815–1914: A Study of Empire and Expansion* Palgrave Macmillan (R. Hyam, 2002) p.xviii © Ronald Hyam 1976, 1993, 2002, reproduced with permission of Palgrave Macmillan; Extract p.55 from *The Empire Project: The Rise and Fall of the British World-System, 1830–1970* Cambridge University Press (J. Darwin, 2009) p.27, Copyright © 2009 Cambridge University Press; Extract p.57 from *Aden under British Rule, 1839–1967* C. Hurst and Co. (R. Gavin, 1975) pp.34–7, Reproduced with permission; Extract 3 p.62 from *Empire, the Sea and Global History: Britain's Maritime World, c1760–c1840* Palgrave Macmillan (Stephen Conway and David Cannadine (eds.), 2007) p.23, reproduced with permission of Palgrave Macmillan; Extract 4 p.62 from *Britain's Imperial Century, 1815–1914: A Study of Empire and Expansion,* 3rd ed., Palgrave Macmillan (R. Hyam, 2002) p.17, © Ronald Hyam 1976, 1993, 2002, reproduced with permission of Palgrave Macmillan; Extract 5 p.62 from *Empire of the Deep: The Rise and Fall of the British Navy* Weidenfeld & Nicholson (Ben Wilson, 2013) p.471, text © Ben Wilson 2013, reproduced with permission from The Orion Publishing Group, London and from Conville & Walsh; Extract p.63 from *The Rise and Fall of British Naval Mastery,* Penguin (Paul Kennedy, 2001) pp.150–51, reproduced with permission; Extract 1 p.72 and Extract 4 p.81 from *Penguin History of the USA* Penguin (Hugh Brogan, 1999) pp.157, 170, Reproduced with permission from the author; Extract 2 p.74 from Christopher Hamner, American Resistance to a Standing Army, teachinghistory.org, the Roy Rosenzweig Center for History and New Media, http://teachinghistory.org/history-content/ask-a-historian/24671 [accessed 23.08.2016], reproduced with permission; Extract 3 p.74 from *Patriots, Settlers and the Origins of American Social Policy* Cambridge University Press (Laura Jensen, 2003) p.51, Copyright © 2003 Cambridge University Press; Extract 2 p.103 from *Why Weren't We Told?* Penguin (Henry Reynolds, 2000) pp.120–21, Copyright © Henry Reynolds 1998, reproduced by permission of Penguin Random House Australia; Extract 3 p.103 from The Fabrication of Aboriginal History, *Sydney Papers,* Vol. 15, No. 1 (Keith Windschuttle, 2003) pp.20–29 and in Lecture to Higher School Certificate History Extension conference, Tom Mann Theatre, Sydney, 26 May 2010, http://www.stolengenerations.info/index.php?option=com_content&view=article&id=229&Itemid=172, reproduced with permission; Extract p.107 from *Turning Points in Australian History* UNSW Press (M. Crotty and D.A. Roberts, 2008) p.2, reproduced with permission; Extract p.111 from *Lord Durham* Clarendon Press (Chester New, 1929) p.322, by permission of Oxford University Press; Extract p.132 from *Empire: How Britain Made the Modern World* Penguin (Niall Ferguson, 2003) p.112, copyright © Niall Ferguson, 2002, reproduced by permission of Penguin Books Ltd and in United States and Canada Copyright © 2003 Niall Ferguson, *Empire: The Rise and Demise of the British World Order and the Lessons for Global Power.* Reprinted by permission of Basic Books, a member of the Perseus Books Group; Extract p.137 and Extract 2 p.145 from *A New History of India* Oxford University Press (Stanley Wolpert, 2009) pp.211,

214 by permission of Oxford University Press, USA; Extract 3 p.150 from *Modern India: The Origins of An Asian Democracy*, 2nd ed., Oxford University Press (Judith Brown, 1994) p.93, by permission of Oxford University Press; Extract p.158 from *Hansard, 14 June 1882, Vol. 270*, pp.1146–47, contains Parliamentary information licensed under the Open Parliament Licence v3.0; Extract p.159 from *The Lion's Share, A Short History of British Imperialism 1850–1995* Pearson Education (Bernard Porter, 1996) p.111, reproduced by permission of Taylor & Francis Books UK; Extract p.163 from *Britain's Imperial Century, 1815–1914: A Study of Empire and Expansion,* 3rd ed., Palgrave Macmillan (R. Hyam, 2002) p.187, © Ronald Hyam 1976, 1993, 2002, reproduced with permission of Palgrave Macmillan; Extract p.169 from *The Scramble for Africa* Abacus (Thomas Packenham, 1991) p.548, Copyright © Thomas Packenham 1991, reproduced with permission from The Orion Publishing Group, London; Extract p.171 from *The River War*, first edition, Vol. ii, Hodder (Winston S. Churchill, 1899) p.195, reproduced with permission of Curtis Brown Group Ltd, London on behalf of the Estate of Winston S. Churchill Copyright © The Beneficiaries of the Estate of Winston S. Churchill.